Library of
Davidson College

BON VOYAGE

The Cruise Guide to the Caribbean

James W. Morrison

Arco Publishing, Inc.
New York

DEDICATION

For Wendy,
who always knows how to sail on
the Song of Norway and the Windsong,
and always the loving sister.

917.29
M879b

Published by Arco Publishing Inc.
219 Park Avenue South, New York. N.Y. 10003

Copyright © 1981 by Arco Publishing, Inc.

All rights reserved. No part of this book may be reproduced, by any means, without permission in writing from the publisher, except by a reviewer who wishes to quote brief excerpts in connection with a review in a magazine or newspaper.

Library of Congress Cataloging in Publication Data

Morrison, James Warner, 1940-
   Bon voyage.

82-147

   1. Caribbean area—Description and travel—
1951- —Guide-books. 2. Ocean travel. I. Title
F2171.2.M67   917.29'0452   80-26848
ISBN 0-668-04865-4 (Cloth Edition)
ISBN 0-668-04851-4 (Paper Edition)

Printed in the United States of America

TABLE OF CONTENTS

Foreword		5
1.	WELCOME ABOARD	7
2.	HISTORY OF SEA TRAVEL	11

First World Travellers • Steamship and Transatlantic Passenger Ships

3. MODERN CRUISE TRAVEL 27
Sea Terms • Steamship Abbreviations • Selecting a Cruise • Cruise Comfort—Space per Passenger • Air/Sea Packages • Air/Sea Program Conditions • Cruise Ship Ticket

4. PLANNING YOUR CRUISE 57
Some Things You Should Know Before You Go

5. CARIBBEAN CRUISE 79
A Caribbean Cruise Itinerary • 20 Days—13 Ports • Is Caribbean Cruising Really for Me • Caribbean Cruise Destinations of Popular Ships

6. LIFE ON BOARD 115
Service on Board • Cruise Accommodations • Dining • Dining Schedule and Menus • Cruise Line Cuisine • Casinos • Tax and Duty Free Shopping • Caribbean Fleet Features

7. ALL ASHORE 161
Shore Program Notes • Example of Shore Tours

8. HEALTH AND SAFETY 175
Additional Safety Precautions

9. **CUSTOMS AND OTHER MATTERS**   **185**
   Insurance • Travel Accident Insurance • Baggage and Personal Possessions Insurance • Trip Cancellation • Traveller's Checks and Foreign Currency • Documentary Requirements • U. S. Passports • Tourist Card • Visa • Special Papers • Health Certificates • U. S. Customs and Immigration • Your Customs Declaration • Prohibited and Restricted Articles • Customs' Pointers • U. S. Customs' Warning

10. **THE CARIBBEAN**   **213**
    A Short History • Trade, Tourists, and Progress • Sports on Land and Sea • Your Legal Status • The Caribbean Nations • Spanish Language Guide

Appendix

A	CARIBBEAN CRUISE SHIPS	288
B	MAJOR CRUISE LINES	310
C	CARIBBEAN CRUISE PORTS OF CALL	312
D	GOVERNMENT TOURIST OFFICES	314
E	PASSENGER SHIP TERMINAL INFORMATION	317

FOREWORD

The interest in cruise travel has been overwhelming. With deregulated air fares, low cost air-sea destinations, and twenty-three cruise ships based in Miami as well as other ships serving the Caribbean, there is a literal boom in cruise ship travel. Cruise ship travel seems to be here to stay.

During the development of this book a vast amount of published and unpublished information concerning cruise travel and tourism was reviewed. The writing of this volume involved a great many contacts with travel agencies, government tourist organizations, air lines, steamship companies and others in ship travel; the author is grateful for their assistance. A particular note of thanks is given to those travel agents who talked at length with the author since air deregulation and to the staffs of those ship lines who provided materials and photographs used in this book. By answering many of the problems included in this text and by offering comments about them, they have made a valuable contribution to the readability, clarity, and validity of the thoughts expressed.

Your travel agent has the latest cruise ship schedules and can be of great assistance in arranging your Caribbean cruise.

JWM

The beach at Peter Island Yacht Club, British Virgin Islands, lying some 75 miles east of Puerto Rico, is a coral and limestone formed island. There are many fine beaches and extensive reefs for scuba enthusiasts who want to explore the depths as well as the wrecks.

Chapter 1

WELCOME ABOARD

Thinking about a Caribbean cruise? This book can help you to plan your holiday. You should have a more enjoyable and meaningful cruise, if, for example, you know about the ports that SUN VIKING will be visiting: Ocho Rios, Willemstad, LaGuaire, Bridgetown, Fort-de-France, St. Thomas, Santo Domingo, and Port-au-Prince. Merely by reading about these Caribbean islands, you will have a greater understanding of your passage and the ports-of-call. It is a good thing to think about the ports when you are considering investing in a cruise vacation.

Examine your ship's itinerary and find out how many hours (days) you will be in the ports. This will give you an idea just how you want to spend your day. In some ports where the ship remains overnight, your ship is your hotel and you can have a "night-on-the-town."

Today's vacation cruises are designed to be carefree, entertainment more than boredom, free of loneliness, and even festive. You can expect several separate lounges with entertainment, a poolside "Happy Hour" bar, slot machines, a gameroom with backgammon, chess and bridge; swimming pools, duty-free gift shop, beauty parlor, medical center, library, theatre, sauna and massage, gymnasium, and religious services. You can play table tennis, swim, shuffleboard, golf, trap shoot or just relax in the sun; or read, play Scrabble, or write a book; or do absolutely nothing!

Your cruise will be a feast—even a midnight snack in your cabin.

A cruise vacation is the very "new wave" of travel; more than 1.5 million passengers are sailing on 23 ships (one-third of the world's cruise fleet) from the Port of Miami. The chances are that this is where you will begin your Caribbean adventure.

I remember, years ago it was different; the ticket for Liverpool was bought, the letter of credit prepared (before the invention of credit cards), and I was ready for my first trip across the Atlantic. There was the ride down to the ocean steamer, getting on board, pushing amid the crowds of passengers and leave-taking friends. Not until the last, and perhaps, tearful leave-taking, and then the liner swings out into the harbor and you realize that you are finally launched on the great ocean—friends and home are left behind as well as the work-a-day world with all its daily pressures, schedules, rules and regulations.

One's first experience upon the great, awful ocean is never to be forgotten. My esteem for that great navigator, Christopher Columbus, has risen one hundred per cent since I have crossed it, to think of the amount of courage, strength of mind, and faith it must have required to sustain him in his venturesome voyage in the frail and imperfect crafts which those of his day must have been.

Two days out, and the great broad sweep of the Atlantic makes its influence felt upon all who are in any degree susceptible. The cruiseship seems to have a regular gigantic see-saw motion, very much like that of the toy ships that used to rise and fall on mimic waves, moved by clockwork, on clocks that used to be displayed in the store windows of jewellers and fancy dealers. Now the bows rise with a grand sweep,—now they sink again as the vessel plunges into an advancing wave,—up and down, up and down, and forging ahead to the never-ceasing, tremulous jar of the machinery. In the calmest weather there is always one vast swell, and when wind or storm prevails,

WELCOME ABOARD

it is both grand and terrible.

The great, vast ocean is something so much beyond anything I ever imagined; The same vast expanse of dark-blue rolling waves as far as the eye can reach; day after day, day after day, the great ship a mere speck, an atom in the vast circle of water, water everywhere. The very wind sounds differently than on land; a cheerful breeze is like the breath of a giant, and a playful wave will send a dozen hogsheads of water over the lofty bulwarks. If ever twelve days seem long to a man, it is during his first voyage across the Atlantic. Fourteen days in the Caribbean today seems too brief a period for words when you are enjoying the luxurious travel of a cruise holiday. It's an all-in-one travel adventure where you can be totally yourself and set your own pace. Every passenger is on board to relax, make friends, and have fun.

Life aboard a Caribbean ship will be special. From the bottle of champagne and basket of fruit you'll find in your well-appointed stateroom on sailing day to the warm smile of your cabin stewardess bringing you your pool robe, you'll be pampered from beginning to end.

A Caribbean vacation with the help of your travel agent and some good personal planning can be a wonderful experience. Study the ships, look at the costs (if you must), and figure out what ports you wish to visit. Prepare for the cruise by reading and organizing yourself.

Learn all you can about the cruise line; the ships in service and the various itineraries. Know about your ship: see how the ship is organized so you know how to go from deck to deck; know where your cabin location is; and know where things are, i.e., restaurants, casino, movies, pool and other important areas of the ship. Read about the islands and ports you're planning to visit. This book gives you some of the answers; the best way to know *all* of the answers is to take a cruise yourself. BON VOYAGE.

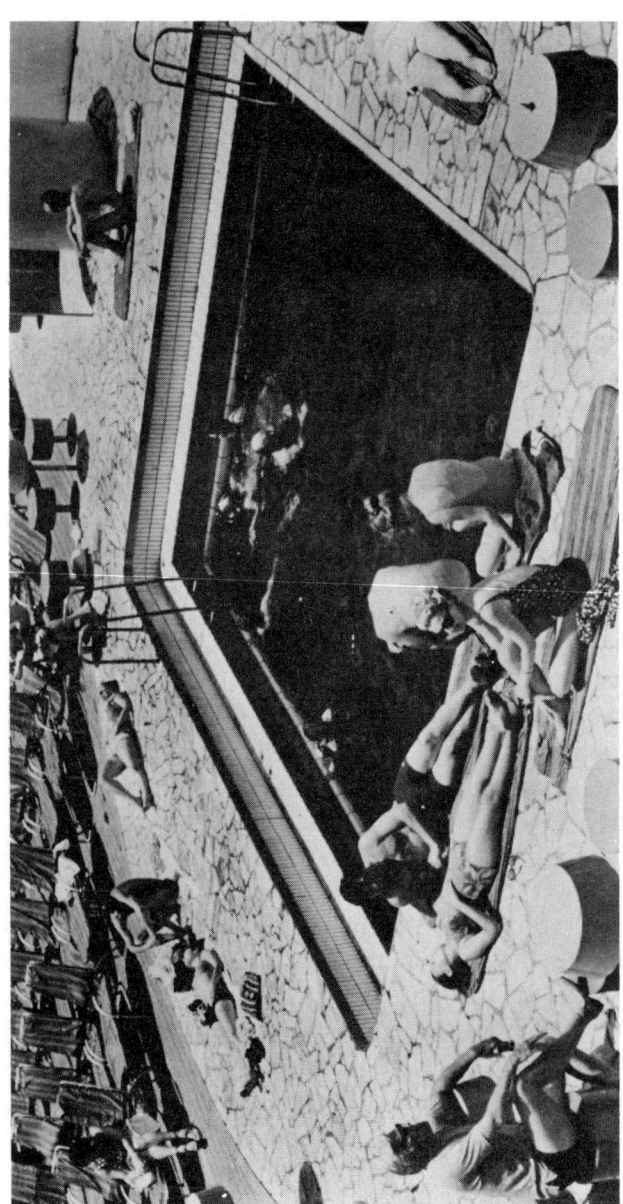

There's nothing quite like relaxing in the warm sun around a sparkling pool to make cruise passengers forget their worldly cares. The Promenade Deck of Holland America's SS STATENDAM offers bars, lounges and a Lido Terrace for a perfect blend of indoor and outdoor living at sea.

Chapter 2

HISTORY OF SEA TRAVEL

FIRST WORLD TRAVELERS

The impulse for the voyages and travels of history did not come without a beginning in antiquity: the Franciscan missionaries to Cathay, the seafarers and marching legions of imperial Rome, the geographers of Alexandria, and ultimately the philosophers of ancient Greece. All of these

True love at sea!

groups and others contributed to the travels of Henry the Navigator, Christopher Columbus and more recently, the voyage of Apollo II to the lunar surface. The great geographers of the ancient world were the Greeks. From their earliest times these people took an interest in their physical environment which was of a far higher order than that of the older worlds along the Nile. In Homer's day, as evidenced by the *Odyssey* and the legend of the Argonauts, the Hellenes sought to learn of the world around them, while their early philosphers tried to solve the problems of the earth's origin and its place in the celestial system.

The story of the great Deluge in the Bible affords us the first more or less authentic account of the building of the original ocean freighter or cruise ship. The specifications of that historic sea going menagerie are worthy of the study of every adult. The ark was to be constructed of gopher wood and divided into many rooms to accommodate all manner of living things. It was to be "pitched within and without with pitch," and this is the fashion after which it was built; in length 300 cubits, in breadth 50 cubits and in height 30 cubits. For easy reckoning, the Hebrew cubit has been accepted as 22 inches, which would indicate that Noah's ark was about 550 feet long with great width of beam and depth. Having no machinery, it was therefore of greater carrying capacity than many of our modern ocean cruise ships. The Ark was a three-decker, but was scantily furnished in the matter of windows and doors. The forty-day voyage established its sea-going efficiency. As the flood receded, instead of sinking to rest in the soft mud of some fertile valley near Bagdad, it went ashore on the top of Mount Ararat, some 17,112 feet above sea level; flood had covered the earth and destroyed every living thing except those with Noah in the Ark. When the waters subsided, the Ark occupied the highest dry dock in the history of maritime adventure.

HISTORY OF SEA TRAVEL

Since the days of Noah, there has been a slow evolution of water carriage by different types of raft and boats with poles, oars and sails for motor power. Tyre and Sidon, on the seacoast of Palestine, were the ports from which the trade of Western Asia sought an outlet to the cities of Europe on the Mediterranean Sea seven hundred years before Christ. It is claimed that Phoenician sailors rounded the Cape of Good Hope fully 2,000 years before Vasca de Gama sailed to India.

The story of the gradual development of transportation, including the great square-rigged ships that sailed every ocean before steam took the wind out of their sails, is one of fascinating adventure and romance.

The Renaissance (14th-17th centuries) was a period of

The 19th Century Coasting Schooner Isaac H. Evans

Santo Domingo's first tourist, Christopher Columbus still stands in Parque Colon (Columbus Park) in the Colonial section of town.
Santo Domingo Tourist Photo

HISTORY OF SEA TRAVEL 15

tremendous economic opportunity and overseas voyages played a large role. The wealth of new lands quickened the economic pace of Europe; the Portuguese and the Spaniards were the first nations to undertake these voyages. The epic figure of the renaissance was the noble and lofty-minded Prince Henry of Portugal, surnamed "the navigator"; he had the vision which launched Portugal on a century of discovery. By patient, methodical exploration, of each Portuguese expedition, Henry collected information to make the work of the next voyage easier. In Sagres, Portugal, Prince Henry and a group of cosmographers, astronomers and physicians worked with the captains and pilots. Several great improvements may be traced directly to the Sagres academy; the first in the art of chart-making, the second in the craft of shipbuilding, the third in the science of navigations, e.g., the compass and astrolabe which permitted the mariners to chart an accurate course on the oceans. Portuguese mariners explored the middle Atlantic and west coast of Africa. In the Atlantic they discovered and settled the Canaries and Maderira, and discovered the Azores. All mankind is indebted to maritime exploration of Prince Henry . . . "If Columbus gave Castile and Leon a new world in 1492, if da Gama reached India in 1498, if Dias rounded the Cape of Tempest in 1486 . . . their teacher and master was none the less than Henry the Navigator."

The second half of the fifteenth century saw more and more discovery; the quest for the Indies inspired men throughout Europe. In 1474 a young man of twenty-three living in Genoa began a very serious correspondence with Paolo Toscanelli, a celebrated Florentine scholar whose hobby was geography, about the possibility of reaching the Orient by a westward passage. Toscanelli, an exponent of the western route to the Indies, encouraged his correspondent Christopher Columbus to make such a voyage.

Columbus, an experienced navigator, believed the world to be a sphere and that he could sail across the Atlantic and reach the shores of Asia. Columbus took his scheme to Queen Isabella and shortly thereafter he set sail from Palos with three ships in August 1492. After a month of very fast sailing, signs of land became evident, and at two in the morning on October 12, Rodrigo de Triana, on lookout on the Pinta's forecastle, shouted, "Tierra! Tierra!"—the New World had been discovered. Christopher Columbus's magnificent plan of reaching the East Indies by sailing westward across the Atlantic was not realized in his lifetime. The Columbus voyage in search of another sea route to India paved the way for the Mayflower and the countless flotillas of sailing vessels that quickly established an ocean highway between Europe and America.

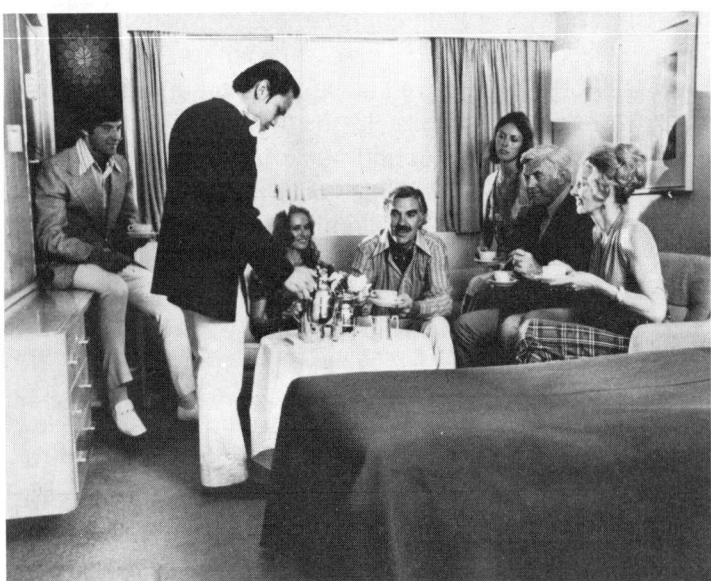

Enjoying afternoon coffee or cocktails with friends in one of the spacious cabins on Holland America's SS STATENDAM is all part of the fun of a cruise.

HISTORY OF SEA TRAVEL

STEAMSHIP AND TRANSATLANTIC PASSENGER SHIPS

The use of steam power in water travel was most successful and enduring. In 1807 Robert Fulton established a successful steamboat line on the Hudson River and by the 1820s steamboats traveled the Great Lakes and the great rivers of America.

THE SAVANNAH
First steamship to cross the Atlantic

From its earliest days the Savannah Steam Ship Company stated that the SAVANNAH's purpose was the establishment of a commercial transatlantic service by steam. She underwent her trials in late February 1819 and advertisements stated that she would sail from New York for Savannah on 27 March, with ample provision for passengers and cargo. In fact, she sailed on 28 March without either and took 222 hours to complete the voyage, of which 37½ were under steam. Three sailing packets left New York for Savannah on the same day as she did, and two of them got there before her.

Towards the middle of April the SAVANNAH proceeded from Savannah to Charleston, South Carolina, mainly in the hope that President James Monroe would agree to travel on her from Charleston to Savannah, but he could not be persuaded to do so. Instead, the ship carried seven farepaying passengers, which was one or two less than she had on the outward voyage. Upon return to Savannah it was decided to advertise a trip to New York during the early part of May, but only three people booked and the trip was cancelled.

The SAVANNAH was the first steamship to cross the Atlantic; she sailed on 20 May 1819 from Savannah, Georgia and her log records that she sighted Cork, Ireland on the 18th of June. The SAVANNAH was a hybrid, for sail and steam, 99 feet long with a 26-foot beam, and registered 350 tons; the paddle wheels were arranged with a series of joints, so that they could be easily detached and hoisted on board, in case of a storm. The eastward run was made mostly under sail; limited fuel permitted use of the engine for only 80 hours. The SAVANNAH had 32 staterooms, but the "terror of steam kept them unoccupied on her maiden voyage." The nautical feat was significant for American ingenuity seized upon the invention of Watt to improve transportation conditions in the new world.

The SAVANNAH proceeded to Elsinore, Stockholm, and St. Petersburg, where she remained a month. She returned to her home port without passengers or cargo, via Copenhagen and Arendal, Norway, and according to most reports the engines were not used until she arrived in the Savannah River. Shortly afterwards she proceeded to Washington to be sold, her engines were removed and she ran as a sailing packet between New York and Savannah until she was wrecked in 1821. Nineteen years elapsed between the SAVANNAH's transatlantic voyage and the first successful

HISTORY OF SEA TRAVEL

attempts by others to start a regular North Atlantic steamship service. In the long run these 1838 voyages were of much greater significance, but credit is, nevertheless, due to the SAVANNAH and her gallant captain and crew for their pioneer transatlantic steamship crossing.

Until the early 19th century, a ship had sailed only when her captain felt he had loaded enough cargo. By 1814, a group of merchants began to operate regular service between Albany and New York City. Each Saturday one packet sailed from each city. Three more lines appeared within a year.

Soon packet service was extended across the Atlantic. In 1818, there was the start of cargo service between New York City and Liverpool by Black Ball Line. In 1840, Samuel Cunard operated regular steamer service between Boston and Liverpool on the BRITANNIA. The 1,135 ton wooden paddle steamer BRITANNIA, commanded by Captain Henry Woodruff, undertook the first mail sailing on 4 July 1840 from Liverpool to Halifax and Boston, her 63 passengers including Samuel Cunard himself. Across the Atlantic, which steam had come to make the great ocean highway, conditions were such that millions needed little urging to take up their belongings and travel to the land of liberty and opportunity. Steamer travel boomed between 1846 and 1849. In the wake of the Irish potato famine, Britain ended its restrictions upon grain imports, thus stimulating the United States wheat exports. After gold was discovered in California (1848), there was more travel by sea to the West Coast.

While most of the early steamships were driven by paddle wheels, the LA PLATA (1852) was one of the last wooden Cunarders with steam heating, a cupola over the saloon to give increased height, two libraries and a comfortable smoking room. There were two funnels and two masts.

After the 1840s the screw propeller was available, the 1,794 ton iron screw ATLAS was completed in 1860 for Liverpool and the Mediterranean service but ran extensively on the North Atlantic. There were accommodations for between 40 and 70 cabin passengers and upwards to 500 steerage. Early ocean steamers also carried sails; steam engines were more reliable at the end of the century.

While sailing packets continued to carry passengers until the late 1860s, British and German companies soon dominated the transatlantic passenger trade. Inexpensive steerage accommodations in the swift steamships encouraged hundreds of thousands of people to immigrate to the shores of America. Sixty days in a sailing ship was to be two weeks in a steamer from England to America.

PS GLENMORE (1895) in her first season

In the last part of the nineteenth century, young Americans, almost unnoticed, were beginning to travel to Europe. These new ocean travellers were not the elite of society, but ordinary people of modest means wanting to see London and Paris, to visit Westminster or Notre Dame,

HISTORY OF SEA TRAVEL 21

RSM TITANIC leaving Southampton April 1912

and to know the culture of the Italians and Germans. It was time when Americans in mass were beginning to travel throughout Europe. The luxury ocean liners required steerage or third class return passengers to fill available quarters. As more and more people reported their inexpensive trips to Europe (probably half the cost of first-class travel), others would travel. This was a time in America when the economy was growing and people could afford to travel modestly.

By international law, any vessel with space for more than 12 passengers is classified as a passenger ship, including freighters with passenger cabins to ocean liners built for speed and luxury. Traditionally, ocean liners are primarily passenger carriers, though they carry mail and some high-value cargo. The most outstanding ocean liner at the end of the 18th century was the first OCEANIC, the prototype of six sister ships of White Star Line. With a large grand ballroom having huge chandeliers (candle lit) and fireplaces, the OCEANIC passengers enjoyed more comforts and services (water taps, steam heat, and room services) than did any other previous transatlantic traveler.

The greatest ocean liner was the MAURETANIA, burning 1,000 tons of coal a day for her turbines of 68,000 horsepower. MAURETANIA and her sister ship, the LUSITANIA, were launched in 1907. The MAURETANIA trial runs were 26 knots; in later years with oil burner and mechanical improvements she had an average speed better than 27 knots. For more than a year the LUSITANIA and MAURETANIA took turns trying to beat each other's records. Both were then fitted with propellers of improved design, the MAURETANIA subsequently proving herself to be slightly faster. In 1909-11 she averaged well over 25 knots in each direction during the course of 44 round voyages. For almost 22 years she remained the fastest liner afloat. She was a liner that introduced elevators, marble statues, private baths, genuine antique furniture and original decorative oil paintings. The MAURETANIA was a lady of elegance and luxurious with beautiful woodwork in her public rooms and corridors and oak panels in her dining saloon. The MAURETANIA could carry 2,165 passengers and a crew of 938. She was always a lovely liner with her four enormous black-topped red funnels. After 28 years of service as a passenger liner, hospital ship and American troop transport, the MAURETANIA as the "White Queen" made her last voyage on the 2nd of July 1935. She was a ship that gained the affection of those who knew her.

1907 LUSITANIA 31,500 tons
Recaptured the 'Blue Riband' for Britain. In 1915 torpedoed and sunk with loss of 1,198 lives. Sister ship of the even more famous MAURETANIA.

HISTORY OF SEA TRAVEL

1914 AQUITANIA 45,647 tons
A larger but slower version of the LUSITANIA. In service until 1949 and crossed the Atlantic nearly 600 times.

The travel business was on the move in the 19th century; anyone with 100 dollars could purchase round trips to Europe. Americans, whose parents had stood at the steerage rail were traveling on the BERENGARIA, AQUITANIA, MAURETANIA, CONTE DI SAVOIA, and ILE DE FRANCE. By June 1929, the BREMEN, a passenger ship with capabilities of a destroyer, had completed her ocean voyage from Cherbourg to Ambrose Light ship in four days, 17 hours, 42 minutes (27.83 knots)—a new transatlantic speed record.

By 1935 there was a gigantic superliner NORMANDIE, a ship without equal, had grace and beauty (with a length of 1,027 feet). The NORMANDIE, 80,000 gross tons with a clipper-type bow, reigned unchallenged on the North Atlantic until Cunard placed the gallant QUEEN MARY in service.

Ocean travel was not confined to the North Atlantic, trans-Pacific passenger liner service from West Coast ports had its beginning in 1867 when the Pacific Mail established side-wheel steamers from San Francisco. The new transcontinental railway considerably helped the West Coast travel business and led to the establishment of mail steamer service between San Francisco and Australia. By 1882, Oceanic Steamship Company operated MARIPOSA and ALAMEDA between San Francisco and Honolulu. By the 1900s there were several lines serving the Pacific Coast and this growth has continued today. The Pacific liners have never attained the size and speed of the highest class of the North Atlantic ocean liners, but they are important in the world's sea lanes. Certainly, Pacific steamers have come a long way from the creaking wooden paddle-wheelers of the 19th century Pacific Mail Line.

Cruising through a calm blue sea in the West Indies and showing off her Promenade Deck is Holland America's 24,500-ton SS STATENDAM.

The largest and fastest ocean liners were built primarily for passenger travel between the United States and Europe. Smaller liners transverse other routes; many specialize in vacation cruises. By the 1970s the world's largest liners were: France's FRANCE (66,348 gross tons, 1,035 feet long, and 111 feet in beam), and Britain's QUEEN ELIZABETH 2 (65,863 gross tons, 963 feet long, 105 feet in beam), used in North Atlantic only during the peak tourist seasons and used in cooler-months as vacation ships in the Caribbean cruise service. The FRANCE relied on spaciousness, elegance, fine food and gracious service to win her share of trans-Atlantic passengers. The UNITED

HISTORY OF SEA TRAVEL

LIST OF TRANSATLANTIC PASSENGER SAILINGS
Eastbound from New York, July 1929[†]

DATE	STEAMER	LINE	DESTINATION
July 1	France	French	Plymouth, Havre
July 2	California	Anchor	Mediterranean Cruise
July 2	Edison	National Greek	Patras, Piraeus, Jaffa, Beyrout
July 2	Laconia	Cunard	Cobh (Queenstown), Liverpool
July 2	Providence	Fabre	Ponta Delgada, Lisbon, Naples, Palermo, Piraeus, Beirut, Malta, Marseilles
July 3	Cameronia	Anchor	Londonderry, Glasgow
July 3	Carmania	Cunard	Plymouth, Havre, London
July 3	Columbus	North German Lloyd	Plymouth, Cherbourg, Bremen
July 3	Estonia	Baltic America	Copenhagen, Danzig, Gdynia
July 3	Homeric	White Star	Cherbourg, Southampton
July 3	Kungsholm	Swedish American	Gothenburg
July 3	Pres. Harding	United States	Plymouth, Cherbourg, Bremen
July 4	De Grasse	French	Havre
July 4	Milwaukee	Hamburg-American	Galway, Cherbourg, Hamburg
July 4	Muenchen	North German Lloyd	Southampton, Boulogne, Bremen
July 4	Republic	United States	Cobh (Queenstown), Plymouth, Cherbourg, Bremen
July 6	Albertic	White Star	Queenstown, Liverpool
July 6	Arabic	Red Star	Plymouth, Cherbourg, Antwerp
July 6	Augustus	Navigazione Gen. Italiana	Gibraltar, Naples, Genoa
July 6	Deutschland	Hamburg-American	Christiansand, Oslo, Copenhagen
July 6	Ild de France	French	Plymouth, Havre
July 6	Minnewaska	Atlantic Transport	Cherbourg, London
July 6	Stavangerfjord	Norwegian America	Bergen, Stavanger, Kristianssand, Oslo
July 6	Veendam	Holland-America	Plymouth, Boulogne-Sur-Mer, Rotterdam
July 7	Aquitania	Cunard	Cherbourg, Southampton

[†] *Typical list of sailings*

STATES was the fastest ocean liner in the world; she set both transatlantic speed records in 1952 (3 days, 10 hours, 40 minutes eastbound; 3 days, 12 hours, 12 minutes westbound). The record-holding UNITED STATES (53,330 gross tons, 990 feet long, and 101½ feet in beam) could accommodate 2,000 passengers and her top speed exceeded 40 knots.

An aerial view of the SS ROTTERDAM, the 38,000-ton, 748 foot-long world cruise liner of Holland America Cruises.

Transatlantic passenger travel includes fast elevators, more deck space, full-size tennis courts, and one class service, but all of this had declined since the Second World War. Cruise passenger service in 1980 is a growing travel business with more than two million passengers on Caribbean cruise ships. By 1990, the Port of Miami alone is preparing to serve four million passengers.

Chapter 3

MODERN CRUISE TRAVEL

World-wide steamship services continue and are an important part of the ocean travel. Trans-Atlantic travel to Ireland, France, England and the rest of Europe from the U. S. (New York) and Canada (Montreal) can be found on these ships: the KUNGSHOLM (Flagship), STEFAN BATORY (Polish Ocean), ROYAL VIKING STAR (Royal Viking), ALEXANDER PUSHKIN (Baltic) and QUEEN ELIZABETH 2 (Cunard).

Intimacy is the byword on Costa Cruise's 12,000 ton WORLD RENAISSANCE where a crew of 240 serves 400 passengers in 215 staterooms. The RENAISSANCE sails year round in a program of 10 and 11 day cruises from Miami through the Caribbean to South America and the Panama Canal. Fly/Cruise packages are available from major cities.

The 25,300-ton SS DORIC on a 7-day "Linger Linger" cruise which docks on Hamilton's Front Street, the heart of Bermuda, for the entire stay from Monday to Thursday. The ship, which many consider to be "The Best to Bermuda" is convenient to everything the fabulous island has to offer, including golf and tennis that can be reserved aboard.   *Home Line Photo.*

The Pacific cruises include Honolulu, Yokohama, Hong Kong, Bali, Cairns, Sydney, Picton, Wellington, Auckland, Papeetee Morrea and return to San Francisco. Trans-Pacific travel for 70 days on CIRCLE PACIFIC (Royal Viking Line) starts at $9,000. A 45-day cruise from Los Angeles to the same places can cost $13,000 for first class travel on the SOUTH SEAS (Royal Viking Line); this, of course, would have superb international cuisine and be a deluxe trip. Ships like SANTA MARIANA and SANTA MERCEDES leave from the west coast ports to Manzanillo, Balboa, Panama Canal (transit), Cartagena, Puerto Cabello, La Guaira, Rio de Janeiro, Sanatos, Parangua/ Rio Grande (optional), Buenos Aires, Strait of Magellan, Valparaiso, Callao, Guayaquil, Buenaventura. Passengers can board vessel at Vancouver or Tacoma. Others leave from east coast ports to South America.

MODERN CRUISE TRAVEL

Not all ships leave from America; there are many outstanding cruises from Europe to the Orient, Europe to Australasia, and Europe to Africa, and these lists can be found in the *Official Steamship Guide*. And, there is "Round-the-World" steamship travel, such as the QUEEN ELIZABETH 2 which begins in Port Everglades, Barbados, Caracas, Salvador, Rio de Janeiro, Montevideo, Tristan da Cunha, Cape Town, Durban, Seychelles (Mahe), Bombay, Colombo, Singapore, Manila, Hong Kong, Kagoshima, Yokohama, Honolulu, Los Angeles, Acapulco, Panama Canal, Cristobal, Caracas, and ends in Port Everglades. The world of steamship travel also includes the local steamboats and ferry services, European river and canal cruises, New England and Virgin Island (Caribbean) schooner cruises, and passenger/freighter travel. A cruise to Martinique, steamship to Cartagena, a barque bound for Barbados, a freighter to Istanbul, ferry to Juneau, or a liner to Bergen are examples of modern cruises. Cruise travel is steaming ahead at full speed after years of concern by steamship lines. Many cruise liners have been sold out six months ahead of their sailings.

SEA TERMS

You should be aware of some of the common nautical terminology in the steamship industry. These terms will help you to investigate the facilities and to know the *bow* from the *stern* of a cruise ship. The vessel you will be boarding is a *ship*, not a boat. The floor on a ship is a *deck;* the stairs are *ladders*, and ladders take you *topside* or *below*. The wall of a ship is the *bulkhead*, and the ceiling is the *overhead*. When you look to the front of the ship you are looking to the *bow;* your right side is *starboard*, your left is *port;* and when you look to the rear, you look *aft* to **stern**. Cruise travel is not in miles-per-hour, but *knots*. **Knots** means nautical miles per hour. A nautical mile is roughly one-seventh longer than a land mile. The length of a nautical mile is 6,080 feet. *Embarkation* means the process of boarding a ship to begin the cruise, and *debarkation* is the process of leaving the ship from voyage. The following list includes a brief glossary of sea terms.

A means a superior class under which boats are registered at Lloyds.

ABOARD means same as on board and used instead of on or in a boat or ship.

ABOUT means when the ship turns around.

ABOVE BOARD means deck above the water line.

AFFINITY CHARTER means the rental of an airplane, train, steamship, bus or sightseeing vehicle on an exclusive basis for the carriage of a common interest group (affinity) with the renter paying a flat over-all rental for the entire vehicle.

AFT means near, toward or in the stern (rear) of a vessel.

AIR-SEA means a cruise or travel program in which one or more transportation legs are provided by air and one or more by sea, including hotel arrangements.

ALLEYWAY means a passageway of the ship.

AMIDSHIPS (or Midships) means in or toward the middle of a vessel, between bow and stern.

ASHORE means on the ground after or before the ship sails.

AVAILABILITY means a conditional status, e.g., space available.

BAGGAGE ALLOWANCE means the volume or weight of baggage that may be carried by a passenger without an additional charge.

BAGGAGE CHECK means stub or claim receipt with a baggage identification number.

BAREBOAT CHARTER means a rental yacht without crew or supplies.

BEAM means the breadth of a vessel at its widest point.

BERTH means a bunk (bed) in a cabin, or the ship's place at anchor or dock.

BOARD means to go aboard or on the ship.

BOARDING PASS means printed pass issued at the check-in or boarding counter when your ticket coupon is taken, giving your flight and seat number.

BOLLARD means an upright metal post on a wharf to which a ship's mooring line may be secured.

MODERN CRUISE TRAVEL 31

BOW means the forward (front) part of a vessel.

BOW THRUSTER means an underwater extension to the bow of a ship designed to reduce pitch.

BREAKWATER means a structure for breaking the force of waves so as to protect a harbor.

BRIDGE means the ship's command center.

BULKHEAD means any of the partition walls used to separate various interior areas of a ship such as rooms, holds, etc.

CHART means a nautical map of seas.

COMPANIONWAY means a set of steps leading from the deck to a cabin or saloon below; also the space occupied by these steps.

COMPASS means the instrument which determines direction.

DEBARK means the abbreviation of disembark which means to land, to go ashore from a ship.

DISEMBARK means to land; to put or to go ashore from a ship.

DOCK means the water area occupied by a ship alongside a wharf. A wharf, often called a dock in common usage, is the structure usually supported upon piling to which the ship's lines are made fast and upon which cargoes are deposited.

DOCKAGE means the charge assessed a vessel for berthing at a wharf, pier or bulkhead. The charge varies with the size of the vessel.

DRAFT (or Draught) means the depth of water a ship draws.

EMBARK means to go aboard a ship to begin a journey.

ESCROW ACCOUNTS means funds placed in the custody of licensed financial institutions for safe-keeping; inclusive tour charter operators maintain escrow accounts.

EXCESS BAGGAGE means baggage that is over free per-passenger allowance, in bulk or weight, and subject to a surcharge by item or weight.

FAIR WIND means a wind blowing in the same direction the ship is traveling.

FATHOM means a measure of length, containing six feet, used chiefly in measuring cordage, cable, and depth of water by soundings.

FORE (Forward) means in or towards the bow (front) of a vessel.

FREEPORT means a restricted zone at a seaport, where duty-free goods are sold.

GALLEY means a ship's kitchen.

GANGWAY means the aperture in a ship's side for the accommodations of persons entering and leaving.

GATE means the airport terminal area where you can check in (if you have not checked in at the front ticket counter), board and deplane.

GROSS REGISTER TON means this is a measure, not of weight, but of the cubical content of the enclosed spaces on a ship, and is the measurement used in giving the size of passenger vessels. 100 cubic feet is equal to one gross register ton.

HELM means a generic term for a ship's steering apparatus.

HOLD means interior of a vessel below decks where cargo is stored.

HOUSE FLAG means the official flag of a shipping line. Usually flown by their vessels when in port and over offices and transit sheds used by them.

HULL means the body or frame of a ship.

KEEL means the chief and lowest support of a vessel. The frame extending along the longitudinal center of the bottom of a ship from bow to stern.

KNOT means a unit of speed, equivalent to one nautical mile (6,080 feet) per hour.

LASH means to bind or tie something with ropes.

LATITUDE means the distance north or south of the equator.

LEE. LEEWARD means the direction away from the wind.

LOG means a daily record of a ship's speed, progress. Also, a device for measuring the speed of a ship.

LONGITUDE means the distance east or west expressed in degrees of the First Meridian.

MANIFEST means a list of the ship's passengers and cargo which must be supplied in every foreign port.

NAUTICAL MILE means a nautical mile is 6,080 feet, compared to a land, or "statute" mile, which is only 5,280 feet.

PACKET means a small mail boat.

PASSPORT means an official government document that proves identity and citizenship of an individual and gives permission to travel abroad.

PIER means a structure built out into the water for use as landing places for vessels.

PORT means the left side of a ship, looking forward.

PORTHOLE means an opening in a ship's side (window).

PROW means the bow of the ship above water.

REGISTRY means the country in which the ship is registered (official nationality of the ship).

RESPONSIBILITY CLAUSE means a portion of a tour brochure which states conditions under which a tour is sold.

MODERN CRUISE TRAVEL 33

SALOON means the main lounge on a passenger ship.

SINGLE PLANE SERVICE means the same as DIRECT FLIGHT.

SINGLE SUPPLEMENT means an additional charge for single accommodations on a tour. (Most brochure prices are for double occupancy.)

STABILIZER means a retractable fin extended from either side of the ship for smoother sailing.

STARBOARD means the right side of a ship looking forward.

STERN means the after or rear end of a ship.

STOPOVER means a stop along the route of a journey (usually 24 hours or more).

STOWAWAY means an illegal passenger.

THROUGH CHECKING means baggage checked through from your departure city to your final destination.

TOUR means a preplanned program of travel employing prepaid reservations of at least one night's hotel accommodations, one sightseeing tour and/or a transfer from airport to hotel, and/or a breakfast.

TOUR OPERATOR means a company that puts together tour packages and sells them either wholesale to a travel agent or directly to the public.

TRAMP SHIP means a cargo ship operating under no regular schedule and connected with no particular trade route. The term is often misconstrued to mean an old ship but it can be a new ship and the terminology has nothing to do with the age or condition of the ship.

UPGRADE means to be changed from a lower class of service or accommodation to a highter one.

VISA means official document issued through the government embassy or consulate of any foreign country, giving a non-citizen authorization to travel and/or stay in that country.

VOUCHER means a document issued by your travel agent or airlines, stating that you have paid for and are entitled to certain accommodations or services. Vouchers are issued for hotels, car rentals, sightseeing trips and other pre-paid vacation features.

WAITLIST means a list of passengers who are waiting for cancellations so that they may be accommodated on a flight or tour that is sold out.

WAKE means the ship's sea tracks.

WEIGH means to lift the anchor from the bottom of the sea.

WEIGH ANCHOR means to raise the anchor.

STEAMSHIP ABBREVIATIONS

These are abbreviations frequently used by the steamship lines. The name of an ocean liner is generally prefixed with several initial letters (SS or MV). A list of ship prefixes, berthing, and ticketing abbreviations follows:

Bibby	"L" Shaped Cabin with porthole
Bth.	With Bath
Conf.	Confirmed
Dbl.	Double Cabin (Two beds or berths)
D/R	Deposit Receipt
E/B	Eastbound
F.	First Class
Guar.	Guarantee
I/S	Inside Cabin
K.I.P. or K.A.I.P.	Keep Alone if Possible
M/M	Mr. & Mrs.
MS.	Motor Ship
MV	Motor Vessel
NRS	No Rate Specified
Opt.	Option
O/S	Outside Cabin
O/W	One Way
Pos.	Positive
P.T.	Port Tax
Q.S.S.	Quadruple Screw Steamship
R.M.S.	Royal Mailship
R/T	Round Trip
SS	Steamship
S & T	With Shower and Toilet
TBA	To Be Assigned (Advised)
Tkt.	Ticket
T, Toil.	With Toilet
Trip.	Triple Cabin (Three beds or berths)
TS	Turbine Ship

MODERN CRUISE TRAVEL 35

TSS .... Turbine Steamship
TV .... Turbo-Vessel
Tour. .... Tourist Class
W/B .... Westbound
W/C Fac. .... Without Facilities
W/Fac. .... With Facilities
W/Show .... With Private Shower
W.L. .... Wait List

AQUARIUS — *Hellenic Mediterranean Lines*

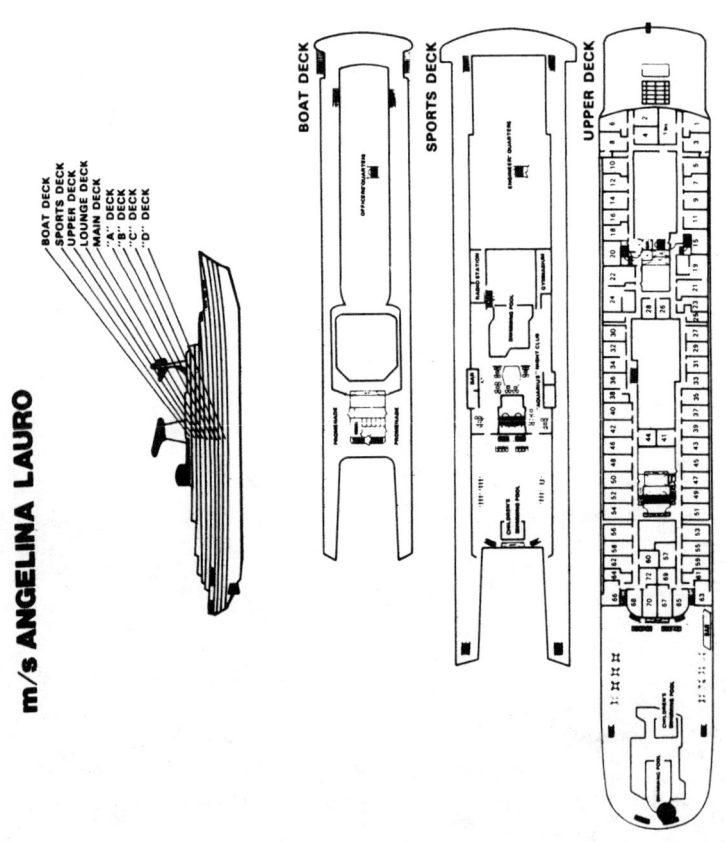

MODERN CRUISE TRAVEL

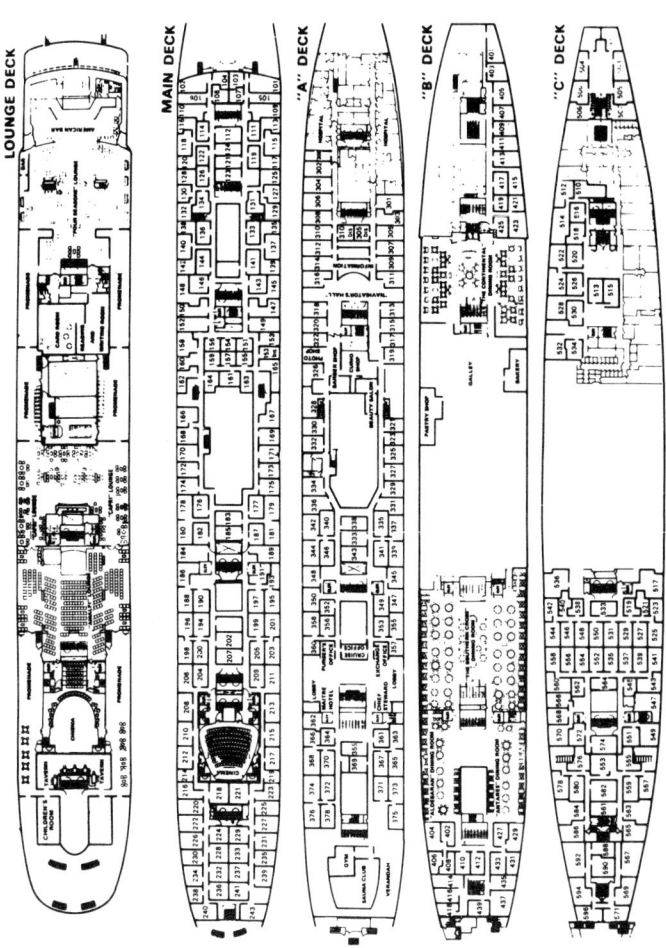

SELECTING A CRUISE

The experienced cruise vacationer will discriminate in the selection of ships. No two ships are the same. Cruise companies want first-time passengers but they want you to come back. The weekend cruise from Miami to Nassau is very different from a week-long Caribbean cruise trip, and so is the more comprehensive around-the-world cruise in 87 days, 19 countries, 22 ports from Port Everglades to Oranjestad, Cartagena, Cristobal, Balboa, Acapulco, Los Angeles, Bombay, Djibouti, Suez, Alexandria, Haifa, Istanbul, Yalta, Odessa, Piraeus, Naples, Villefranche, Lisbon, and back to Port Everglades, four months later.

When returning from a cruise, you say a number of things about your voyage, for example:

"Food is good but commercial, portions small, and there are no midnight buffets; coffee shop is available for purchasing snacks."

"Lower decks provide best ride but lesser views; other decks have views but experience more motion and sometimes noise, expecially near disco."

"Lido deck and pool are usually busy with breakfast, lunch and lounging; two dining rooms easily hold full complement of passengers, and the menus are identical in both dining rooms and non-listed items often are available."

"Ship is smooth riding, beautifully decorated in public rooms, has excellent children's play area, fine plumbing, large baths; deluxe cabins and suites have Italian tile floors. Cuisine is excellent and varied, international, features daily Lido Deck lunch buffet

MODERN CRUISE TRAVEL 39

Eating on board a luxury cruise ship is an exciting time. Transportation has combined with the skill of the world's menus that boggle the imagination and tempt the palate. Foods you never attempt to prepare at home and which are much too expensive to order in a restaurant appear on nearly every bill of fare. When and where else can you order two helpings of caviar? Where else will you be faced with the tough choice of Salsiccia di Francoforte, Prosciuttella di Napoli or Cosciotto d'agnello, Menta at the same meal?

What do you suppose they're serving tonight? Chicken Cordon Bleu? Shrimp Scampi? Souffle Grand Marnier au Froid?

and usual midnight buffet."

"Top deck lounge is done in beautiful Scandinavian modern style and a favorite gathering place. Expensive, good for sophisticated travelers looking for something different."

"Short cruises are a bit hectic with their multiple stops and short stay in Istanbul, and some of the offbeat islands have relatively little interest for shore excursions."

"All cabins have lower beds and insides are larger than outsides. All cabins have ample closets but those above and below lounges may be noisy."

"Staff comes from 30 nationalities and service can range from excellent on down, depending on language and other uncertainties."

"Cabins are roomy, well appointed, but best in higher priced upper decks; lower-rated passengers must dine in former tourist class dining room."

"The main drawback is dark decor and somewhat uncomfortable furnishings, narrow twin beds in staterooms."

"Facilities include ample deck space, adequate pool, dignified widely varied cabins with wood paneling, all well appointed. The public areas are spacious and well decorated. The ship features 24-hour cabin service."

"Linens are not always in the best condition and

MODERN CRUISE TRAVEL

On board ship relaxing. *Royal Viking Line Photo*

towels were inclined to be skimpy. Shore programs and entertainment were on the mediocre side."

"All accommodations have air conditioning, 2-channel stereo, phones, and suites have TV."

Steamship travel literature is attractive, colorful, hyperdescriptive and can be misleading. Cruise brochures sell "Ship Board Excitement." It is important not to mis-read the materials, including cancellations and refunds information. A cruise brochure typically contains a deck plan in order to designate the exact location of any given cabin on the ship. The cabins on the lower decks are the cabins which are generally economy. The higher up on the ship a passenger goes for his accommodation the higher the cost.

Rates: ss ROTTERDAM
Fall Entertainment Festival at Sea

Category	DESCRIPTION	U.S. $ PER PERSON FALL (Sept. 2 thru Nov. 4)
A	OUTSIDE DOUBLE CABINS DELUXE: Extra large, extra comfortable cabins with sitting room alcove, separate wardrobe room. Possibly the most deluxe cabins on any cruise ship anywhere.	$820
B	OUTSIDE DOUBLE ONE ROOM SUITES: Luxurious staterooms with twin beds and sitting area.	770
C	OUTSIDE DOUBLE ROOMS: Beautiful staterooms with twin beds and space for entertaining.	750
D	OUTSIDE DOUBLE ROOMS: Beautiful staterooms with twin beds and space for entertaining.	715
E	OUTSIDE DOUBLE ROOMS: Beautiful staterooms with twin beds and space for entertaining.	690
F	OUTSIDE DOUBLE ROOMS: Staterooms with twin beds.	670
G	INSIDE DOUBLE ROOMS: Comfortable rooms with twin lower beds.	635
H	INSIDE DOUBLE ROOMS: Comfortable rooms with twin lower beds.	605
I	ECONOMY OUTSIDE DOUBLE ROOMS: Upper and lower beds, with sea view.	570
J	ECONOMY INSIDE DOUBLE ROOMS: Upper and lower beds.	545
K	ECONOMY INSIDE DOUBLE ROOMS: Upper and lower beds.	510
L	ECONOMY INSIDE DOUBLE ROOMS: Upper and lower beds.	460
M*	OUTSIDE SINGLE ROOMS: Charming sea view staterooms with lower bed.	820 & 745
N*	INSIDE SINGLE ROOMS: Lower bed.	675 & 645

*Prices vary according to cabin number.

Rates: ss STATENDAM
Fall Entertainment Festival at Sea

Category	DESCRIPTION	U.S. $ PER PERSON FALL (Sept. 2 thru Nov. 11)
A	DELUXE OUTSIDE DOUBLE ONE-ROOM SUITES: Elegant, extra large, extra comfortable bedrooms with sitting room alcove, bath and shower.	$815
B	OUTSIDE DOUBLE DELUXE ROOMS: Luxurious extra-large rooms with twin beds, vanity and closets, full bathroom; table and chairs allow you to entertain friends in comfort.	795
C	LUXURY OUTSIDE DOUBLE ROOMS: Superb, spacious staterooms with twin beds. Private shower and bath.	745
D	LUXURY OUTSIDE DOUBLE ROOMS: Superb, spacious staterooms with twin beds. Shower and/or bath.	725
E	LUXURY OUTSIDE DOUBLE ROOMS: Superb, spacious staterooms with twin beds and shower.	700
F	SUPERIOR OUTSIDE DOUBLE ROOMS: Luxurious staterooms with twin beds, shower and/or bath, and space for entertaining.	675
G	OUTSIDE DOUBLE ROOMS: Luxurious staterooms with twin beds, shower and/or bath, and space for entertaining.	655
H	OUTSIDE DOUBLE ROOMS: Sofa converts to comfortable double bed.	640
I	INSIDE DOUBLE ROOMS: Twin beds, shower and/or bath.	625
J	ECONOMY OUTSIDE DOUBLE ROOMS: Two-porthole rooms with upper and lower beds, shower and/or bath.	615
K	INSIDE DOUBLE ROOMS: Sofa converts to double bed; shower.	580
L	ECONOMY INSIDE DOUBLE ROOMS: Upper and lower beds, shower.	550
M	ECONOMY INSIDE DOUBLE ROOMS: Upper and lower beds, shower.	510
N	ECONOMY INSIDE DOUBLE ROOMS: Upper and lower beds, shower.	460
O*	OUTSIDE SINGLE ROOMS: Two-porthole rooms with lower bed, shower and/or bath.	820 & 745
P*	INSIDE SINGLE ROOMS: Lower bed, shower.	675 & 645

*Prices vary according to cabin number.

MODERN CRUISE TRAVEL 43

Though the cabins on the upper decks are the highest in cost, they are not always the ones with the smoothest ride. Due to the stabilizing unit that most ships have in their hull, the cabins located on the lower decks give the smoothest ride. Cabins can be provided on an inside or an outside basis.

Brochures give essentially general information on embarkation, travel documents, sightseeing tours, and other passage contract information. See your travel agent for more details.

The Atlantic Coast stretches for miles of pure white sand and crystal sea for cruise line passengers. Willie Alleyne Assoc. Photo Ltd., Bridgetown, Barbados, W.I.

CRUISE COMFORT — SPACE PER PASSENGER

Is it better to be on a big cruise ship or a small one? The best size is a matter of choice. There are certain advantages on a world luxury liner like the SS NORWAY (66,348 gross registered tons) but smaller ships have the ability to visit unique areas. How much space per passenger is the question? For example, the BOHEME will carry about 500 passengers but the gross registered tons (GRT) is 11,000, the ship offers 22 GRT per passenger (See Space Per Passenger Chart), whereas the BRITANIS has 24,350 GRT and with 1200 passengers its space index is only 20.3. The higher GRT Index number indicates more space per passenger.

Big ships have more to offer, i.e., more public rooms (night clubs, casinos, shops, pools and other special feature rooms). Smaller ships are more "intimate" and offer less entertainment. Ships with 25,000 or more GRT are considered big, and under 10,000 GRT is small. In terms of passengers, over 900 passengers is big, and under 400 capacity is small.

A bigger ship is better when it comes to ride. If you are sensitive to motion, remember that bigger ships roll and pitch less than smaller ones in the same weather. Seasickness can be aggravated by any feeling of being "closed in"; the huge public rooms of bigger ships counteract this factor.

Size does have its drawbacks. There are many small ports the giants just can't reach because they're too big. At some very popular larger ports, the big ships have to anchor (deep water berth) out in the harbor, putting passengers ashore in tenders.

Tendering is a slow process, and if there are any snags it can take an hour or more to get ashore. The SS NORWAY carries three super-tenders holding 350 passengers each

MODERN CRUISE TRAVEL

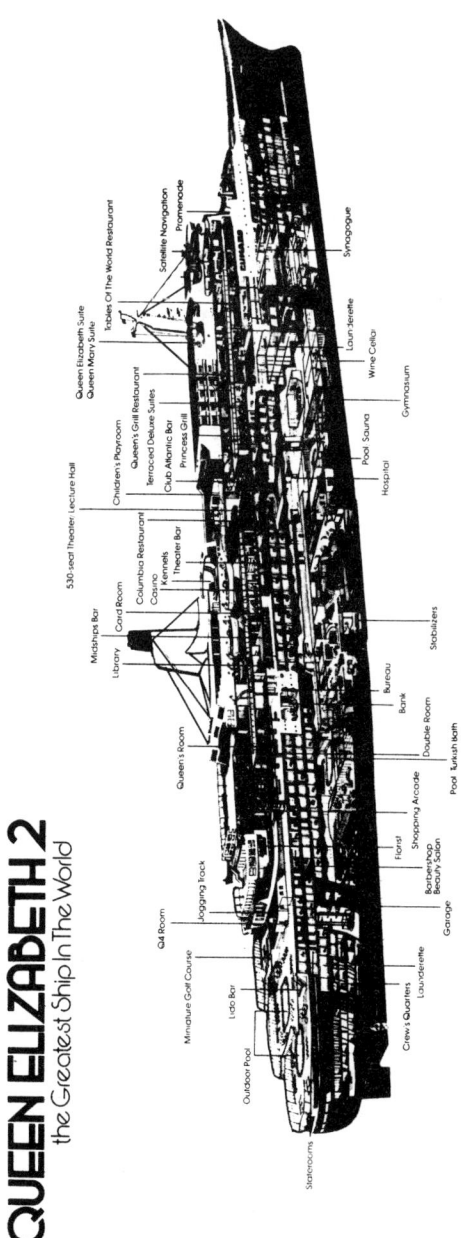

Two roundtrips of each tender will completely unload the 2,000-passenger ship in the Out Island, St. Thomas, and San Juan stops.

CARIBBEAN SPACE PER PASSENGER INDEX CHART

SHIP	GRT[1]	Passengers	Space Index[2]
AMERIKANIS	19,377	650	29.8
AQUARIUS	4,800	297	16.2
BOHEME	11,000	500	22
BRITANIS	24,351	1,200	20.3
CARIBE	11,000	480	22.9
CARLA C	20,477	748	27.4
CARNIVALE	27,250	950	28.7
CUNARD COUNTESS	17,495	750	23.3
CUNARD PRINCESS	17,495	750	23.3
DANAE	15,560	465	33.5
DORIC	25,300	720	35.1
FAIRSEA	25,000	830	30.1
FAIRWIND	25,000	830	30.1
FESTIVALE	38,175	1,144	33.4
GOLDEN ODYSSEY	10,500	460	22.8
ISLAND PRINCESS	20,000	622	32.2
KAZAKHSTAN	16,600	330	50.3
MARDI GRAS	27,250	906	30.1
MERMOZ	13,800	550	25.1
NORDIC PRINCE	23,000	1,040	22.1
NORWAY	66,348	2,000	33.2
OCEANIC	39,241	1,034	38
ODESSA	14,000	470	29.8
PACIFIC PRINCESS	20,000	622	32.2
QUEEN ELIZABETH 2	67,139	1,640	40.9
ROTTERDAM	38,000	1,050	36.2

[1] GRT (Gross Registered Tons) — a measure of space, not weight. One GRT equals 100 cubic feet of enclosed space. Passengers capacities are based on two persons per double cabin (excluding third and fourth beds).

[2] SPACE INDEX is the GRT/passenger ratio — an approximate guide to spaciousness that has some effect on passenger comfort. The higher the index, the more spacious.

MODERN CRUISE TRAVEL

SHIP	GRT	Passengers	Space Index
ROYAL VIKING SEA	22,000	500	44
ROYAL VIKING SKY	22,000	500	44
ROYAL VIKING STAR	22,000	500	44
SKYWARD	16,250	724	22.4
SONG OF NORWAY	23,005	1,040	22.1
SOUTHWARD	17,000	738	23
STARWARD	15,500	742	20.9
STATENDAM	24,500	800	30.6
STELLA MARIS	4,000	212	18.9
STELLA OCEANIS	6,000	318	18.9
STELLA SOLARIS	18,000	650	27.7
SUN PRINCESS	17,000	700	24.3
SUN VIKING	18,500	750	24.7
VEENDAM	23,500	666	35.3
VERACRUZ	10,595	737	14.8
VICTORIA	14,917	500	29.8
VISTAFJORD	25,000	660	37.9
VOLENDAM	23,500	679	34.6
WORLD RENAISSANCE	12,000	528	22.7

Built in West Germany in 1968, the MS CARIBE displaces 11,000 gross tons, is 441 feet long, 70 feet wide midships and can carry 480 passengers with a cruising speed of 20 knots. The GRT/passenger space index is 22.9.

48 BON VOYAGE

AIR/SEA PACKAGES

For years the airlines and shiplines were seeking the same passengers traveling the oceans. Steamships lost the trans-Atlantic travel when people could reach far destinations in a few hours by air.

The 39,241-ton SS OCEANIC, whose number of repeaters are the largest of any ship in modern cruise annals, will again offer passengers a choice of 2 days and nights in Nassau or a day in Bermuda in addition to a day and night in Nassau. While the Spring and Summer sailings feature either the one-port and two-port itineraries, all Autumn cruises call at both ports. While there are many reasons for the consistent popularity of the OCEANIC among one-week vacationers, travel experts attribute Home Lines' reputation for high cruise standards as the major factor. This is especially apparent in the quality of cuisine and in the dedicated service of the well-trained Italian personnel. Worth noting, too, is the fact that all double cabins have 2 lower beds. Home Line Photo

MODERN CRUISE TRAVEL

As air travel grew, it brought with it the decline of the passenger ship industry.

Gradually, the steamship industry was forced to change its view of itself and, in turn, its public image. No longer were passenger ships viewed as a means of transportation, but rather the idea of vacationing at sea began to take hold.

Ironically, a key factor in the successful development of this concept was the growth of air travel. What once had been the harbinger of doom for the cruise industry, now became its passport to a new vitality. The growth of air markets led cruise companies to join with airlines to enable people who live far from port cities to be within a few hours of a cruise vacation.

Since steamships were no longer required for transportation, the idea of vacationing at sea became a new travel opportunity. More than two million Americans are cruising in the Caribbean. Most cruise lines are experiencing high occupancy rates and are finding it increasingly difficult to meet consumer demands. Things are so busy that the cruise lines are looking for new ships and the Port of Miami has become the biggest cruise port in the world. Miami has nine passenger terminals and has launched a $40 million port expansion. The "new" Port of Miami is located in tranquil Biscayne Bay facing the heart of Miami. This cruise capital is only a few minutes from the famous resort hotels and motels in Miami and Miami Beach and from the Miami International Airport.

The typical air supplement for roundtrip air transportation from Baltimore to Miami)Ft. Lauderdale) is $60, and no matter where you live in the United States, Canada or Mexico, steamship lines have made it easy for you. Passengers fly aboard regularly scheduled airlines and are met on arrival by a uniformed steamship line representative who escorts them by private motor coach directly to the ship. The Air/Sea Caribbean package price may require an "add-on" of $60 for someone from Quebec, or free from Savannah. The steamship line writes the tickets (air and sea tickets) for the passenger.

AIR/SEA CRUISE ADD-ON AIR FARE COST SAMPLE

	Mexico	Canada & Alaska	Caribbean	Trans-Panama and 14-Day Caribbean†
Ottawa, Ont.	$190	$190	$110	Free
Palm Springs, Calif.	Free	Free	*110	Free
Paso Robles, Calif.	Free	Free	*100	Free
Pensacola, Fla.	150	165	Free	Free
Philadelphia, Pa.	150	165	60	Free
Phoenix, Ariz.	Free	50	150	Free
Pittsburgh, Pa.	150	150	60	Free
Portland, Ore.	25	Free	250	Free
Prince George, B.C.	190	150	**125	Free
Providence, R.I.	150	165	60	Free
Quebec, Que.	225	250	175	Free
Raleigh, N.C.	150	190	50	Free
Regina, Sask.	190	90	190	Free
Reno, Nev.	Free	Free	**125	Free
Richmond, Va.	150	190	60	Free
Roanoke, Va.	190	190	90	Free
Rochester, N.Y.	150	165	90	Free
Sacramento, Calif.	Free	Free	**125	Free
St. Louis, Mo.	90	125	60	Free

*From Los Angeles Airport) Transportation to & from Los
**From San Francisco Airport) Angeles or San Francisco airports not included.

†1. *These rates represent supplementary charges for computing Air/Sea package prices. They are not air fares. 1979 prices.*
2. *The Air/Sea program is applicable to all cabin categories from cities for which the air supplement is shown as "Free." The Air/Sea program is not otherwise acceptable to categories M, N & P.*
3. *Only full-fare, complete cruise passengers are eligible for the Air/Sea program.*

MODERN CRUISE TRAVEL   51

Salt Lake City, Utah	25	25	190	Free
San Antonio, Texas	60	125	60	Free
San Diego, Calif.	Free	Free	110	Free
San Francisco, Calif.	Free	— —	125	Free
San Jose, Calif.	Free	— —	**125	Free
San Juan, P.R.	290	290	60	Free
San Luis Obispo, Calif.	Free	Free	*110	Free
Santa Ana, Calif.	— —	Free	*110	Free
Santa Barbara, Calif.	Free	Free	175	Free
Santa Maria, Calif.	Free	Free	*110	Free
Sarasota, Fla.	150	165	Free	Free
Saskatoon, Sask.	190	90	190	Free
Savannah, Ga.	150	165	Free	Free
Seattle, Wash	25	Free	250	Free

Pan Am Boeing 747SP on Air/Sea Tour Flight to the Caribbean.
Pan American World Airways Photo

AIR/SEA PROGRAM CONDITIONS

Air/Sea Tour: In addition to the services and facilities included in the cruise fare, any Air/Sea tour includes roundtrip, coach air transportation between the originating air/sea city and the port of embarkation, and ground transfers to and from the ship. Passengers are required to use flight schedules (may be a regularly scheduled air carrier) and routings specified by the cruise line if they wish to utilize the ground transfers arranged by cruise line. The airlines are independent contractors and the line is not responsible for their conduct. The cruise line will not be responsible for any expenses or other consequences resulting from a change or delay in the vessel's schedule, or a change or delay in schedule or routing made by a passenger, travel agent or airline.

Air Transportation: Civil Aeronautics Board certificated scheduled and charter airline services will be used. In the case of charter flights, no stopovers will be permitted. The cruise line reserves the right to substitute charter flights for scheduled flights and scheduled flights for charter flights, without prior notice. Changes in airline routings will be at cruise line's discretion and the line reserves the right to change them to facilitate consolidation of groups of passengers, or for any other reason. If due to airline schedules, the cruise line is unable to provide same-day service to or from a cruise with an Air/Sea package flight, the cruise line assumes no responsibility for additional expenses incurred by the passenger.

The Air/Sea packages have been so well received that today approximately 85% of the passengers arrive at the embarkation city by way of the air/sea package. In many respects, the popularity of air/sea programs now being offered by the steamship lines is responsible for the current boom in the cruise industry. These packages offer

MODERN CRUISE TRAVEL 53

cruises to Americans who otherwise might never have considered a vacation at sea. Americans seem to be enjoying the "new vacation option," because statistics show cruise lines enjoy one of the highest repeat passenger factors in the travel industry. Passengers have passed the word to neighbors, friends and relatives so that now demand for cruises is increasing.

With more and more people cruising and enjoying it, travellers can benefit by the complete program which includes the airfare and cruise fare as well as well as all the meals, entertainment, and activities aboard ship, plus transfers between the airport and pier.

Ferryboats connect the colorful harbor in downtown Ford-de-France, capital of Martinique; cruise line customers enjoy local hospitality. French West Indies Photo.

Most steamship lines use only scheduled air carriers for passengers and can offer the same stopover privileges available to any air passenger using the same tariff. The cruise lines have combined these stopover privileges with two-night sightseeing tours, e.g., West Coast passengers returning from a Caribbean cruise stopover in New Orleans.

What has happened is that cruising suddenly has seized the public's imagination. The television series "Love Boat," in particular, has excited younger people and those from the landlocked midwestern states who were little acquainted with cruising. While the new converts to cruising lost their hearts to "Love Boat," just as many have come to realize that cruising is good travel value.

Miami and Port Everglades, Florida aren't the only cruise ports available, and clients can wander elsewhere to board steamships, e.g., San Juan, New Orleans, Martinique, Tampa, Baltimore, New York and Boston.

CRUISE SHIP TICKET

Be sure to read the Conditions for Carriage of Passengers as set forth in the Passage Contract Ticket. The acceptance of the ticket constitutes acceptance of those terms and conditions. Among other rights reserved, the line may choose not to accept or retain any person as a passenger. The steamship line's responsibility does not extend beyond their own vessels and before passengers board or whenever passengers leave it, any arrangements made by or for them are at their own risk.

After you have purchased your ticket, the cruise line will send you a "Confirmation/Deposit Receipt" which will tell you Flight Information, Cruise Data; i.e. name of ship, departure time, departure location, and cabin assignment; Costs, including fare, port taxes and miscellaneous costs; and any other information you require.

The following is a sample of a ticket of a recent Caribbean cruise:

MODERN CRUISE TRAVEL

SITMAR CRUISES		PASSAGE CONTRACT TICKET NOT TRANSFERABLE		PASSENGER'S COUPON not good for passage		COUPON **7**	SC/ N⁰ 501768	
SHIP	VOYAGE N:	FROM	TO	SAILING DATE	LOCAL TIME		PIER AND LOCATION	
T.S.S. **FAIRWIND**	**PE/204**	**PEV**	**PEV**	**APR 08'78**	**7 PM**		**2 FT. EVERGLADES**	
NAME OF PASSENGERS		AGE	NATIONALITY	DECK	ROOM	BED	FARE BASIS	CURRENCY FARE
STRNAD, MR. J.		A		**ACAPULCO**	193		I/7	$ 705.00
MRS.		A		**ACAPULCO**	193		I/7	$ 705.00
				FINAL SITTING			TOTAL FARE(S)	$1410.00
HOME ADDRESS				AGENT VALIDATION				
CRUISES UNLIMITED GROUP				AGENT **CRUISES UNLIMITED TRAVEL**				
AIR/SEA/DCA				**CHEVY CHASE, MD.**				
IT SIT CAR 78				ADDRESS			TAXES AND PORT FEES	26.30
ISSUED IN CONNECTION WITH								
DATE	TICKET No		FARE	DATE OF ISSUE			GRAND TOTAL	$1436.30
SHIP FLIGHT							AGENT'S CODE	
				SIGNATURE For SITMAR CRUISES Inc. AS AGENTS ONLY **NW**				**GR-5**
ENDORSED TO:	DATE:							
SIGNATURE:	VALUE:							

IMPORTANT: Passengers should read the terms of this Passage Contract which are incorporated into, and form part of this Contract which is binding upon the parties by acceptance of same by the Passenger. The terms of this Passage Contract supersede all representations which may have been made by anyone on behalf of the Carrier.

Sitmar Cruise Ticket — FAIRWIND

A view of Courland Bay from Fort James, Trinidad.

Chapter 4

PLANNING YOUR CRUISE

SOME THINGS YOU SHOULD KNOW BEFORE YOU GO
Accommodations

You may be interested in knowing why there are differences in fares. A ship's staterooms are rated according to type and location of accommodation. Fares are based on two to a room per person basis. You should obtain a brochure that describes each kind of stateroom.

Royal Caribbean Cruise Line's SUN VIKING sails into the Port of Miami after a 14-day cruise. SUN VIKING alternates with her sister ship NORDIC PRINCE offering Royal Caribbean vacationers two-week cruises every Saturday year-round from Miami.

Bon Voyage Party

If you wish to have a Bon Voyage party in your stateroom, the cruise line can supply alcoholic beverages, ice, glasses, and soft drinks if advised one week in advance of sailing. This is a Customs regulation. You may bring your own alcoholic beverages aboard. Your room steward will make ice, soft drinks, and glasses available to you at nominal prices.

Rendezvous Lounge/Casino

Casino open ONLY at sea. Roulette, Blackjack, "21" and other games of chance are usually available. Slot machines—nickel, dime and quarter slot machines are also available. Most ships in the Caribbean offer gambling.

Gift Shop

The gift and duty-free shops aboard ship offer, for sale, alcoholic beverages, cigarettes and many gift items from around the world. There are also sundries for sale. The gift shop is open ONLY at sea. Times should be posted for ordering cigarettes and liquor which are then delivered to your stateroom during the last night of your cruise.

Personal Properties

Aboard ship, travelers checks, credit cards, and cash are accepted. It is impossible to cash personal checks on most ships.

Photographs

PRIOR to sailing, the ship's photographer is generally available to take pictures in black-and-white for your hometown paper at no charge. Simultaneously, he will photograph in color . . . a nice "bon voyage" memento which you may purchase. Before you leave, secure the address of your hometown newspaper where you would like the photo sent. Use the smaller weeklies, as the large metropolitan newspapers very seldom use these

PLANNING YOUR CRUISE 59

photographs. Throughout the trip, the photographer will be taking color pictures which you may purchase. Be sure to get those you want before the end of the cruise. Once your cruise is over, the negatives are destroyed.

Queen's Lounge on Holland America's SS ROTTERDAM.

Foreign Cameras, Jewelry, and Other Items

If you are bringing with you foreign-purchased items, it is wise to declare these with U. S. Customs prior to boarding. Otherwise, have your sales slips with you as proof of prior purchase.

What Clothes do I Pack for the Caribbean?

If you go by air, you are of course limited by baggage restrictions and your wardrobe is necessarily restricted. On a cruise, you can take along as many suitcases, and even steamer trunks as you wish, at no additional charge. The following is a suggested basic wardrobe for a 2-week cruise that is based on the experience of many vacationers (formal clothes are treated separately). Keep in mind, that if you're cruising during cold months you will need warm clothes for the first day out and the last day coming back.

Dress

While casual attire is in order during the day both on ship and shore, for the Captain's Cocktail Party, Welcome Aboard (first night) and Farewell Dinner (last night) formal dress or dark suit is suggested. On some evenings casual attire is appropriate, including sport shirts or leisure suits for the men and slacks for the ladies. On other evenings, gentlemen are requested to wear jackets and ties in the dining room and lounges; for ladies, dresses and pantsuits are appropriate. Evening wrap or light, dressy sweaters will be welcome on the breezy decks at nights. On a 14-day cruise, visiting 5 ports, you can plan to dress up approximately 5 evenings.

Your clothing should be light, casual, easy to care for, and comfortable. The ship's laundry and valet service can handle them neatly and quickly for your convenience.

You can use shorts, sandals, halters or knit shorts for shipboard play hours. Don't forget your swim suit, terry robe and shower clogs for going to and from the pool.

For the Ladies

Cocktail-lengths are the overwhelming favorites in formal wear, although floor-length gowns are very chic. Your stole? Yes! A dramatic evening shawl? By all means! And if you have a glamorous theatre coat, wonderful!

Items to Remember

3 swim suits, 2 beach jackets, beach shoes, 2 play sets.

1 or 2 dressy sweaters, befurred or bejeweled, to toss over your shoulders in air conditioned public rooms.

1 warm and 1 lightweight pair of slacks; 3 pairs of

PLANNING YOUR CRUISE

Bermudas; 2 casual sweaters; 6 casual outfits (coordinated separates, sun dresses, sleeveless blouses, lightweight skirts). Take several pairs of nylons of the same shade. Robe, slippers, dressy and casual shoes. And be sure to take along a head scarf or two!

To the Ladies—A Hint About Sportswear Coordinates

The unusual flexibility provided by color coordinates have made them the "must" of a travel wardrobe. Select a basic color. Add a second color that picks up your basic choice, with accessories in a single color to wear with both. For a 2-week cruise, pack the following:

In your basic color:
- 1 skirt
- 1 jacket
- 1 jumper
- 1 pair slacks
- 1 cardigan sweater
- 1 soft pattern blouse
- 1 matching pattern skirt
- 1 soft style solid blouse

In your accent color:
- 1 skirt
- 1 pair shorts
- 1 solid sport blouse
- 1 pattern blouse

... and voila! ... combinations unlimited for an ensembled look!

For the Men

Cabana set, 2 additional swim trunks, beach jacket, beach shoes, rubber-soled canvas shoes if you participate in active deck sports.

Pair of winter slacks, 3 pairs lightweight slacks, 2 Bermudas (if you wear 'em); raincoat; sleeveless sweater, 2 or more sport jackets, a casual jacket, 2 lightweight summer suits.

2 long sleeved **sport** shirts, 4 short sleeved; 5 business dress shirts (less **if they**'re wash and wear), 6 neckties. Lightweight robe, **slippers**; dressy and sport shoes.

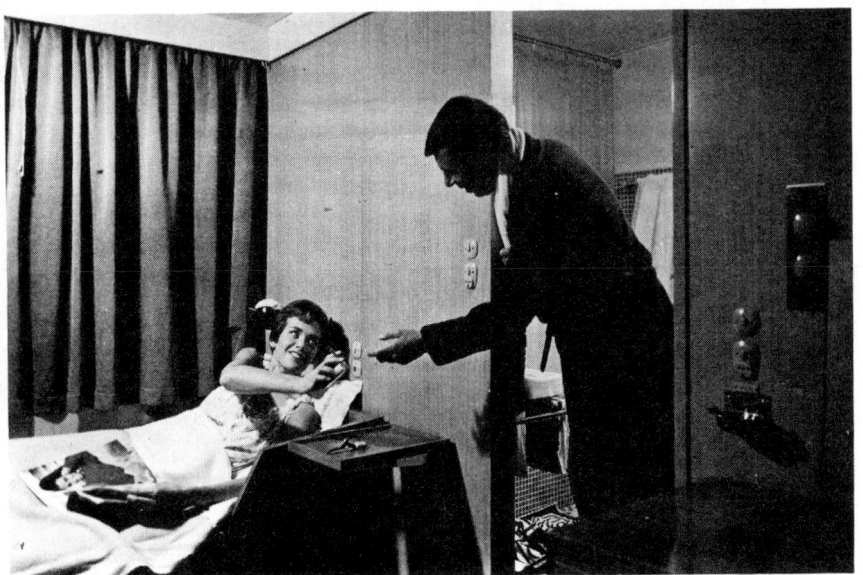

Cruise passengers after an active day are ready for sleep in their comfortable cabin.

Additional Suggestions From Sunshine to Children

You may want to take along sunglasses, suntan lotion, a costume for the ship's carnival masquerade (if there is one) lens shade and light meter for your camera (have it checked before you leave to avoid missing shots you'll treasure). The ship's gift shop, however, has most of the essentials for your trip, should you forget one or more.

Take along as much wash-and-wear as you can as well as plastic clothes pins. You'll shower often and your cabin is air conditioned, so bring a lightweight but warm flannel or terry robe. If you're a golf addict, bring along your clubs. There are good golf courses in most ports and charges are nominal. Also, arrangements can sometimes be made with your Cabin Steward or through the Purser for children's nursery and playroom services.

PLANNING YOUR CRUISE

Baggage

There is no set limit to the amount of personal baggage that you may bring aboard the ship. It is to be understood that baggage means wearing apparel and effects necessary to and appropriate for your personal comfort and convenience. Most passengers find that suitcases are sufficient for their clothing requirements.

Remember that two suitcases (44 lbs.) per person may be taken on the airplane plus one carry-on which must fit under the seat. Remember that the tour operator is not usually responsible for loss or damage to tour participant baggage. The liability of the carrier for loss or damage to personal baggage is usually limited to the actual value of such baggage, but not more than approximately $400.00 per passenger in the case of unchecked baggage or other property.

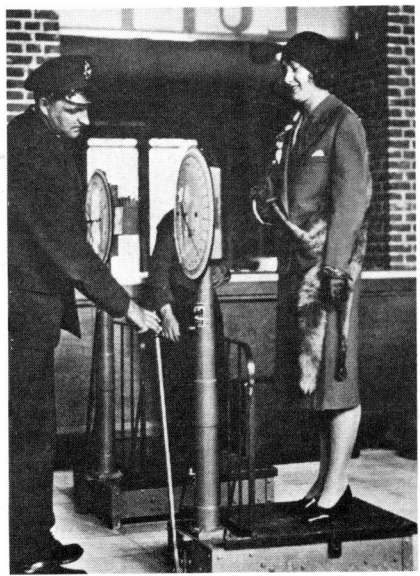

You can take more baggage on your cruise trip than you can on an international airline flight.

To avoid baggage being lost or misplaced, be sure that each piece, including the smaller articles that you may be carrying, has a tag securely attached. Baggage tags will be supplied with your ticket. Additional tags may be obtained through your travel agent or cruise line, or on arrival at pier from porters. Baggage tags and labels should clearly indicate the passenger's name, cabin number, ship, and sailing date.

There are porters at the airport and the pier, but hand luggage, valuables and breakable items must be hand carried by the passenger. A cruise line does not accept responsibility for any personal items, nor for any luggage not under its direct care on board.

Baggage responsibility and insurance is your business. Cruise lines make every effort to assist its passengers to safeguard their belongings, but in the absence of negligence on its part, passenger's belongings are at all times at "owner's risk." The cruise line is not responsible for or liable for damage, loss or theft of baggage or personal effects. Insurance may be purchased at the pier or ask your travel agent for full details.

Cameras, Jewelry, and Other Valuables

It is not possible for the ship or the company to accept responsibility for cameras, watches, jewelry or other valuable articles which you may own. While in port there are many visitors and other persons in the pier area and aboard ship who may, inadvertently or otherwise, pick up the wrong bag, camera, or other items. It is strongly recommended that your valuable items to which you attach special importance be kept under your own control at all times. However, you may place valuables in a "free" safe deposit box located in the Purser's Office. Passengers do this personally and there is no inventory or check-up made by the company. For this reason, the cruise lines do

PLANNING YOUR CRUISE

not accept any responsibility for the contents delivered. Should baggage be damaged or lost due to the line's fault, claims must be made in writing to the Chief Purser or Pier Manager prior to leaving the disembarkation pier. A line's liability for such claims is usually limited to $250 per passenger.

Personal Funds

Most veteran travelers prefer to carry their personal funds in the form of traveler's checks which are accepted for expenses incurred on board ship and by shops, hotels, and other places of business on shore. Since the amount of U. S. currency that the ship is permitted to carry is limited, it will be appreciated by the line if you will bring a reasonable amount of U. S. currency in denominations not larger than $10.00. While U. S. currency is accepted in many of the shops ashore, it is not always possible for them to make change in U. S. currency. Therefore, to avoid the inconvenience caused by obtaining change in local money, it is suggested that you carry suitable quantities of U. S. currency in $1.00 and $5.00 denominations. Personal checks are not usually cashed or accepted on board.

Cruise Rates

The nice thing about a cruise fare is that it is practically all inclusive: shipboard transportation, accommodations reserved and paid for, meals and entertainment on board, the services of the cruise staff, and landing and embarkation facilities at ports of call. Cruise rates do not include shore excursion or sightseeing, port taxes, gratuities, liquor, wines, mineral water or other beverages and other items not included in the regular bill of fare on board; the expense of passport and visas, if required.

Pets
No pets such as dogs, cats or birds can be accepted.

Physical Disability
Any physical disability that may require special attention or treatment must be reported when reservation is requested. Passage may be refused anyone whose state of health or physical condition renders them, in the opinion of the line, unfit for travel, or anyone whose condition may constitute a danger to themselves or another passenger.

Sailing Day
Embarkation and pier location will be stated on your ticket. Your cruise ship will sail promptly at the appointed time from (most likely) the New Port of Miami on Dodge Island, a short taxi ride from hotels, airports, bus and railroad stations. Embarkation will take place several hours prior to sailing. Porters are available on the pier to assist you with baggage. Passengers are requested to arrive at the pier as early as possible within the scheduled boarding hours. In any event, you should board the ship no later than one hour before the actual sailing time.

Automobile Storage Facilities
These facilities are usually available at every major port. The City of Miami Seaport Parking Lot, for example, will store passengers' cars for the duration of the cruise at a rate of $2.00 per day. This is an attended, park-and-lock lot adjacent to the pier on Dodge Island, from which the ship sails. Reservations aren't required. However, cruise passengers should identify themselves as such when parking.

The cruise lines do not operate any storage facilities for cars. The information above is provided as a service to passengers who wish to drive to the pier and store their

PLANNING YOUR CRUISE

cars for the duration of the cruise. Neither the cruise lines nor the vessel are able to accept any liability in connection with such arrangements.

Debarkation

When arriving at the various ports of call, the local authorities must clear the ship before passengers are allowed to go ashore. The cooperation of the passengers is requested in NOT crowding the foyer or the stairways since this interferes with the work of the crew members assigned to secure the gangway and consequently delays the land procedure. You should plan to wait in comfort in the public rooms until an announcement is made over the public address system that debarkation can commence.

The day you leave on a Caribbean cruise will be the beginning of your new way of life.

Reservations

Requests for seating in the dining room may be made in advance through your travel agent. Passenger's wishes are usually followed to the extent possible. Actual table assignments will be made by the Maitre d'Hotel upon boarding and are usually confirmed prior to the time of embarkation.

Deck chairs are reserved on some ships and if this is the procedure, reserve your chairs and decide whether you want sun, shade, solitude, or companionship. The Chief Deck Steward will help with the decision. Deck chair charges are less than $10.00 per week on cruise ships. Ships that do not charge, do not reserve deck chairs.

Beauty parlor appointments can be made in advance (day, date, and time) with your travel agents or on the ship. Reservations are usually made in advance for Bon Voyage Parties.

Cabin Service

You will have a Cabin Steward assigned to you for your entire voyage. He (or she) will care for your comfort and respond to your service calls. If you have any questions while on board, chances are he can answer them. A cabin key will be given to one passenger in each cabin who'll be responsible for it and return it before debarkation.

Cruise Director and Cruise Staff

Providing continuous entertainment for every taste is the concern of the Cruise Director and Staff. A whole spectrum of fun awaits you aboard, from sports events in the morning to outstanding late night-club shows. In between there are lectures on the ports, card games, shuffleboard, ping-pong, bingo, games, dancing, a full casino, movies, and of course the major show event of every evening. If there's anything the staff has missed,

PLANNING YOUR CRUISE

ask them; but it may be difficult to think of something!

Activities Bulletin

The daily program of entertainment and sporting events is available to all passengers. All activities are conducted in the public rooms or on the decks reserved for the use of the passengers. In order that all passengers may take full advantage of these activities, all events will be announced in a daily paper and/or posted on the bulletin board.

Sun Line Cruise's Dining Room.

Snack Time

You can literally eat around the clock if you want. In addition to the three hearty main meals, you can enjoy mid-morning bouillon, afternoon tea, and a delicious midnight buffet. There's also hamburgers and hot dogs throughout the afternoon.

Purser's Office

Passengers are asked to apply to the Purser's Office

for any questions or desired information or for cashing Traveler's Checks. Office hours (subject to change according to the requirements of the service) are 8:00 a.m. to 8:00 p.m.

Change of Cabin

Changes in quarters (if others are available) may be arranged only through the Purser or Cashier on the pier. Receipt for any monetary difference paid for such a change will be given to the passenger by the Purser or Cashier who will note it on the passenger's ticket.

Duty-Free Shops

So called because items carried in these miniature department stores are free from import tax, and of course, are much less expensive. It's a good idea to check the cost of items in the duty-free shop before purchasing the same item in port, since, due to low overhead, the shop on board sells many items at prices lower than the shops ashore. Remember, that by law, the shops must be closed in port (though orders will be taken), so buy your diamond or toothbrush while at sea.

Medicine

A qualified and experienced doctor is available on board. Passengers are entitled to free medication for sea sickness, treatment by the ship's surgeon for injuries which occur on board and contagious or suspected contagious diseases subject to compulsory report.

Medical examinations may be held in the consulting room or in the cabin. For cases other than those mentioned, a professional fee will be charged.

Passengers using a doctor's prescription, vitamins or other medication of any kind should bring an ample supply as these may not be readily available either aboard

PLANNING YOUR CRUISE

ship or in ports-of-call. Commonly used medications are kept on board and may be purchased at the office of the ship's surgeon.

Tobacco Products

A wide assortment of cigarettes, cigars and pipe tobacco can be purchased from the duty-free shop.

Lost and Found

Items lost on shipboard should be reported to the Purser's Office. Likewise, any article found by a passenger should be turned into the same office. If a found article is not claimed before the ship returns, or if you leave an item in your cabin, it will be sent to the company's headquarters and may be obtained through inquiry there.

Ship-to-Shore Telephone

Your cruise ship will be equipped with modern, high-stability radio-telephone systems which make possible connections with the telephone systems ashore. By law, there is no service from the ship while it's in port.

Wireless Service

Radiograms may be sent from abroad to wireless stations throughout the world. Likewise, persons wishing to send passengers messages aboard the ship may do so. Unless the passenger requests that incoming messages be delivered upon receipt, radiograms arriving during the night will not be delivered until 7:30 a.m. Shorebound night radiograms will be accepted at any time at reduced rates for delivery in the United States the following morning.

Birthdays and Anniversaries

Passengers celebrating their birthdays and wedding

anniversaries during the cruise are kindly requested to advise the Maitre d'Hotel and the Cruise Staff.

Package Delivery
Should you purchase items in port and wish them delivered to you on board ship, they should be addressed as follows:

Passenger's Name _____
Ship _____
Cabin No._____
_____ (day) _____(date)

Sauna Bath and Health Club
You can have an opportunity to experience the true continental sauna and a stimulating massage at nominal charge on your cruise.

Liquor Restrictions
Passengers are not usually permitted to bring their own wines and liquors into the public rooms or on deck. These must be consumed in the individual's stateroom.

Wines Available
Should you desire a bit of "bubbly" or any other type of wine, just ask for our extensive wine list. The Wine Steward will take your order and bring you your choice of the many fine wines available at moderate prices.

Accident Prevention
Please read and comply with the safety instructions posted in the cabin.

Fire Precautions
For everyone's safety, passengers are kindly asked to adhere to these fire safety rules:

PLANNING YOUR CRUISE

1. Don't smoke in bed.
2. Don't throw lighted cigarettes, cigar butts or matches overboard. They can start a fire by slipping through portholes or side doors. Please extinguish cigarettes, cigars, or matches in ash trays located throughout the ship.
3. Don't use irons or other electrical appliances, other than razors, in your cabin.
4. Please do not run on the ship, and please walk carefully when the deck is wet.
5. Do not permit children to run or play unattended, or to sit or play on stairways.
6. Do not remove safety hooks from furniture.
7. Be careful to step over doorsills when entering or leaving bathrooms and cabins.
8. Use the berth ladder to enter upper beds. Make certain the ladder is securely placed.
9. Passengers should familiarize themselves with the notice in their staterooms regarding emergency station and life boat number, and must participate in the fire and boat drills.

Emergency Drills

You will go through an Emergency Drill soon after embarking on the ship. If at any time you hear the emergency signal, get your life preserver and go to your "Muster Station." You'll find the location of your station by reading the instructions posted in your cabin. From there, the Captain and his officers will direct you. Emergency drills are performed in the interest of passenger safety, and are in accordance with the rules of the International Convention for Safety of Life at Sea, signed in London in 1948.

Life Preservers

Make sure at embarkation that there are life preservers

in your Cabin. Your Cabin Steward can show you the location of the life preservers in your cabin, and how to wear them.

Safety Precautions

Be sure you do not have fireworks, matches, gunpowder, gasoline, or cartridges in your baggage. Do not smoke in bed. Do not throw lighted cigarettes, cigar butts or matches overboard because they may fly into an open window or porthole. Please use ashtrays located throughout the ship. The use of hair dryers, blowers, irons or other electrical appliances is not generally encouraged. The only exception is an ELECTRIC RAZOR which may be plugged into the plate indicated in your stateroom.

Dangerous Articles

Passengers are not allowed to bring on board weapons, firearms, ammunition, explosives or other dangerous goods without written permission from the owners or their managers.

Drain Pipe Obstruction

Please do not throw any extraneous objects into wash basins or toilet bowls. It is impossible to repair outboard outlets at sea or in foreign ports.

Shore Excursions

Lectures will be given to inform passengers about the ports of call and tours that are available on shore. If you're interested in going on one of the tours, early arrangements sould be made.

Should you require any information regarding tour itineraries ashore, or literature on points of interest to visit while you're there, generally the Cruise Staff and Purser's Office will be happy to assist you.

PLANNING YOUR CRUISE

In Port

While in port, your ship is still your home and you may leave it or return to it at any time of day or night. You are entitled to the same meals and snacks while in port as at sea, at no extra charge.

A cruise ship comes into a Caribbean port for one night's berth.

Language is No Barrier

You will not encounter any language barrier in the Caribbean Islands.

Island Hospitality

Almost without exception, residents of the Caribbean Islands are friendly people, anxious to serve you. They recognize the importance of tourism to their island economy and are happy to see us. An important thought here to keep in mind—no matter how brief our visit, we're still visitors in someone else's home and we hope to be invited back again.

So Now You're a Sailor!

In the days when clipper ships ruled the seas, time was indicated by the ringing of the ship's bell. Since the watches were relieved every four hours, the bells were rung accordingly. For instance, at 12:30 one bell was struck, at one o'clock two bells, and so on until four o'clock, at which time eight bells were struck. This indicated the change of watch and the cycle of bells would start again. It is a nautical custom of bygone days which has survived up to the present time.

Tipping

Tipping is always a personal matter. This is an individual decision. When such gratuities are extended, the amount should be based on the quality and manner of service, along with the overall length of the voyage.

On cruises of less than two weeks, dining room and cabin service gratuities are usually extended at the end of the voyage. More than two weeks, most passengers prefer to handle them on a weekly basis. However, gratuities are normally extended for bar and deck services at the time they are provided.

Many first-time cruisers are unfamiliar with shipboard tipping. We, are, therefore, offering suggested guide-lines.

1. Room Steward—Keeps your stateroom clean; supplies clean towels, soap, ice; turns your bed down at night; takes care of your personal requests for special room service. We suggest $1.50 to $2.00 per day per person.
2. Dining Room Waiter—You will have the same waiter for the entire voyage. He will be serving you three times a day. We suggest $2.00 per day per person.
3. Busboy—Sets and clears your table; keeps you supplied with beverages, dressings, butter, rolls and assists the waiter in serving. We suggest from $1.00 to $1.50 per day per person.

PLANNING YOUR CRUISE

4. Wine Steward—Bartenders, Lounge Waiters—Tip a percentage, just as you would ashore. Stateroom tabs cannot be run, as charges are usually submitted per drink ordered.
5. Maitre d'—The Maitre d' is there to see that the dining room runs smoothly. If you require special service, he will be happy to take care of your requests. Your tip is your personal thank you for his extra service.

Tipping is usually taken care of the last night of the voyage.

Buck Island National Park on St. Croix is a member of the U. S. National Park System. It consists of beaches with picnic facilities and two marked underwater trails.

Trunk Bay, on the island of St. John, the smallest of the three major United States Virgin Islands, is considered to have one of the most beautiful beaches in the world.
St. John, over three-quarters of which is a national park, is only minutes away from St. Thomas by ferry boat and a "must" on every visitor's list.   *Fritz Henle Photo*

Chapter 5

CARIBBEAN CRUISE

The Caribbean. Gloriously warm and soft year-round. Where clear waters reflect the sun like a tourquoise prism and edge fabled islands where sandy beaches form silken powder plateaus ringing forests of palm green, poinsettia red and parrot yellow.

Above, cloud puffs are kissed by off-shore breezes. Cruising these waters, it's often been said, is like sailing into a never-never land. One day melts gently into the next. Worries fade. Pressures lighten. And the most important moment becomes the one you're experiencing right now. Yes, there are reasons so many travelers choose the Caribbean as a destination year after year.

For the Americas, it all began in the Caribbean Sea. In 1492, Christopher Columbus wrote, "I saw so many islands that I hardly knew to which I should go first." French, Dutch, Spanish, British, and Danish explorers soon followed him. Your ports of call help you to experience the variety of Caribbean life: different landscapes, different rhythms, and different languages to experience and enjoy.

A Caribbean cruise can be the most relaxing vacation that you will ever experience. Unlike air travel, there is no constant packing and moving about to visit foreign places. There are no expensive taxi rides from airports to hotels. No worries about schedules from day to day. Your cruise ship is your hotel and it takes you where you want to go. A cruise vacation offers unlimited opportunities — you can be alone to relax, to read, or to your privacy, or you can share experiences with hundreds of different people. It is well to remember that the great cruise vacation ships have a tradition of gracious living and superb dining. A grand feature of cruising is that when you sit down to dine you review a menu with no prices. Your fare includes pratically every expenditure aboard ship.

When you check inflation and rising air fares, a cruise is no longer an expensive vacation. Cruise fares are all-inclusive: the fare covers transportation to all ports you go, the equivalent of resort hotel accommodations, all meals, and most entertainment activities. On a cruise, everyone eats the same meals, enjoys the same entertainment, is waited on to the same degree. The price affects only the type and location of your cabin. When you vacation in the Caribbean Sea, the cruise itself is the primary destination; the ports of call are a "bonus" that enhance the total experience. Your holiday begins the moment you walk up the gangway.

Surfers ride the last waves of the day as evening falls.

CARIBBEAN CRUISE

Where in the Caribbean to go? While all the islands of the West Indies have much in common... wonderful climate, lush vegetation, exotic sights, carefree living... each has a fascination all its own. Some are very British (Nassau, Bermuda, Barbados); others reflect the British accent more casually (Jamaica, the melting pot of Trinidad with its Hindu-Chinese—African culture); still others show the influence of Holland (Curacao, Aruba), France (Haiti, Guadeloupe, Martinique); Spain (Puerto Rico, Panama, Venezuela); and Denmark (Virgin Islands).

Any island you select is a good one, and to get the full flavor of the Caribbean, experienced vacationers generally plan a holiday cruise that includes visits to several islands. For instance, on a vacation of 20 days (13 ports) or 7 days and 5 ports, there is time to explore the old-world cultures and their varied blendings of traditions and their breath-

There's ample space aft for sun-worshipping aboard the GOLDEN ODYSSEY.

taking beauty. You can do all of this with a well-planned Caribbean cruise. As you cruise, you unwind and acclimate yourself gradually to the warm sun and relaxing pace (no sudden "shocks" to your nervous system), and by the time you reach your first island, you're already sun-tanned and in the right mood to welcome its exotic sights and exciting activities.

In such a pleasant atmosphere of clean accommodations, smartly decorated lounges, cozy bars and refreshing pools, you will certainly want to share your enjoyment with old and new acquaintances aboard. Jump into the pool and cool off, or sip a tall drink and just relax.

CARIBBEAN CRUISE

A CARIBBEAN CRUISE ITINERARY — 20 Days — 13 PORTS

1ST DAY, SUNDAY, MIAMI (DODGE ISLAND)
Your cruise into the colorful history of the Caribbean begins with the mid-afternoon sailing.

2ND DAY, MONDAY, AT SEA
... and what better way to unwind after the flurry of farewells at home, to settle into your comfortable quarters and begin to investigate — and to enjoy — the many amenities and the warm hospitality the ship offers. These days will be spent in the lee of (and often within sight of) the many Bahama Islands as the ship sails the storied Old Bahama Channel. If the southern sun is kind, you should already be revelling in its warm glow around the pool.

3RD DAY, TUESDAY, HAITI, CAP HAITIEN
Steeped in legends of an almost fanatic domination by self-proclaimed King Henry Christophe, Haiti today sits serenely in the tropical sun, a beautiful isle of verdant green valleys and hazy blue mountains. You may wish to wander the narrow streets by the wharf, where hastily-conceived shops laden with carved mahogany reflect at once an art both primitive and contemporary, but unerringly with a style strictly Haitian. The village of Milot is but a short distance away. From here you may witness the twin wonders of the Sans Souci Palace — Christophe's private residence erected in mock imitation of the French Court of Versailles, or view the majestic Citadel, an impregnable fortress perched 3,000 feet above the plain, considered to be one of the greatest wonders of the Western Hemisphere. The center of Cap Haitien is crowned with an aluminum-domed cathedral surrounded by homes with wrought-iron balconies. A tradition of voodoo ceremonies and cockfights. Warm friendly people speaking French and Creole in a central market featuring native straw work and masterpieces of wooden sculpture and world famous primitive paintings. Dramatic mountains, superb white beaches and brilliant flowers.

4TH DAY, WEDNESDAY, PUERTO RICO (SAN JUAN)
Welcome to the "Crossroads of the Caribbean" — island of beauty, happiness and old Spanish charm. Throughout your stay you find the people, like the weather, warm and appealing. Blessed by the benevolence of nature, San Juan is today a brilliant anachronism —

Tourists visiting the 18th-century Whim Greathouse on St. Croix in the United States Virgin Islands enjoy photographing this restored sugar mill. Its blades still revolve gracefully in the gentle trade winds, as they did two centuries ago. *Fritz Henle Photo*

CARIBBEAN CRUISE

the best of Old Spain back-to-back with a Miami Beach modernity — each facade promising much, fulfilling much. Stroll the glowing grey cobbled streets of the Old City for superlative shopping in centuries-old buildings, the pleasures of dining to the soft thrum of a muffled guitar. For those who prefer, the "swinging life" is a short taxi ride away — a world of Broadway shows, beaches, bikinis and the tugging temptation of sophisticated gambling casinos. A leap into the jet set present of luxury resort hotels, spectacular Las Vegas type stage shows, superb restaurants and elegant international casinos. Here, at the height of the season, plenty of time for a late, giddy evening ashore. A trip back through time as you pass turreted Morro Castle to enter the harbor Ponce de Leon described so vividly —"Que Puerto Rico!", ("What a rich port!"), that it became the name of the country. A short drive away from the ethereal world of El Yunque Rain Forest National Park with its sparkling waterfalls, lush vegetation and misty mountains. The pulsating energy of growth and glitter that gives an intriguing contrast to the charm of another era.

5TH DAY, THURSDAY, VIRGIN ISLANDS (ST. CROIX)
Like her sister island St. Thomas, in the U. S. Virgin Islands, St. Croix is a former possession of Denmark, but is quiet and pastoral. The ruins of great plantations recall the days when St. Croix rivalled Barbados as the great Caribbean's sugar producing center. Its tiny capitol, Christiansted, is a Beautifully preserved Danish port. Picturesque costumes can still be seen. The town square and waterfront areas are officially classified as a National Historic Site. Twenty short years ago, an indolent island lazing in the sun, today St. Croix is a Mecca for the shopper, for it is, remember, one of the few duty-free ports where merchandise is selected by Americans for Americans — and the taste is uncannily unerring. Remember, too, the double customs allowance for those shopping here, making the bargains doubly-so. Here, however, the tempo is a more tranquil one, the beaches broader and better, and the village of Frederiksted an appealing lethargic one. Ample time to cross the island to the quaint town of Christiansted where the mood remains a relaxed Danish one. In mid-afternoon the ship sails for still another Caribbean.

6TH DAY, FRIDAY, DOMINICA and MARTINIQUE (ROSEAU and FORT de FRANCE)
Little-known and even then confused with the Dominican Republic, Dominica is perhaps the most ruggedly beautiful island in this world

Fresh Dominican fruit drinks cool off a warm Santo Domingo day, just outside the oldest cathedral in the western world, Santa Maria la Menor.

CARIBBEAN CRUISE

of beauty. Mountains scrape the tropic skies, shrouded in virgin rain forests (over half are still "Crown Lands"), criss-crossed by 365 roaring rivers. No neon gloss or glitter here — the glories of nature reign unsullied and supreme. In Fort de France the flavor is French, with all the good in life that this implies — superb cuisine, fine free port shopping, a lilting 'upbeat' in daily life. Historically, the island attracted world attention twice — as the birthplace of Napoleon's Empress Josephine and as the site of once-deadly Mount Pelee which, in its final eruption, wiped out the entire city of St. Pierre. For you, these events pale in the present-day beauty and vivacity of the island. Sailboats gliding around a chain of islets lead the way to what could be the verdant peaks of a sea-buried mountain. Martinique has a poised French manner to complement her serene location. The birthplace of Empress Josephine is the home of a noble people. Their pride is justified by the island's beauty — the kind you "drink in" — and recall on gray winter days.

7TH DAY, SATURDAY, AT SEA
Another indolent day today to laze in the tropical sun and enjoy the gracious service and amenities aboard your cruise ship.

8TH DAY, SUNDAY, VENEZUELA (LA GUAIRA)
A modern cosmopolitan city of spacious avenues and handsome public buildings, La Guaira is merely a reflection of the vast changes and modernity, which have, as a result of its vast wealth, transformed the face of Venezuela in recent years. Gateway to the pulsating capital city of Caracas, just minutes away (ten miles), the winding serpentine motor road affords a breathtaking view as you climb to an altitude of 3,000 feet where Caracas is nestled in a valley between the high Andes Mountains. Here you gaze at skyscrapers, the boulevards, the fine residential areas, and feel the modern pace of this great city. Special sights: The National Capitol, the Birthplace of Simon Bolivar, and the Pantheon, Bolivar's resting place. Also, the fabulous Centro Bolivar, Officer's Club and Tamanaco Hotel. Our early morning arrival will afford all cruise guests the opportunity to spend the day in this elegant capital city, to enjoy the superb scenery, clubs, restaurants... to visit the magnificent historical museums and monuments at the birthplace of the liberator, Simon Bolivar. The literal highpoint of your visit, however, may be the 7,000 foot ascent on the Teleferico cable car to the summit of Mt. Avila, for a breathtaking view of the glittering city and vast ocean beyond.

9TH DAY, MONDAY, CURACAO (WILLEMSTAD)
Your first Dutch treat will be sailing through the middle of town past the Queen Emma pontoon bridge to Willemstad's harbor. But you'll get a better view of the city's Dutch confectionary charm on foot. That way, you can shop and enjoy its unique pastel houses and gabled shops that date back to 1708. Be sure to shop Heerenstraat. It's the Fifth Avenue of the islands. For a shopping break try one of the outdoor sidewalk cafes in the city square. Our evening departure allows ample time for every interest, every pleasure. Dedicated shoppers will find Willemstad an affordable treasure trove. Sun-and-sea guests will head for the unspoiled and remote beaches. For photographers, boundless interest and opportunities at every picturesque turn. "Little Holland" is its appropriate nickname. And many things to see: the floating fruit & vegetable market; the world's second largest oil refinery; a synagogue built in 1732; the Jewish Cemetery, the oldest in the Western Hemisphere; and "Chobolobo" Mansion, the home of Curaçao liqueur.

10TH DAY, TUESDAY, AT SEA
Again the delight of a lazy day at sea as we sail on to the San Blas Islands with arrival there scheduled for early afternoon.

11TH DAY, WEDNESDAY, PANAMA (SAN BLAS ISLAND)
San Blas Islands are inhabited by almost pureblooded aborigines of Carib origin. The men work mostly on the mainland, while the women tend the crops and stitch the exquisite colorful applique needlework they sell to visitors. To call them "Panama" is misleading for the 365 Mulato Islands lying off the San Blas archipelago are unique in this day and time, beholden to no one but themselves. Aside from the superb scenery, the "sightseeing" here is in our visit with the Cuna or San Blas Indians. These small and attractive people seem worlds away from anything else in these seas. They strongly resemble Asiatics, with slanted eyes and Mongoloid features, their nose rings and colorful costumes also of another world. Our visit here is a rare one in travel. Then leaving the San Blas this evening, we set our sights on our next landfall, Cristobal.

12TH DAY, THURSDAY, PANAMA (CRISTOBAL)
This is the Gulf of Panama side of the Canal, and administrative headquarters for the Canal Zone. It's contemporary, historic, primitive. A city where ultra-modern buildings stand beside Spanish colonial

CARIBBEAN CRUISE 89

"Electric mules" tow the MS GOLDEN ODYSSEY through Miraflores Locks, Panama Canal.

churches and forts. Where Indians from the jungles still lead an ancient unchanged life. Panama's destiny has been ruled by its geography. Since Balboa measured the short span from Caribbean to the Pacific, the land has alternately been wooed and warred upon by those who would control such a strategic and valuable road of commerce. Its gold-laden ports were pillaged by pirates and a variety of foreign interests sought the near-miracle connecting of the oceans. Not until early this century did the U. S. finally accomplish the awesome undertaking and the whole world of shipping and trade was changed forevermore. "Sightseeing" here means a visit to watch the Canal in operation, but there are other pleasures and rewards as well — Colon's shops are laden with temptations from the world over and there are opportunities — as well as the time — for photographic strolls.

13TH DAY, FRIDAY, COLOMBIA
San Adres Island . . . a cruising first! On even the largest of maps, the tiny eden-like island of San Andres appears a pinpoint dot; with its neighbor, Providencia, the total land area is only 27 square miles. Our visit here precedes and presages the touristic development which seems inevitable, for these islands are pure South Seas, with virgin white sand beaches and reefs, the inhabitants also out of time and place as direct descendants of English buccaneers and pirates. The visit here is without planned program — perhaps only a stroll with the satisfying sense of personal discovery or the finding of your own private beach for an afternoon swim.

14TH DAY, SATURDAY, AT SEA
Once again, the sheer release of relaxation in a day to deepen your tan, continue your round of bridge or simply to ruminate over the glories you have seen and the incredible highlights which still lie ahead.

15TH AND 16TH DAY, SUNDAY – MONDAY, GUATEMALA (SANTO TOMAS de CASTILLA)
These two days offer the opportunity for treasures in travel never before found on a Caribbean cruise — time (and the planned programs) to experience every facet of the glory that is Guatemala — the sublime scenery of both its coastal plains and its highlands, the colonial art and architecture and, foremost, the daily life and ritual of its proud Indian population. For, while conquerors have come and gone, the land is still an Indian land and its pride in that fact is reflected in every aspect of its culture. City sophistication exists but

CARIBBEAN CRUISE

Guatemala remains an agrarian nation, the insular quality of its communes attested to by the fact that, even today, there are 22 different languages spoken within the country. The smiling farmer, tilling his fields or strolling the marketplace, differs little from his Mayan or Quiche ancestor — and the grandeur of the landscape remains the same, untouched and inviolate. (In addition to the inland overnight excursion for all guests who sign for the Optional Shore Excursion package, there will be still more extensive Special Optional Shore Excursions to include Antigua and Chichicastenango, plus the possibility of continuing by air to the greatest of Mayan sites, Tikal, then on the Merida, Uxmal and Chichen Itza — rejoining the cruise at Cozumel.

17TH DAY, TUESDAY, HONDURAS (PUERTO CORTES)
Virtually undeveloped with regard to tourism, Honduras remains one of the seldom-visited countries in Central America. Puerto Cortes will mark the point of departure for those guests who wish to visit the interior of the country, a mountainous terrain covered with dense jungle and home of an almost pure Indian population, anachronistically set aside from the times of the twentieth century. The fabulous Mayan city-ruins of Copan, which once thrived around the time of Christ and fell as quickly and mysteriously as it had arisen, may be visited by chartered aircraft for those who wish. For details of this and other excursions, consult the Optional Shore Excursion booklet.

18TH AND 19TH DAY, WEDNESDAY AND THURSDAY, MEXICO (COZUMEL ISLAND)
Little known to American travelers, the island of Cozumel has understandably been kept their own secret by knowledgeable Mexican and Central American sophisticates who have sought — and found — their own version of a holiday paradise. It is proving such a touristic magnet that more — and better — hotels spring up each year and an Acapulco-style future seems sure. The better beaches are two miles north of the little port town of San Miguel; complete informality is the keynote. (A special excursion will be offered by regularly scheduled aircraft from the island of Cozumel for those guests wishing to visit the vast Mayan city-ruins of Chichen Itza on the Yucatan Peninsula. Departure will be by air the morning of the second day, returning in the early evening.)

20TH DAY, FRIDAY, AT SEA

Inevitably "all good things must come to an end" but today stretches before you without urgency — a day for leisurely packing and the rounds of parties with friends before tomorrow morning's arrival.

21ST DAY, SATURDAY, MIAMI

Arrival has been considerately planned for just-after-breakfast. The thought of continuing homeward travel is warmed by the knowledge that few travelers before you have ever seen so much, in such comfort and in so short a time, of the fascinatingly different "worlds" of the Caribbean.

Costa Cruises emphasize elegant dining and continental service. Costa's 10 and 11 day cruise ships maintain a ratio of 3 stewards to every 5 passengers.

CARIBBEAN CRUISE 93

In downtown Pointe-a-Pitre on the French West Indies island of Guadeloupe, the traditional French greeting of a kiss on both cheeks is as common a sight as it is in Paris.
*Photo by **Rose Fu**jimoto, The Clement-Petrocik Company*
French West Indies Tourist Board

IS CARIBBEAN CRUISING REALLY FOR ME?

According to the Cruise Line International Association these are some of the most-asked questions and answers about vacations at sea.

ABC's *Love Boat* (PACIFIC PRINCESS) brings you a shipboard setting of fantasy and the instant romance of a vacation cruise.

"Beautiful," you say. But as you watch, you wonder... "Is cruising really for me?"

And it's small wonder that you wonder. Between the make-believe world of the midnight movie and the real life pleasures of contemporary cruising, stands a mountain of misconceptions.

I need to get the most I can from my money. Isn't cruising more expensive than other kinds of travel?

On the contrary. Cruising represents one of the best travel values available. Break down the cost of a cruise and compare it to what you'd spend on room, meals, transportation and entertainment for a similar vacation on land. All these things — and many more — are included in the price of your cruise ticket. You will also save money on your drinks and gifts for the folks back home, since these items aboard ship are sold at duty-free prices.

Of course, there are different cruises for different budgets. The main factor in determining the price of a cruise is its duration, and there are itineraries ranging in length from three days to three months. Just tell your travel agent how much you wish to spend, and he'll recommend the ship that is right for you.

I'm budget conscious and would have to purchase less expensive accommodations. Won't I be treated as a second-class citizen?

On a cruise, everyone eats the same meals, enjoys the same entertainment, is waited on to the same degree. The price affects only the type and location of your cabin, so select within your means and have a ball. (It is important, however, to differentiate between a cruise and a trans-Atlantic crossing. The latter often may offer two classes of service, just as air travel does.)

I can only afford an inside cabin. Isn't that to be avoided?

That common misconception dates back to the days before air-conditioning, when no porthole meant no ventilation. Today, every ship is completely climate controlled, so your cabin is as comfort-

CARIBBEAN CRUISE

able as those "outside." You have to get along without a view, but the watching is better from up on deck, anyway.

I am an avid reader; should I bring my latest best sellers?
The ship's library has the latest New York Times best-sellers. There are plenty of hard and paperback books, as well as magazines, available to read. A 14-day voyage offers the opportunity to read several novels. Usually the public rooms, deck areas and library have very comfortable chairs and good light for leisure reading. Your stateroom will have an easy chair for a more private reading area.

I live 1,000 miles from the nearest cruise port. Can I get there from here?
Yes. From anywhere in North America, you are never more than a few hours from a cruise. Your travel agent can advice you about the availability of fly/cruise packages — so can make individual flight arrangements for you — from virtually every major North American airport to points of cruise departure in all parts of the world. Most often, the fly/cruise packages represent a considerable savings in airfare and include complimentary transfers and baggage handling between airport and pier.

If I travel that far, I don't want to spend all my time on a cruise. Are there any combination packages available?
Several. Many lines offer a choice of pre- or post-cruise land packages which may be purchased at the same time you book your voyage. And in many instances, your air ticket will include return options, such as free or minimal-cost stop-overs, that enable you to make your own arrangements through your travel agent.

I don't have a lot of fancy clothes. Won't I need a whole new wardrobe?
No. Just pack as you would if you were going to any resort destination. Cruise ships are casual by day and most encourage you to do your own thing in the evening. As at home, attire is dictated by the occasion; you'll probably want to dress up for the captain's cocktail party (dinner jackets and gowns are popular, but rarely required), and dress down for the island night or luau. There's only one rule: Be comfortable.

I'm always in a hurry to get where I'm going. Won't ship travel be too slow for my taste?

When you vacation at sea, the cruise itself is the primary destination; the ports of call are a "bonus" that enhance the total experience. Your holiday begins the moment you walk up the gangway!

Vacation planning makes me nervous. Aren't there a lot of details to attend to?

Travel agents book 96% of cruises sold in North America; yours will handle all the arrangements necessary to get you from doorstep to gangway, and furnish a lot of other helpful hints besides. Chances are he's experienced many cruises first-hand, and can tell you all the ins and outs of getting fore to aft. And his services cost you nothing; his compensation comes from the cruise lines.

But not all cruises are alike. How will I know an individual ship's passport requirements, embarkation procedures, and other important details?

Virtually every company publishes a comprehensive brochure containing such information. Study it carefully and, if you still have questions, consult your travel agent again. He will get you an answer directly from the cruise line.

I'm single, and usually travel alone. Will I feel comfortable?

Absolutely. Cruising is ideal for singles because of the wide variety of activities designed to help people get acquainted; some are planned specifically with the unattached in mind. Most ships offer some single accommodations, while others publish special one-person rates for their double cabins, or will try to find you a roommate if you prefer.

There are three of us who travel together. Can we share the same cabin?

Most ships offer accommodations with extra beds for third and/or fourth persons . . . and often these additional passengers qualify for reduced rates. You can obtain exact prices from your travel agent.

I'm afraid of getting seasick. Isn't this a common problem?

Not really. Improved stabilizers on modern ships, advance availability of accurate weather information, and development of effective

CARIBBEAN CRUISE

SUN PRINCESS calls at Saint Thomas, U.S. Virgin Islands.

Codrington College, St. John-Christopher Codrington was born in Barbados in 1668. He was entered at Christ Church, Oxford in 1685 and later elected to a Fellowship at All Souls, Oxford.
When his father died, he succeeded him as Captain General and Governor of the Leeward Islands. He served 30 years. He retired to this estate in 1703 and died there seven years later.
Six years after his burial at St. Michael's Cathedral, Bridgetown, Barbados, his body was exhumed and shipped to England to be deposited in the Ante Chapel of All Souls, Oxford, where it is marked by a single stone lettered "Codrington."
This college was founded under his will dated 1702 and was opened in 1745, thus its nearest rival in the Western Hemisphere is New Brunswick Theological Seminar founded in 1784.

CARIBBEAN CRUISE

preventive medication have, for the most part, eliminated the incidence of motion sickness.

I am concerned about becoming ill. Are there facilities for treatment?

Every vessel maintains a shipboard hospital staffed by a doctor and nurse, with medication and equipment readily available to handle most emergencies.

I can't afford to be out of touch. How can my family or business contact me?

Every ship is equipped with radio to originate or receive calls while at sea, and your cruise company retains agents in every port of call who will be pleased to relay messages. A list of the latter usually is available upon request.

Several couples in our neighborhood traditionally vacation together. Do cruise lines accept group bookings?

Most do — sometimes at reduced rates, depending upon how many persons are involved. Policies vary from line to line, but your travel agent can get details for you. Because group arrangements are coordinated by the ship's staff, cruising is an easy and relaxed way for people to travel together — for business as well as pleasure.

Business? Are there meeting facilities aboard cruise ships?

Most cruise lines will be pleased to make public rooms available for meetings when they are not in general use, and their group departments will work with you to design a schedule that is compatible with the ship's. In many instances this includes access to audio/visual equipment. Meal functions, of course, are never a problem, and if your agenda calls for a private cocktail party, it's always nice to see your company logo carved in ice as a centerpiece.

I know very little about foreign cuisines and wines. How will I know what to order?

Your waiter will be glad to explain anything the menu doesn't about the variety of different and exotic international dishes which are a shipboard tradition, and your wine steward will be equally helpful in recommending the proper accompaniment. If your tastes tend to the conservative, you are also certain to find an ample selection of meat-and-potatoes style standbys, with which you can quaff an ice-cold beer.

I've heard there are different "sittings" for meals. What does that mean?

A few ships accommodate all passengers in the dining room at one time. Most, however, offer two sittings — which differ only as to schedule — and will take your request to dine early or late at the time of booking. But consider this decision carefully; you'll want to leave room for the midnight buffet.

I eat lightly during the day. Must I partake of a full lunch?

Most ships offer casual poolside buffets or barbecues in addition to a full-course lunch in the dining room, and nobody will complain if you care to splurge one day and try both.

I'm on a restricted diet. Can the ship accommodate me?

If properly notifed in advance, most cruise companies will make arrangements for salt free, low carbohydrate, kosher and other special menus. Just be sure to advise your travel agent when you book your cruise.

I'll be celebrating my wedding anniversary during the cruise. Can special arrangements be made?

Definitely ... usually a cake will be provided with the compliments of the cruise line. And if you wish to make the occasion even more memorable, orders may be placed in advance for champagne, canapes, flowers and other extra touches. Similar arrangements can be made for honeymooners, or for bon voyage parties if friends and family are seeing you off. Once again, all you need to do is advise your travel agent.

I have a tendency to gain weight. What can I do?

Join in the morning calisthenics class or walk-a-thon, make good use of the ship's exercise equipment, use the staircase instead of the elevator, or skip the second dessert. Better still, worry about it when you get home. Who wants to watch the waistline on a vacation?

I'm an active person. Won't the days be boring?

Hardly. Ships offer full and varied programs of organized activities, from dance lessons to skeet shooting, cooking demonstrations to backgammon tournaments, with just the right amount of relaxation in between. Or, you can get off on your own to jog, swim, work out in the gym or stretch out in the sauna.

CARIBBEAN CRUISE

I'm a quiet person. Will I be forced to participate?

Never. You'll find many peaceful places on your ship to read, write postcards home, or simply bask in the sun. The choice of taking part is yours.

I'm a night person. Is there anything to do?

Virtually every evening you'll find quality entertainment in the night club, first-run movies in the cinema, and dancing in the lounges and discos. Many ships also feature casinos where you can try your luck at the slot machines or gaming tables. And you won't want to miss the special events like talent night, masquerade (you may bring your costume or make one aboard ship, utilizing suggestions and materials provided by the cruise staff), and other features which are part of the grand camaraderie of cruising.

I like to meet people who have similar backgrounds and interests to mine. Will I find them?

Most definitely. Just let your travel agent guide you. Some ships cater to a particular clientele, others to a broader mix . . . but there's a cruise for just about anyone. Many lines offer sepcial interest cruises that guarantee you'll find what you're looking for in terms of both people and programming. Sign up early for those; because they enjoy a specific following, they sell out in a hurry.

I like to spend my time in meaningful pursuits. Aren't cruises nothing but fun and frivolity?

Not at all. Shipboard activities encompass a broad range of educational and cultural programs, often presented by well-known guest lecturers. Some are designed purely for enrichment, others for practical application. Many relate directly to the destinations the ship will visit, to encourage greater understanding of and interaction with the people who live there.

I like to move around. Won't I feel confined?

Confined to what? Not only are cruise ships bigger than they look, but it takes some people two full days just to discover all the amenities. If you will test yourself with a few reflective moments at the rail of a ship at sea, you'll find that "fear of confinement" is quickly replaced by the freest feeling in the world.

I like to travel with my family. Are there activities for children?

Only if they enjoy swimming, and deck games, and movies, and, of course, eating! Truth is, children are literally enchanted by shipboard life . . . it's a self-contained world of continuous things to do. During holiday seasons, there are many supervised programs planned especially for them. And no matter when you travel, cruise personnel will always pitch in to look after the youngsters while mom and dad relax. Best of all, children sharing a cabin with adults often may travel at substantially reduced rates; your travel agent will give you specific details.

I want to see as much as I can. Wouldn't I be better off on a tour?

In most instances, a cruise is a tour, encompassing several destinations in a given region such as the Caribbean, Mediterranean or South Pacific. And it's the only kind of tour allowing you to take your hotel room with you (no frequent packing and unpacking), offering you continued access to all conveniences while traveling from palce to place, and guaranteeing that the level of services will remain constant. What better way to see the world . . . or any part of it!

I like variety in my vacations. Aren't all those islands alike?

No more so than Paris is like Rome, or Tokyo like your hometown. Within the limitations imposed by operational considerations, ship itineraries are deliberately designed to take you to different kinds of destinations. And by its very nature, a cruise offers an interesting and balanced contrast between shoreside experiences and life at sea.

I think travel should be an educational experience. Since most cruise calls are brief, aren't they also superficial?

On the contrary. They provide a capsule introduction to a place, highlighting the best it has to offer. Shore excursions for cruise passengers focus on the most representative aspects of a culture, and direct you to the sights of greatest historical and archeological significance. It's an excellent way of determining whether you wish to return some day for a longer stay.

I like exotic, out-of-the-way places. Can I visit those aboard a cruise?

Ever been to Dominica? Or Mykonos? Or Ketchikan? Try to reach them other than on a cruise. The unique logistics of ship travel

CARIBBEAN CRUISE

make it possible to visit areas otherwise inaccessible as vacation destinations.

I feel uncomfortable in exotic, out-of-the-way places. Are there cruises to more highly developed locations?
How about Acapulco, Caracas and Venice, to name just a few? Itineraries are strictly a matter of personal preference; convey yours to your travel agent, and he'll recommend the best cruise for you. There's an ample selection to choose from.

I'm not a sightseer or shopper, and don't care where I go. Can't I just get away to relax?
For you, cruising is made to order. No matter how appealing a destination, the ambiance of a ship at sea is still the focal point of a cruise, and many experienced cruisers never disembark. Should you choose to remain aboard while in port, you'll find a full range of activities and services always available.

I am an incurable dreamer. Will I find instant romance?
Who knows? There's no setting more romantic than a ship at sea in the moonlight; in fact, many lovers of long standing find it the perfect place to rekindle old flames. But this is one of the few pleasures we don't promise to provide. You're on your own!

When shall I vacation in the Caribbean?
The answer is easy: any time you have a vacation . . . the Caribbean is ALWAYS in season! Of course, winter time is a super magnet for Caribbean travel (who can blame you for wanting to trade in cold blasts and snow for the islands' warm sun and sandy beaches!). But a great many others have discovered that the West Indies is a year-round paradise . . . fall, winter, spring and summer.

Yes, summer, too! Temperatures in the West Indies don't fluctuate drastically with the seasons as they do up North. In most instances, you'll find that, favored by the cooling Tradewinds, summers there are more comfortable than those of New York.

What should I wear?
Summer clothing may be worn during most of the cruise. Recommended: light-weight sports clothes, bathing suits and other beach attire.

Will I find it hot or cool; what are the temperatures in the Caribbean?

CARIBBEAN WEATHER

	JAN	FEB	MAR	APR	MAY	JUN	JUL	AUG	SEP	OCT	NOV	DEC
Bahamas	72°	72°	73°	75°	78°	81°	82°	82°	82°	80°	76°	74°
Bermuda	63°	63°	63°	65°	70°	75°	79°	80°	78°	74°	69°	65°
Antigua	76°	76°	77°	78°	79°	80°	80°	81°	81°	80°	79°	77°
Barbados	77°	76°	77°	78°	80°	81°	80°	80°	80°	80°	79°	78°
Cuba	72°	72°	74°	76°	84°	81°	82°	82°	81°	79°	75°	74°
Dominican Republic	75°	76°	76°	77°	79°	80°	80°	82°	80°	79°	78°	76°
Haiti	76°	77°	78°	79°	80°	82°	82°	82°	81°	80°	78°	77°
Jamaica	77°	77°	77°	79°	80°	82°	82°	82°	81°	81°	79°	78°
Netherlands Antilles	79°	80°	80°	81°	83°	83°	83°	83°	84°	83°	82°	82°
Puerto Rico	75°	75°	75°	77°	79°	80°	80°	81°	81°	80°	79°	76°
Trinidad and Tobago	78°	78°	79°	80°	81°	80°	80°	80°	80°	80°	80°	79°
Virgin Islands	77°	77°	77°	78°	80°	81°	82°	82°	81°	81°	79°	77°

What are Port Taxes?

The following port taxes or charges are typical: Miami—$2.00 per adult and $1.00 per child under 12; St. Maarten—$3.00 per adult and $1.50 per child under 12; San Juan—$2.50 per adult and $2.50 per child under 12; St. Thomas—$2.00 per adult and $2.00 per child under 12. These taxes will be collected upon ticket issuance or by the Purser's Office on board if they have not been paid prior to embarkation. Any addition or increase in taxes which may be levied by any government must be borne by the passenger.

So what ship should I choose for my cruise?

As you have probably found out from reading the various travel ads, there are many claims and counter claims among the various steamship lines as to why their particular ships are best for a Caribbean cruise. How do you choose the ship that really gives you most for your money? Experienced Caribbean vacationers will tell you to read between the lines... to disregard claims and concentrate on the 5 chief qualities that distinguish a true cruise ship:

CARIBBEAN CRUISE

THE SHIP

1. Is the ship expressly designed for cruising? Or is it one that changes from business travel to cruise service, with temporary makeshift installations to make it look the part?

THE LINE

2. Is the line really experienced in Caribbean cruising or is it one that is primarily a transatlantic carrier, and enters Caribbean waters only occasionally?

THE ACCOMMODATIONS

3. Are all the cabins modern, of first class calibre. Do they all have private bathroom facilities and individual air conditioning controls or are these facilities limited only to the higher-rate staterooms?

THE SERVICE

4. Is the ship personnel specifically trained to meet the very particular requirements of American vacationers strictly for pleasure?

THE CRUISE STAFF

5. Are the people who run the ship's entertainment and activities program a permanent team or merely a temporary group hired for a few cruises?

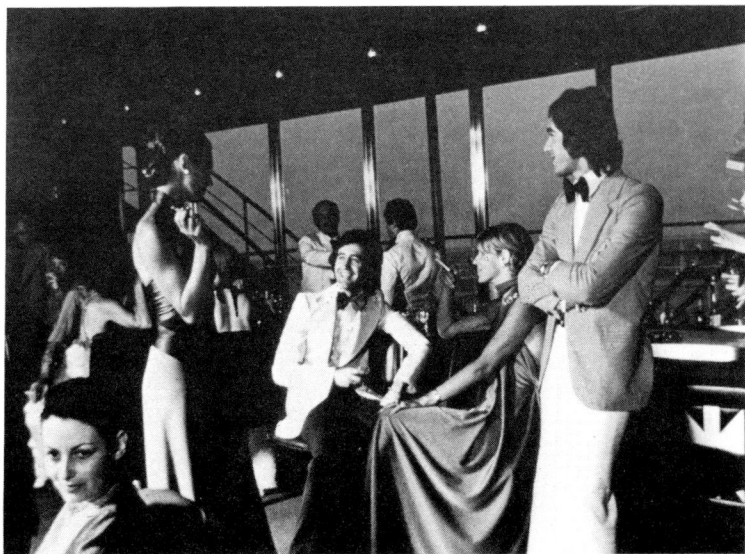

First night at sea on a Sun Line Cruise.

What to buy where in the Caribbean?

Practically the entire Caribbean is a bargain-lover's paradise. Liquor, perfume, merchandise from Europe and the rest of the world are to be found here at duty-free prices that are considerably lower than at home. Native products, too, are considerably lower than at home. Native products, too, are most interesting and reasonably priced.

Some examples of what to buy:

CURACAO, ARUBA: Europe's most renowned lines of silverware, watches and jewelry; china and glassware; perfume; liquor; table linens from both Europe and the Orient; photographic equipment; transistor radios; some continental fashions for men, women and children.

ST. MAARTEN: This lush, mountainous island, half Dutch and half French, has become a shopper's haven. The most famous stores of the Dutch West Indies now have branches here, and French perfumes sell at bargain prices.

NASSAU, BERMUDA: Primarily products from Great Britain: English china, men's and women's cashmere sweaters; slacks, Bermudas. Liquor.

GUADELOUPE, MARTINIQUE: these islands are specially known for bargains in perfumes and other French imports.

JAMAICA: Similar to Nassau, plus a special emphasis on silverware, china and glassware ... as well as the native products in their famous Straw Market. Perfume, too.

BARBADOS: A very extensive selection of English china, silver and glassware, plus a wide variety of domestic casual fashions, Hong Kong Dynasty fashions, men's ready to wear and made to measure clothes, liquor, perfume.

HAITI: Liquor, perfume, Continental gifts, jewelry, silverware, watches ... plus the island's famed specialties: unusual glowing mahogany woodenware and native Haitian art.

ST. THOMAS, V.I. Just about everything ... in great abundance. Liquor, perfume, silver, china, watches, linens, glassware. Sweaters from England and the continent. Domestic casual fashions (alterations same day). Plus ... high-style ready to wear and accessories that equal the selections of Paris, London and Rome.

CARIBBEAN CRUISE

A regular visitor to many Caribbean ports—STELLA OCEANIS (Sun Line Cruises) has 18,000 gross tonnage, carries 630 passengers on 14 day cruises. Has 8 decks, 2 swimming pools, air conditioned, stabilized. Additional facilities include: Monte Carlo room; gymnasium/sauna; children's playroom; beauty salon; duty-free boutique; hospital; cinema/theatre; discotheque; library/card room.

CARIBBEAN CRUISE DESTINATIONS OF POPULAR SHIPS

This is a listing of your favorite ships as they sailed December 1979, including embarkation port, destination and length of cruise.

( ) Cruise length shown in parens; (*) asterisk indicates length of cruise may vary.

AMERIKANIS — COSTA LINE INC.: Dec. 22 until Apr. 5 San Juan to Caribbean every Sat. (7).

AQUARIUS — HELLENIC MEDITERRANEAN: Dec. 22 until Apr. 5 San Juan to Caribbean every Sat. (7).

BOHEME — COMMODORE CRUISE LINE: Year round Miami to Caribbean every Sat. (7).

BRITANIS — CHANDRIS LTD.: Dec. 24 until Oct. 27 San Juan to Caribbean every Mon. (7).

CALYPSO — PAQUET CRUISES: Jan. 6 until May 11 Miami to Caribbean every Sun. (7); May 18 Miami Transcanal to Vancouver (19); Jun. 6 until Sep. 19 Vancouver to Alaska every Fri. (7); Sep. 26 Vancouver Transcanal to Miami (21).

CANBERRA — P & O PASSENGER DIVISION: Nov. 11 Southampton to Canary Is./Mediterranean (16); Dec. 16 Southampton to Caribbean (24).

CARIBE — COMMODORE CRUISE LINE: Nov. 17 until Apr. 19 Miami to Caribbean every Sat. (7).

CARLA C. — COSTA LINE INC.: Year round San Juan to Caribbean every Sat. (7).

CARNIVALE — CARNIVAL CRUISE LINES: Year round Miami to Caribbean every Sun. (7); Dec. 14 Norfolk to Caribbean (8).

CUNARD COUNTESS — CUNARD LINE LTD.: Year round San Juan to Caribbean every Sat. (7).

CUNARD PRINCESS — CUNARD LINE LTD.: Nov. 17 until May 17 San Juan to Caribbean every Sat. (7); May 24 San Juan Transcanal to Vancouver (19); Jun 12 until Aug. 28 Vancouver to Alaska every Thu. (7); Sep. 4 West Coast Ports Transcanal to San Juan (24*).

CARIBBEAN CRUISE

DANAE — COSTA LINE INC.: Jan. 12 until Mar. 15 San Juan to Caribbean every Sat. (7); May 17 until Oct. 4 Venice to Mediterranean (14).

DAPHNE — COSTA LINE INC.: Dec. 15 until Apr. 5 San Juan to Caribbean every Sat. (7).

DOLPHIN — PAQUET CRUISES: Until Jun. 2 Miami to Bahamas every Mon. (4), every Fri. (3).

DORIC — HOME LINES: Until Mar. 23 Port Everglades to Caribbean (9-13*); Apr. 5 until Oct. 18 New York to Bermuda every Sat. (7).

EMERALD SEAS — EASTERN STEAMSHIP LINES: Year round Miami to Bahamas every Mon. (4), every Fri. (3).

FAIRSEA — SITMAR CRUISES: Until Mar. 29 L.A. to Mexico (7-11) and L.A./San Juan Transcanal (13, 14).

FAIRWIND — SITMAR CRUISES: Until Mar. 29 Port Everglades to Caribbean (7-14*); Dec. 15, 30 & Feb. 2, 16 Pt. Everglades/Acapulco Transcanal (13, 14).

FEDERICO C. — COSTA LINE INC.: Jan. 11 until Mar. 14 Miami to Caribbean (10, 11); Jul. 31 until Sep. 29 Genoa to Canary Islands (10).

FESTIVALE — CARNIVAL CRUISE LINES: Year round Miami to Caribbean every Sat. (7).

FLAVIA — COSTA LINE INC.: From Nov. 5 Miami to Bahamas every Mon. (4), every Fri. (3).

GALILEI — ITALIAN LINE CRUISES INT'L.: Until Jun. 14 Port Everglades to Caribbean every Sat. (7).

GOLDEN ODYSSEY — ROYAL CRUISE LINE: Nov. 23 Piraeus/Las Palmas to Caribbean (24); Dec. 18 until Mar. 4 Curacao/Acapulco/Miami Transcanal (9, 10).

ISLAND PRINCESS — PRINCESS CRUISES: Until May 31 San Juan/Los Angeles Transcanal (14); From Sep. 20 Los Angeles/San Juan Transcanal (14).

KAZAKHSTAN — BLACK SEA SHIPPING COMPANY: Dec. 22 until May 24 New Orleans/Tampa to Caribbean (7, 14).

MARDI GRAS — CARNIVAL CRUISE LINES: Year round Miami to Caribbean every Sun. (7).

MERMOZ — PAQUET CRUISES: Dec. 10 La Guaira to Caribbean (10); Dec. 21 until Apr. 6 Miami to Caribbean (10).

NORDIC PRINCE — ROYAL CARIBBEAN CRUISE LINE: Until Feb. 16 Miami to Caribbean (14).

OCEANIC — HOME LINES: Until Nov. 10 New York to Bahamas/Bermuda every Sat. (7); Dec. 20 until Mar. 20 New York to Caribbean (9-13*); Mar. 29 until Oct. 18 New York to Bahamas/Bermuda every Sat. (7).

ODESSA — BLACK SEA SHIPPING COMPANY: Dec. 22 until May 24 New Orleans to Caribbean every Sat. (7); Jun. 1 New Orleans Transcanal to Vancouver (20); Jun. 22 until Sept. 7 Vancouver to Alaska every Sun. (7); Sep. 15 Vancouver Transcanal to New Orleans (20).

QUEEN ELIZABETH 2 — CUNARD LINE LTD.: Nov. 3 New York/Boston to Caribbean (12); Dec. 21 New York/Pt. Everglades to Caribbean (14); Jan. 4 New York/Norfolk to Caribbean (12); Jan. 17 New York/Pt. Everglades/Los Angeles Around the World (80); From Apr. 1 Transatlantic crossings New York — Southampton/Cherbourg; Apr. 6 New York/Pt. Everglades to Caribbean (14); Apr. 26 Southampton to Canary Islands (8); May 9 & Jun. 6 New York to Caribbean (8); Jul. 18, Aug. 16 & Sep. 21 New York to Caribbean (7); Aug. 29 Southampton to Canary Islands (7); Oct. 9 New York to Bermuda (4); Oct. 24 New York to Caribbean (7).

ROTTERDAM — HOLLAND AMERICA CRUISES: Until Nov. 10 New York to Bahamas/Bermuda every Sat. (7); Nov. 17 & Dec. 22 New York to Caribbean (18, 17); Jan. 9 New York/Pt. Everglades/Los Angeles Around World (100).

ROYAL VIKING SEA — ROYAL VIKING LINE: Nov. 14 S.F./L.A. Transcanal to Port Everglades (17); Dec. 8 Port Everglades to Caribbean (7); Dec. 15 Port Everglades to South America (28); Jan. 12 Pt. Everglades/Los Angeles Around the World (87); Apr. 8 Port Everglades to Caribbean (13); Apr. 21 Port Everglades to British Isles (10); May 1 until May 31 Southampton to North Sea/British Isles (10); Jun. 13 until Aug. 22 Copenhagen to Norway/Baltic (14); Sep. 5 Southampton Transatlantic to New York (8); Sep. 13 New York to Maritime Provinces (14); Sep. 27 New York/Pt. Everglades Transcanal to Los Angeles/San Francisco (21); Oct. 17 Los Angeles/San Francisco to South America (57).

ROYAL VIKING SKY — ROYAL VIKING LINE: Dec. 16 San

CARIBBEAN CRUISE

Francisco/Los Angeles to Hawaii (24); Jan. 9 & 26 S.F./L.A./Pt. Everglades Transcanal (33, 18); Feb. 12 Los Angeles/San Francisco to Orient (70); Apr. 23 San Francisco/Los Angeles Transcanal to N.Y. (19); May 13 & 27 New York to Maritime Provinces (14); Jun. 10 New York Transatlantic to Copenhagen (10); Jun. 20 until Aug. 1 Copenhagen to Norway/Baltic (14); Aug. 15 Copenhagen to Black Sea (25); Aug. 27 until Oct. 5 Piraeus to Black Sea (13); Oct. 18 & 31 Piraeus to Mediterranean (13).

ROYAL VIKING STAR — ROYAL VIKING LINE: Nov. 8 Piraeus Transatlantic to Port Everglades (13); Nov. 21 Port Everglades to Caribbean (4); Dec. 3 Port Everglades Transcanal to L.A./S.F. (18); Dec. 20 Los Angeles/San Francisco to Mexico (18); Jan 7 Los Angeles/San Francisco to South Pacific (45); Feb. 22 until Mar. 28 S.F./L.A./Pt. Everglades Transcanal (17-35); Mar. 28 S.F./L.A./ Pt. Everglades to Black Sea (75, 42); May 26 Port Everglades Transcanal to Los Angeles/San Francisco (18); Jun. 13 until Aug. 22 San Francisco/Los Angeles to Alaska (14); Sep. 5 San Francisco/Los Angeles to Orient (54); Oct. 29 San Francisco/Los Angeles Transcanal (35).

SAGAFJORD → NORWEGIAN AMERICA LINE: Nov. 17 until Jan. 5 Port Everglades to Caribbean (14-20*); Jan. 29 Port Everglades Around the World (91); May 4 until Oct. 19 Genoa to Mediterranean/Black Sea (14).

SANTA MAGDALENA — DELTA LINE: Year round West Coast Ports around S. America (64*) and Pacific Coast (9*).

SANTA MARIA — DELTA LINE: Year round West Coast Ports around S. America (64*) and Pacific Coast (9*).

SANTA MARIANA — DELTA LINE: Year round West Coast Ports around S. America (64*) and Pacific Coast (9*).

SANTA MERCEDES — DELTA LINE: Year Round West Coast Ports around S. America (64*) and Pacific Coast (9*).

SKYWARD — NORWEGIAN CARIBBEAN LINES: Year round Miami to Caribbean every Sat. (7).

SONG OF NORWAY — ROYAL CARIBBEAN CRUISE LINE: Year round Miami to Caribbean every Sat. (7).

SOUTHWARD — NORWEGIAN CARIBBEAN LINES: Year round Miami to Caribbean every Sat. (7).

STARWARD — NORWEGIAN CARIBBEAN LINES: Year round

Miami to Caribbean every Sat. (7).

STATENDAM — HOLLAND AMERICA CRUISES: Until Nov. 10 New York to Bermuda every Sat. (7); Nov. 19 until Mar. 24 Miami to Caribbean (10, 11).

STEFAN BATORY — POLISH OCEAN LINES: Dec. 22 London to Canary Islands (14); Jan. 5 London to Caribbean (31); Mar. 14 London to Black Sea (37).

STELLA MARIS — SUN LINE CRUISES: Dec. 20 until Mar. 21 San Juan to Caribbean/South America (14).

STELLA OCEANIS — SUN LINE CRUISES: Dec. 21 until Feb. 29 San Juan to Caribbean/ South America (14).

STELLA SOLARIS — SUN LINE CRUISES: Dec. 21 until Feb. 22 Galveston to Caribbean (12, 15*).

SUN PRINCESS — PRINCESS CRUISES: Until Nov. 17 Acapulco/Los Angeles to Mexico (7); Nov. 24 Los Angeles Transcanal to San Juan (14); Dec. 8 until May 3 San Juan to Caribbean every Sat. (7); May 10 San Juan Transcanal to Los Angeles (14); May 24 Los Angeles to Nowhere (2); May 31 until Sept. 13 Vancouver to Alaska every Sat. (7); From Oct. 4 Los Angeles/ Acapulco to Mexico (6).

SUN VIKING — ROYAL CARIBBEAN CRUISE LINE: Year round Miami to Caribbean (14).

SUNWARD II — NORWEGIAN CARIBBEAN LINES: Year round Miami to Bahamas every Mon. (4), every Fri. (3).

VEENDAM — HOLLAND AMERICA CRUISES: Nov. 11 until Apr. 27 Miami to Caribbean (14); May 11 Miami Transcanal to Vancouver (20); May 31 until Sep. 20 Vancouver to Alaska every Sat. (7); Sep. 27 Vancouver Transcanal to Miami (23).

VERACRUZ — BAHAMA CRUISE LINE: Until Nov. 24 Tampa to Mexico every Sat. (7); Dec. 1 Tampa to Caribbean (14); Dec. 14 until Apr. 18 Montego Bay to Caribbean (14).

VICTORIA — CHANDRIS LTD.: Dec. 24 until Apr. 14 San Juan to Caribbean every Mon. (7); May 17 until Oct. 18 Genoa/Venice to Mediterranean (14).

VISTAFJORD — NORWEGIAN AMERICA LINE: Nov. 2 Barbados to South America (23); Nov. 25 Barbados to Caribbean (7); Dec. 2 until May 10 Port Everglades to Caribbean (6-18*); May 24 Port Everglades to North Sea (13); Jun. 7 until Aug. 16 Hamburg

CARIBBEAN CRUISE 113

to Norway/Scandinavia/Baltic (14); Oct. 7 Cuxhaven Transatlantic to Port Everglades (18).

VOLENDAM — HOLLAND AMERICA CRUISES: Nov. 6 Miami to Caribbean (5); Nov. 11 until Mar. 30 Miami to Caribbean every Sat. (7).

WORLD RENAISSANCE — COSTA LINE INC.: Year round Miami to Caribbean (10, 11*).

SS EMERALD SEAS—an elegant ocean liner, Lanai suites and double staterooms, bath, TV, music channels. Ballroom, lounges, theatre, entertainment, parties. Lido deck and pool, game rooms, gift shop. Fine food and service. Step ashore sightseeing, shopping and tropical night life in Nassau and relaxing daytime sailing to Freeport for more sightseeing and shopping.

An evening's entertainment is part of your floating resort life aboard ship in the Caribbean.

Chapter 6

LIFE ON BOARD

Cruising is a way of life — the good life. All passengers are V. I. P.'s with one-class of service. Your ship is fully air-conditioned, and has swimming pools, and there's enough going on every day to fill the ship's newspaper. At night, you'll find your floating holiday resort becomes a kind of ocean-going showboat, with music, dancing, and cabaret. For sheer comfort and relaxation, shipboard life is hard to beat with great food and friendly efficient service.

Purser's Lobby—ISLAND PRINCESS

So who goes cruising? Nice people. People like us. Moms and Dads go, with the kids; honeymooners go; four pretty girls from the typing pool save up and share a cabin; old timers celebrate their anniversaries and share a luxury suite; businessmen go, and get to know their wives again; lone wolves go, and get to know everyone, dieters go, and lose it, old folk, young folk, babies, joiners-in and count-me-outers, everybody goes, and they ALL have a wonderful time. That's the general idea, but how does it *work*?

Take any day at sea. It begins as early as you like, or as late. An early morning cup of tea from your cabin steward or stewardess followed by a brisk walk around the deck. OR with a lazy lie-in and a good old-fashioned, leisurely breakfast in the restaurant, time to eat your way through eggs and bacon, toast and marmalade and coffee while you plan your day. You can do everything — or nothing.

Deck quoits, tennis, shuffleboard, Bingo, and bouncing in and out of the pool, and joining in on everything... OR hot bouillon on the Promenade Deck, and a gentle stroll; cool drinks by the pool, a game of Bridge, visit the hairdresser, letters to write, books to read, and hour upon golden hour to spend, dreaming in the sun.

At sea, you live it your way. If you want to talk, there's always someone; if you want to be alone, then that's no problem either.

There's never a dull moment aboard your cruise ship. Life can be as active or as slow-paced as you like. There are bridge lessons and tournaments by experienced instructors, dance classes, outdoor deck competition, port lectures, language classes or that relaxing deck chair by the pool with a long, cool drink. There is an endless variety of things to do and partake in. Everyday you will receive a morning newspaper listing all the activities, their times and locations for that day.

In the evening, the ship becomes a floating nightclub.

LIFE ON BOARD

Professional entertainment in the lounge, many times headed by big-name entertainers, first-run movies in the theater (and sometimes an old favorite), and late-night dancing to a four-piece orchestra or music in the discotheque are just a few of the evening activities to enjoy.

On some evenings, the passengers become the show. There is the masquerade ball or a talent show with prizes going to the winners. Both of these prove to be very popular with the passengers, both old and young alike.

All cruise ships have at least one swimming pool, with many having two and sometimes three. Gymnasiums and saunas are there to help you take off those few pounds gained at dinner the night before. There is skeet shooting and, for golf addicts, many cruise ships have golf driving with the largest range in the world — the open sea!

The combination of all of these activities, plus the excellent service, food and accommodations, the fascinating ports-of-call, new-found friends and total relaxation make cruising a very rewarding experience and create fond memories to be cherished the rest of your life.

The nice thing about your cruise fare is that it is practically all-inclusive. The fare includes accommodations reserved and paid for, your transportation by ship, use of the ship as a hotel in port and at sea, all meals (usually 5 a day) and all entertainment on board.

A Typical Day on Board

It's your vacation, so you can be active, or as relaxed as you like.

Every evening, a schedule of the following day's activities is delivered to each cabin.

Sample Day

Time	Activity	Location
6:30 am	Eye-opener coffee is served	Promenade
7:45 am	Breakfast is served (Main seating)	Dining Room
9:00 am	Breakfast is served (Late seating)	Dining Room
9:00 am	Slot Machines open	Casino
9:30 am	Exercises and deck hike	Sun Deck
10:00 am	Coffee, rolls & bouillon	Lido Deck
10:30 am	The Shore Excursion Office is open for sale of tour tickets	Upper Deck Forward
10:30–11:15 am	Your cruise staff will be available to help you with materials and ideas for the Crazy Hat & Masquerade Party	Showplace
10:45 am	Learn to "do the Hustle" with Debbie	Mardi Gras Club
11:15 am	Ports-of-call briefing with your Cruise Director	Showplace
Noon	Luncheon is served (Main seating)	Dining Room
Noon–3:00 pm	Complimentary hamburgers & hot dogs	Lido Deck
12:30–1:30 pm	Fun & games in the sun	Pool Deck
1:30 pm	Luncheon is served (Late Seating)	Dining Room
2:00 pm	Current Feature Length Movie (Movie repeated at 4, 6 and 8 pm)	Cinema
2:00–3:00 pm	Horseracing "Daily Double" $$$	Showplace
2:00–3:00 pm	Calypso music	Poolside
2:30 pm	Trapshooting	Upper Deck, Aft
2:30 pm	Bridge Tournament begins	Riverboat Club
2:45 pm	Games available (Scrabble, Password, Chess)	Promenade
3:00 pm	Grandmother's Bragging Party	Mardi Gras Club
3:30 pm	Visit to ship's bridge (please meet promptly at the Purser's Office at 3:30)	
3:45 pm	Plank Jousts	Poolside
4:00 pm	Tea is served	Lido Deck
5:15 pm	Musical cocktail time	Riverboat Lounge
6:00 pm	Dinner is served (Main seating)	Dining Room
7:00 pm	Full Gambling Casino opens— Try your luck!	Casino
7:15 pm	Musical cocktail time	Riverboat Lounge
8:00 pm	Dinner is served (Late seating)	Dining Room
8:30 pm	Dancing to the tunes of Mark V	Mardi Gras Club
9:00 pm	It's Jackpot Bingo Time for mountains of money $$$	Showplace

LIFE ON BOARD

10:00 pm	Registration for the Crazy Hat & Masquerade Party	Riverboat Lounge
10:30 pm	The Crazy Hat & Masquerade Party begins	Showplace
12:30 am	Midnight Buffet is served	Dining Room
12:15 am	MIDNIGHT SPECIAL Cabaret Show featuring Harold Wand	Mardi Gras Club
12:00–'til...	"The Good Time" entertains into the whee hours	Fly-Aweigh Disco
1:30 am	Late night Buffet is served	Promenade
2:00 am	Fly-Aweigh and Casino still going strong	

An Exercise Room is a Fun Place.

Widely known as the "Happy Ship", the FAIRWIND is your floating hotel for the enjoyable days and nights as she sails into balmy tropical waters. Everything about her is designed for carefree vacation living and you are invited to make the most of her spacious decks, pool areas and the beautifully appointed lounges.
Of course the sun and the sea are yours to enjoy during the cruise, just stretch out in your deck chair and let the sun and the seabreezes chase your cares away.

Please feel free to make use of all the facilities made available for your comfort, pleasure and convenience.

Above everything else, it is the "People" who man the "FAIRWIND" who make your dream vacation come true. Attentive cabin stewards and stewardesses to cater to your needs, the gracious restaurant staff who serve in a manner which makes dining a delight, with tempting dishes prepared by master chefs. Also, the friendly personnel in attendance in the public rooms and at the bars will cater to your wishes.
An experienced cruise staff will conduct indoor and outdoor activities inviting your participation and supply top flight entertainment.

On board "FAIRWIND" the emphasis is on ease and comfort, so completely relaxing and unwinding that everything is easy to get used to in no time at all.

Captain Rodolfo POTENZONI, Chief Purser Angelo GHIGGINI, Cruise Director Tony NOICE and his Staff, and the Hospitable Italian Officers and Crew extend sincere wishes for a wonderful Cruise vacation and promise to make this a most memorable vacation.

LIFE ON BOARD

Highlights of Main Activities During the Cruise

SUNDAY, APRIL 9, 1978 — AT SEA
  Dance Class
  Welcome Talk and Port Information
  Bingo
  Muster Drill for all Passengers
  Dance Music and Movie
  Captain's Welcome Cocktail Party and Dinner
  Showtime and Late Cabaret
  Dress: FORMAL

MONDAY, APRIL 10, 1978 — CAP HAITIEN
Arrival: 8.00 a.m. — Departure: 3.00 p.m.
  Tours Ashore
  Horse Races
  Singles Party
  Dance Music and Movies
  Showtime and Late Cabaret
  Ladies Night
  Dress: INFORMAL

TUESDAY, APRIL 11, 1978 — SAN JUAN
Arrival: 2.00 p.m. — Departure: 2.00 a.m. (after midnight)
  Tours Ashore
  Visit to the ship's bridge
  Travel talk on Ports
  Dance Music and Movies
  Dress: INFORMAL

WEDNESDAY, APRIL 12, 1978 - St. THOMAS
Arrival: 8.00 a.m. — Departure: 4.00 p.m.
  Tours Ashore
  Service Clubs Meeting
  Bingo
  Masquerade Carnival
  Late Cabaret
  Dress: INFORMAL or COSTUME

THURSDAY, APRIL 13, 1978 - AT SEA
  Bridge Tournament
  Ship's tournaments on deck
  Visit to the ship's bridge
  Gala Kentucky Derby
  Showtime and Late Cabaret
  Dress: FORMAL

FRIDAY, APRIL 14, 1978 - NASSAU
Arrival: 1.00 p.m. — Departure: 7.30 p.m.
  Disembarkation talk and briefing on tipping etc.
  Tours ashore
  Snowball Bingo
  Showtime
  Dress: CASUAL

SATURDAY, APRIL 15, 1978
  Arrival at Port Everglades, Florida

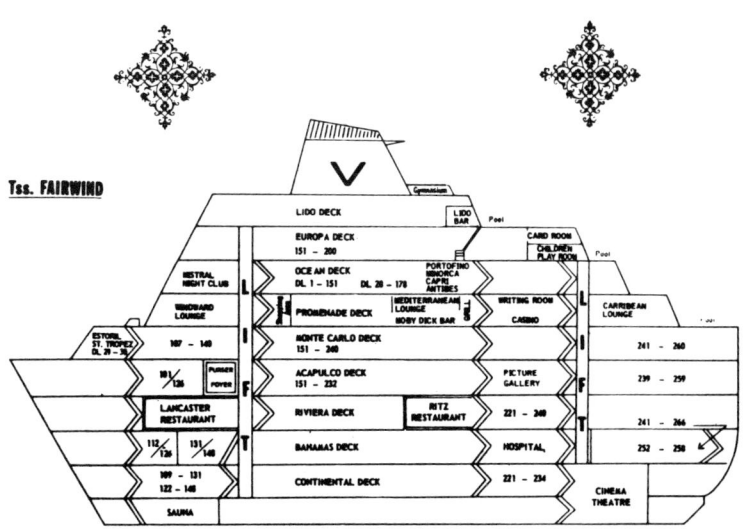

The above advanced program is for general information only and is subject to last minute changes. For detailed events,
Please see "The New on The Wind" which will placed in your cabin every night — Thank You.

Today's Activities

SUNDAY, APRIL 9, 1978
Sunrise 5.51 * Sunset 6.12

8.00 a.m.	THE GOLF RANGE OPENS. Come and practice your swing.
9.00 a.m.	CATHOLIC MASS will be celebrated in the Cinema by Rev. Thomas Butler.
9.30 a.m.	MORNING EXCERCISES – Promenade Deck.
9.55 a.m.	HIGHLIGHTS OF THE DAY – Broadcast over P.A. System and on Radio Channel 4.
10.00 a.m.	INTERDENOMINATIONAL DIVINE SERVICE with Rev. Thomas Butler – Cinema.
10.00 a.m.	COMPLIMENTARY DANCE CLASS with Jamie and Jackie – Windward Lounge.
10.00 a.m.	SCRABBLE, CHESS AND CHECKERS TOURNAMENTS in the Mediterranean Lounge.
10.15 a.m.	COMPLIMENTARY GOLF CLINIC with Rick – Promenade Deck, Fwd.
11.00 a.m.	**INFORMAL TRAVEL TALK ON OUR APPROACHING PORTS OF CALL.** By the Cruise Director, Tony NOICE, plus details on the shore excursions and latest U.S. Customs Information. This will take place in the Windward Lounge and also projected on TV and broadcast on radio channel 4.
2.30 p.m.	ITALIAN LESSON with Georgiana in the Mediterranean Lounge.
2.30 p.m.	PING PONG TOURNAMENT – Meet at the table on the Promenade Deck, Fwd.
2.45 p.m.	BRIDGE MEETING – Interested passengers are invited to join our Bridge Experts, Col. and Mrs Sommers in the Card Room, on Riviera Deck, Fwd.
3.45 p.m.	**GENERAL MUSTER OF PASSENGERS FOR EMERGENCY DRILL – In accordance with the Iternational Convention of the Safety of Life at sea, all passengers are obliged to attend this important and compulsory Muster. Please follow the instruction given by P.A. System.**
4.15 p.m.	AFTERNOON MUSICAL TEA with Dan Lanning at the Piano – Mediterranean Lounge.
4.15 p.m.	**B I N G O** – Windward Lounge.
4.30 p.m.	SHUFFLEBOARD TOURNAMENT – Meet on Lido Deck.
5.00 p.m. - 8.00 p.m.	TUNE IN ON RADIO CHANNEL 2 FOR SIX HALF HOUR NOSTALGIC MUSIC.
5.00 p.m. - 6.00 p.m.	CALYPSO MELODIES with "The Calypso Quartet" in the Caribbean Lounge.
6.00 p.m. - 6.45 p.m.	MUSICAL COCKTAIL TIME
7.45 p.m. - 8.30 p.m.	with "The Roger James Trio" in the Caribbean Lounge.
	C A P T A I N ' S C O C K T A I L P A R T Y
6.00 p.m. Main Sitting	The Master of the vessel, Captain Rodolfo POTENZONI, cordially invites
7.45 p.m. Final Sitting	all passengers for Welcome Aboard Cocktails in the Windward Lounge.
7.45 p.m. - 8.45 p.m.	MUSICAL COCKTAIL TIME with Dan Lanning at the Piano in the Mediterranean lounge.
9.00 p.m. - 12.00 Mid.	MUSIC FOR YOUR DANCING with "The Quintet" in the Windward Lounge.
9.00 p.m. & 10.45 p.m.	**G A L A W E L C O M E S H O W**
	Starring: DAVID MASTERS "The Funnyman from Fiddler on the Roof"
	JEAN BONARD "An Enchanting Song-Stylist"
	BERNIE FIELDS "Virtuoso of the Harmonica"
	Accompanied by "The Quintet" in the Windward Lounge (2nd show also on TV)
10.00 p.m. - 1.30 a.m.	MUSIC FOR DANCING with "The Roger James Trio" interludes by "The Calypso Quartet" in the Caribbean Lounge.
10.00 p.m. - 12.00 Mid.	PIANO MELODIES with Dan Lanning in the Mediterranean Lounge.
11.00 p.m. - 3.00 a.m.	THE MISTRAL NIGHT CLUB opens. Music by "The Fair-Ones"
12.30 a.m.	**LATE SHOW CABARET**
	Starring: RON MARRIOTT "A new fashioned song & dance man" – Music by "The Fair-Ones"
	THE SUGGESTED ATTIRE FOR THIS EVENING IS: F O R M A L (This applies in all lounges until the wee hours)
TODAY'S MOVIE:	The Cinema is situated on the Continental Deck, Aft. Please use aft elevators.
8.30 p.m. & 10.30 p.m.	"THE ONE & ONLY" Rated: PG – Duration: 98 minutes Starring: Henry Winkler and Kim Darby (Shown also on TV)
N O T E :	There will be a meeting of the NRTA / AARP Group with your escort, Anita, this morning at 10 o'clock in the Mistral Lounge, Ocean Deck, Fwd.
MEDICAL SERVICE OFFICE :	Bahamas Deck, Aft. From: 9.00 a.m. to 11.00 a.m. and from 3.30 p.m. to 5.30 p.m. CALL ANY TIME – DIAL 700 – NIGHT TIME: ONLY EMERGENCY
N O T E :	Our golf range can ONLY be reached by taking the stairway up from Monte Carlo and Acapulco Decks, all the way forward

MEAL HOURS

6.30 a.m. - 7.30 a.m.	COFFEE FOR EARLY BIRDS will be served on Promenade Deck	
7.30 a.m. - 9.30 a.m.	BREAKFAST will be served in both Restaurants	
7.30 a.m. - 10.30 a.m.	CONTINENTAL BREAKFAST served in your cabin - Contact your cabin steward	
11.00 a.m.	BOUILLON will be served on Promenade Deck	
12.00 noon - 1.30 p.m.	POOLSIDE SNACK FOR SUN LOVERS with Calypso Quartet - Prom. Deck aft	
12.00 noon	LUNCHEON - MAIN SITTING - will be served in both Retsaurants	
12.00 noon - 2.00 p.m.	NEAPOLITAN PIZZA will be served in the Grill Promenade Deck, midship	
1.30 p.m.	LUNCHEON - FINAL SITTING - will be served in both Restaurants	
4.15 p.m.	AFTERNOON TEA - will be served in the Mediterranean Lounge	
6.45 p.m.	**WELCOME GALA DINNER MAIN SITTING** will be served in both Restaurants	
8.30 p.m.	**WELCOME GALA DINNER** FINAL SITTING will be served in both Restaurants	
11.00 p.m. - 2.00 a.m.	PIZZA - The Grill, Prom. Deck, midship (sorry, pizza is NOTSERVED in the cabin)	
12.00 mid - 1.00 a.m.	MIDNIGHT BUFFET will be served in the Ritz Restaurant, Riviera Deck aft	
1.30 a.m.	SNACKS FOR THE NIGHT OWLS will be served in the Mistral Night Club	

ACTIVITIES FOR JUNIORS "YOUTH CENTRE" EUROPA DECK AFT - Centre Hours : 9.00 a.m. to 12.00 Midnight

CHILDREN'S PROGRAM :

9.00 a.m.	Meet the counselors and explore the ship		4.00 p.m.	Ice Cream
10.00 a.m.	Cartoons		4.30 p.m.	Bingo-Win a Prize!
11.00 a.m.	Arts and Crafts- Making Yarn Animals		8.30 p.m.	Paper Design
1.30 p.m.	Supervised Swimming		9.30 p.m.	Story Time

TEENAGER'S PROGRAM :

9.00 a.m.	Soda a Go-Go opens		4.00 p.m.	Ice Cream
10.00 a.m.	Teen meeting to learn about the ship		4.30 p.m.	Music and Games
11.00 a.m.	Teenage Ping Pong Tournament		8.30 p.m.	Dancing and More!
1.30 p.m.	Swimming and Pool Games- Lido Pool		10.30 p.m.	Late Feature Movie

---

T.S.S. FAIRWIND

MASTER
Captain RODOLFO POTENZONI C.S.L.C.

SHIP'S STAFF

Chief Engineer GIORGIO DORIGO	Staff Captain DOMENICO TRINGALE	Chief Purser ANGELO GHIGGINI
Staff Engineer ANTONIO VAUDO		Chief Surgeon FILIBERTO ZADINI M.D.

HOTEL DEPARTMENT

Maitre d'Hotel MARIO ANSELMI	Chief Steward UGO BENEDETTI Chef de Cuisine STEFANO GADALETA	Chief Cabin Stewards FRANCO ROSSINI ROBERTO PORCELLA

CRUISE STAFF

Social Directress/Director GEORGIANA MAGOLIE JUDI BARLOWE RICK ADAMS BERNIE FIELD	Cruise Director TONY NOICE Asst. Cruise Director RON MARRIOTT Piano Vocalist NICK MESSINA	Children's Co-ordinator MAUREEN RICKER Children's Counselors ALICE WELCH CYNTHIA RUTKOWSKI PENNY CRADDOCK PAULINE PAPLAS
Dance Team HENRY & MARIA HOFFMAN	Entertainers DAVID MASTERS JEAN BONARD KAY CAROLE JAMIE & JACKIE McVICAR	
Bridge Lecture COL. AND MRS SOMMERS		Ship's Orchestras "THE QUINTET" THE FAIR-ONES ROGER JAMES TRIO CALYPSO QUARTET
Catholic Chaplain BUTLER Rev. THOMAS		

SERVICE ON BOARD

Cruise lines pride themselves in the quality of service that they have provided aboard their ships. The many ships of Italy, France, England, Greece, Germany and the Scandinavian countries each had a crew as distinctive as the ship itself. Many cruise lines have built their reputations on the service provided by their experienced crews.

With economics and labor unions being what they are today, however, many lines have been forced to abandon the one-nationality crew aboard their vessels. It is not unlikely to find a Norwegian cruise ship staffed by Norwegian officers and a service crew made up of Bahamians, Haitians, Italians and Koreans. Holland American Cruises has been able to retain their Dutch officers, but the majority of the service crew are Indonesian, trained at Holland America's own training school in Java.

A few cruise lines have been able to retain their one-nationality identity aboard ship. Sitmar Cruises and Costa Line are exclusively Italian; Royal Cruise Line and Sun Line Cruises are Greek; and Pacific Far East Line is American.

Whatever cruise line you eventually chose, you are assured of excellent service by the crew. Your room steward is always at hand to provide you with fresh towels and linens, to make the beds and tidy the stateroom, or to get that extra bucket of ice for an evening party. On practically all ships, room service is available so that you can order an extra sandwich before retiring at 2 A. M.

Everywhere on the ship there is someone at your service.

CRUISE ACCOMMODATIONS

Once the decision has been made as to where you want to go, on what ship and how long, then you can choose your stateroom. When the stateroom category has been chosen, the cruise line will, in most cases, give a choice of

LIFE ON BOARD

This stateroom offers luxurious comfort for a couple's fourteen day cruise to the Caribbean islands.

staterooms within that particular price category. Occasionally the cruise line will be unable to give you a cabin in the category of your choice, and will instead, give you a RATE GUARANTEE. This is based on an anticipated reservation turnover and guarantees that you will have accommodations at sailing time, equal to or better than the chosen rate. A stateroom number is usually assigned 2 to 3 weeks prior to sailing. **Travel Tip. Never turn a guarantee down — you may get superior accommodations at medium or minimum rates.**

Your stateroom, your home away from home, has been designed for comfort and relaxation. Cruise ship accommodations can be what you expect, if you know where you want to be and how much relaxing and entertaining space you require. Remember that vacation vessels were specifically designed for your needs. The cruise stateroom is your personal living space, any hour of the day or night. Your stateroom is really two rooms in one. By day, it is a sitting room, and a perfect place to entertain friends or just relax, read or prepare for the day's activities in comfort. At night, a plush couch becomes a comfortable bed. Your stateroom may be equipped with a two-channel radio, private telephone, wall-to-wall carpeting, air-conditioning, light console on each bed and private bathroom. In short, all the comforts of home. In deluxe cabins, a separate large sofa, color TV and a refrigerator/bar unit may be featured. Your stateroom will probably have standard American electric current and sockets, so you can use your hair dryer, electric razor or any lightweight appliance without the need for a troublesome electric converter. Some cruise ships are older than others, and may be equipped with only 220 D. C. current which will require a converter, obtained from the purser. Your travel agent can advise you on this in plenty of time. There is always someone available, day or night, to answer your smallest request. From the color brochures, you know that there are differences in rooms based on fares. A ship's staterooms are rated according to type and location of accommodation. Fares are usually based on two to a room per person basis. In recent times, it sometimes seems that more and more passengers are being carried in smaller and smaller cabins, particularly on the non-luxury ships. With new ships under construction and older ships like the SS NORWAY back in service, you can easily find comfortable accommodations, even lavish living, if you are willing to pay for it.

Your stateroom has a limited amount of space available due to marine construction techniques and will not be as large as a conventional hotel room, but it is usually comparable in amenities and comforts offered.

On a modern vacation ship, staterooms will feature

LIFE ON BOARD

several types of bed arrangements. The smallest room available (and usually the least expensive) normally has an upper and lower berth and located on the lower decks of the ship. The beds are not as long and wide as those found in hotels and a ladder is used for access to the upper berth.

With few exceptions, most cruise ships marketed in the West have all their staterooms with two lower beds. These are arranged one of two ways: the standard side-by-side arrangement with a night stand or dresser in between; or in an "L" shape, with one bed against an outside bulkhead and the other against an inner wall. In addition to providing greater space, "L" shape bed arrangements allow staterooms to become sitting rooms by day so that occupants may entertain guests without the appearance of a bedroom.

Modern elegance is the dominant motif of all GOLDEN ODYSSEY staterooms.

Outside double room on Holland America's SS ROTTERDAM.

A limited number of staterooms on some ships have double beds and are usually found in the higher-priced categories or suites and located on the upper decks. Natural light in a stateroom is provided by portholes or windows. On newer cruise ship, outside staterooms will often have two portholes.

All staterooms aboard new deluxe cruise ships have private bathroom facilities. Compact as they are, the bathrooms include a toilet, vanity, and a shower and/or tub bath. Tub baths are usually found in the suites and higher-priced staterooms. Other features found in staterooms are dressers, mirrors, abundant drawer and wardrobe space, individual air-conditioning controls and a multi-channel radio. A few cruise ships even have closed-circuit TV, so that entertainment from the lounge or movies from the theater can be viewed in the privacy of the stateroom.

The price of accommodations on a cruise ship, generally,

LIFE ON BOARD

is determined by the following factors:

Size — Number of square feet of living area in the stateroom.

Location — Forward to aft (the most desirable being midships, slight forward, where motion and vibration are at a minimum).

Decks — Most passengers prefer the higher decks (although the higher decks do not necessarily provide the most comfortable sailing); lower-priced accommodations are usually on the lower decks which are rarely below the waterline on new ships.

Inside or Outside — Staterooms with portholes always cost more than those without. On newer ships, inside and outside staterooms on the same deck can be equal in size,

Sumptuous outdoor deck buffets are a highlight of GOLDEN ODYSSEY cruises. Both buffet and served cuisine are specially tailored to meet the tastes of the discriminating American passenger.

but those with portholes bring higher fares and those with windows instead of portholes are priced even higher.

Bed — Arrangement (upper and lower berths, two lower beds, "L"-shaped arrangement, or a king-size double bed).

Bathroom Facilities — With a very few exceptions, all ships feature staterooms with private bathrooms. Those staterooms with bathtubs are priced higher.

Proximity to Public Areas — Closest to dining room, lounge and other public rooms are normally higher priced.

DINING

Dining at sea becomes a pride of culinary delights. Cruise ship dining rooms compare with the best restaurants ashore. Every night the chefs outdo themselves creating delicious specialties; they vie for your compliments with course after course of irresistible temptations. From hors d'oeuvres to soups, fish, pasta, roasts, poultry, salads and sherbets to extravagant desserts, followed by a presentation of cheeses and fresh fruits. To complement your dinner, you have a choice of distinguished wines from one of the world's great wine cellars. Some lines have a small charge for wine.

For the Welcome Aboard Dinner following the Captain's Cocktail Reception, and at your ship's Farewell Dinner, you'll have the chance to wear your most festive fashions. Special nights will bring the flavor and charm of foods from foreign lands, and other evenings may feature Caribbean and Continental specialities.

Your dining room will surround you with gracious decor. You'll find crisp linen clothes and fresh-cut flowers on the tables. Friendly solicitous waiters are always nearby to service you. You can even request a table in either a smoking or non-smoking area. Simply state your preference in advance.

Between dinner time and midnight, the sea air works

LIFE ON BOARD 131

wonders on your appetite, and you're ready for the bountiful Midnight Buffet — a superlative array of meats, fish, salads, fruits and delectable desserts.

All delicious reasons why so many passengers find it a joy to come to dinner while vacationing in the Caribbean.

On some vacation vessels the dining room is large enough to serve everyone at a single, relaxed seating. It may be high on an upper deck, and walled with windows, where the *piece de resistance* at every meal is a horizon-to-horizon view.

Costa's MS WORLD RENAISSANCE relies on the expertise of 15 chefs and assistants each schooled in various phases of the culinary arts. During an 11 day cruise, Costa chefs handle an average of 12,500 pounds of meat, fish and poultry; 16,200 pounds of fruit and vegetables and 7,400 pounds of pasta.

DINING SCHEDULE AND MENUS

Table reservation: Seats in the main restaurant dining room will be assigned by the Maitre d'Hotel after embarkation or at the time of booking.

Meals Schedule: The following is typical for the serving of meals.

> Breakfast: Open sitting, from 7:30 to 9:30 a. m. In the cabins breakfast will be served from 7:30 to 10:30 a. m.
>
> Bouillon: Served at 11:00 a. m. on deck (optional service)
>
> Lunch: First sitting, 12:00 noon; second sitting, 1:30 p. m.
>
> Tea: Served at 4:40 p. m. on deck
>
> Dinner: First sitting, 7:00 p. m.; second sitting 8:30 p. m.

Midnight Buffet is always available. You may help yourself to anything from just coffee to a full course buffet.

Any deviation from the above schedule will appear in the Daily Shipboard Activities.

Wines: A choice selection of the finest wines is available at moderate prices. Orders will be accepted by the Wine Stewards.

Weather permitting, there is also a buffet luncheon on deck.

Evenings in the islands are special. You will enjoy before-dinner cocktails with your friends. Your ship's saloon bar is always open. Then sit down to a graciously served candle-light dinner in the open-air saloon. Along with wine served in pewter goblets, charcoal-broiled filet mignon, fresh caught lobster and paella, you will savor the exotic cuisine of the West Indies. Delight in soursop soup, dasheen, tannia and calalu, prepared according to native recipes, then, for dessert, papaya, banana flambé and sapodilla. This gourmet repast will set your mood for an

LIFE ON BOARD

after-dinner liquor and a fine evening ahead.

This is always a choice of distinctive bars which enable you to change the scene daily to observe an ancient maritime custom and lift your glass as the sun goes over the yardarm — at unbelievable low prices. Take in the afternoon action around the swimming pools from the vantage spot where drinks are served, have an early evening cocktail before dinner, join your friends around the circular bar, and have your night cap at an intimate club bar. Don't forget the captain's cocktail party, gala welcome aboard dinner, welcome aboard cabaret show, and dance to your favorite melodies before the midnight buffet is served.

If you wish to have a Bon Voyage party in your stateroom, the cruise lines can supply alcoholic beverages, ice, glasses, and soft drinks. Please advise the line one week in advance of sailing; there is a Customs regulation if you do not have the week's notice. You can usually bring your own alcoholic beverages aboard. Your Room Steward will make ice, soft drinks and glasses available to you at nominal prices.

Let them entertain you. Or visit a night club, disco or theater during a Costa Cruise aboard the FLAVIA. Theme cruises geared to a variety of special interests are scheduled throughout Costa's cruise season.

Typical Menus

The food is always delicious, plentiful and varied. Along with breakfast, lunch and dinner you can expect mid-morning snacks with bouillon, complimentary hamburgers, hot dogs or pizzas by the pool, an afternoon tea and two dazzling, well-laden midnight buffets. All meals include diet selections for weight watchers. Special dietary needs (diabetic, salt free, kosher, etc.) are available with two weeks advance notice.

Breakfast

You may have a *full* breakfast in bed any day you wish.

Chilled Juices
Grapefruit
Prune
Orange
Tomato
Apple

Express Breakfast
Orange Juice
Scrambled Eggs
Crisp Bacon
Toast
Beverage

Cold Cereals
Corn Flakes
Rice Krispies
Frosted Flakes
Special K
Puffed Rice
Bran Flakes

Fruits
Half Grapefruit
Baked Apple
Orange Sections
Grapefruit Sections
Stewed Prunes
Melon in Season
Kadota Figs

Hot Cereals
Cream of Wheat
Oatmeal

Eggs
Boiled (To Your Order)
Eggs Benedict
Poached
Fried
Scrambled

Fish
Panned Scotch Kippers
 and Onions
Smoked Nova Scotia Lox &
 Cream Cheese
Smoked Sable Fish

Upon Request, Served with White Grits or Hash Brown Potatoes

From the Grill
Hickory Smoked Ham
Sugar-Cured Ham
Hot Pancakes
Country Style Sausage
Corned Beef Hash
French Toast
(Served with Honey,
Maple Syrup or Jellies)

Omelettes
Plain
Ham
Diced Onion
Cheese
Jelly
Minced Lox

LIFE ON BOARD

Most people find it more congenial to join friends in the dining room.

BON VOYAGE

Assorted Roll Basket
Toast

Beverages

Coffee　　Milk　　Postum　　Tea　　Sanka　　Hot Chocolate

Luncheon

Chilled Juices
Apple Nectar
Apricot Nectar
Tropical Fruit
　Punch
Pear Nectar
Cranberry
Peach Nectar
Apple
Orange

Soups
Jamaican Kidney Bean
Puree Mongol Aux
　Croutons
Puree of Stock, Semonlina
Consomee Imperial
Beef Broth with Rice
Cream of Chicken A
　La Reine
Oxtail Soup
Cream of Celery
Bean and Bacon
French Rose (Tomato
　and Onion with Dry
　Sherry)

Entrees

Combination Ham & Cheese Sandwich
Corned Beef Sandwich
Club Sandwich
Cold Roast Beef Sandwich
Broiled Chop Steak, Mushroom Sauce
Golden Brown Filet of Sole, Tartar Sauce
Old-Fashioned Beef Stew
Hungarian Goulash, Broad Noodles
Baby Beef Liver (Pan-Broiled with Browned Onions)
Boneless Chicken Gourmet
Chicken Tetrazini Au Gratin with Spaghetti
Baked Pork Chops
Lasagne Neapolitan
Broiled Baby Pompano
Finnan Haddie
Shrimp Newburg, Bed of Rice
Mushroom Omelet
Spanish Omelet
Western Omelet
Cheese Blintzes with Sour Cream

LOW CALORIE DIET SPECIALS

Tuna Fish Salad, Garni
Fresh Fruit Jello (side order of Cottage Cheese or Sherbet)
Shrimp Salad Supreme, Garni
Chopped Liver Platter, Garni
Chicken Salad Supreme, Garni

LIFE ON BOARD

Vegetables

Whipped Potatoes
Oven Browned Potatoes
Buttered Carrots
Broccoli Newburg
Buttered Corn Niblets
Harvard Beets
French Cut Green Beans

White Rice
Creamed Onions
Carrots and Peas
Brussel Sprouts
Buttered Noodles
Rutabagas

Salads

Creamed Cole Slaw
Lettuce and Sliced Tomato
Potato Salad

Sliced Cucumber
Green Beans, Vinaigrette
Beet Salad

Desserts

Freshly Baked Pastries
Ice Cream
Sherbert

Fruit Jello
Pudding

Beverages

Coffee and Tea . . .
  Hot or Iced
Postum

Sanka
Hot Chocolate
Milk

Dinner

Appetizers

Island Delight (Crushed Pineapple, Coconut Flakes and Rum)
Venice Petite
Melon in Season
Conch Cocktail
White Grape Juice
Eggs A La Reine
Herring in Cream Sauce
Grapefruit Au Rum
Hearts of Artichoke, Vinaigrette
Quiche Lorraine
Smoked Oysters

Berries Espagnole (Seasonal Berries in Malaga Wine)
Red Burgundy Grape Juice
Sardines on Toast Points
Huevos Diablo (Deviled Egg)
Maine Lobster Cocktail
Pineapple Supreme
Shrimp Cocktail
Chopped Livers Gourmet
Antipasto
Fresh Squids, Italienne
Fruit Cup Maraschino

Soups

Bahamiam Conch Chowder
Pepper Pot
Potato Soup
Chicken Pfarfel
French Onion Soup
  Au Croutons
Green Turtle Soup Au Sherry
Caldo Gallego (Spanish Bean Soup)

Lentil Soup
Gazpacho Andaluz (Chilled Spanish Vegetable Soup)
Green Split Peas Au Croutons
New England Clam Chowder
Minestrone Parmesan
Zuppa Di Pesce
Shrimp and Lobster Bisque
Petite Marmite

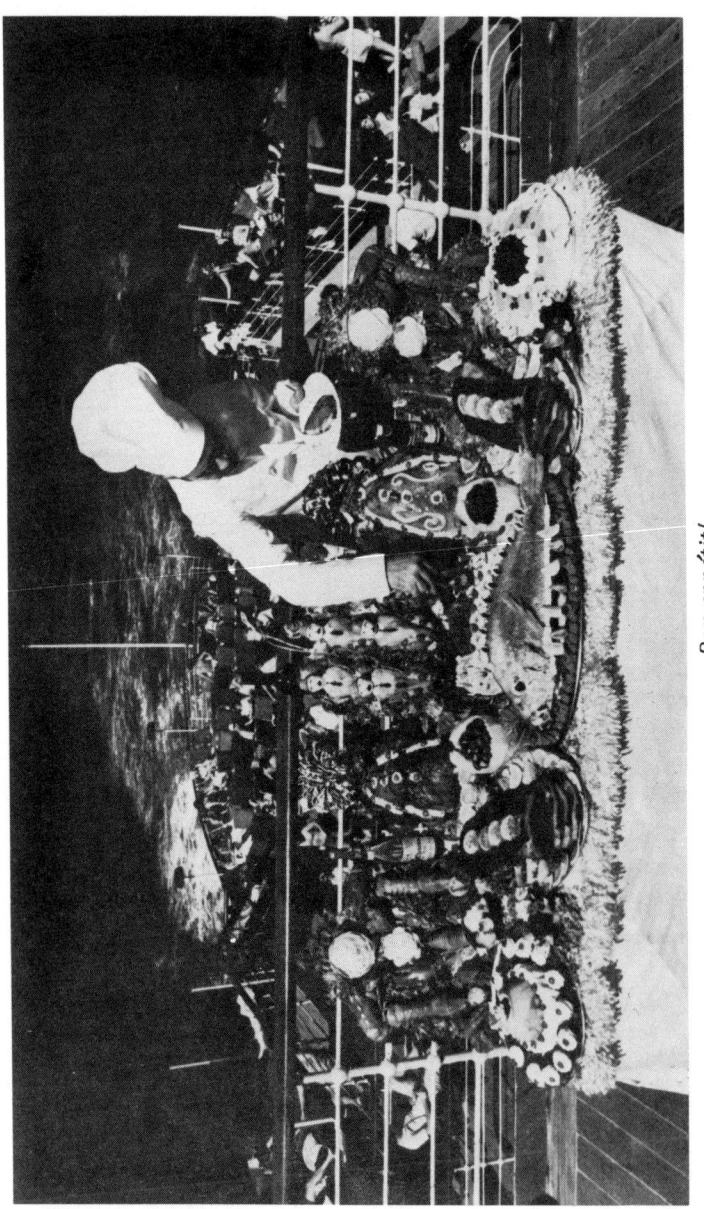

Bon appétit!

LIFE ON BOARD

Entrees

Baked Short Ribs of Beef,
   Champigonons
Steak Concord
Chicken Marengo
Broiled Filet Mignon
Chicken Schonbrunn
Austrian Veal Schnitzel
Baked Filet of Dolphin,
   Paprika
Broiled Red Snapper Filet,
   Montego
Merluza Madrilena
Roast Long Island Duckling
   A L'Orange
Crabmeat Au Gratin,
   New Orleans
Roast Pork Caribbean
Sliced Tenderloin of Beef,
   Bordelaise
Stuffed Vermont Turkey
Baby Flounder, Gourmet
Chinese Pepper Steak
Broiled Filet of Dover Sole
Breaded Pork Chops

Frog Legs Osborn
Poulet Maraschino
Veal Scallopine Marsala
Broiled Shrimp Scampi
Baked Filet of Cod
Baked Turbot Filet, Lemon
   Butter
Steak on a Sword
Roast Leg of Lamb, Trinidad
Chicken Curry
Paella Valenciana
Palomilla Steak Barcelona
Ham Steak Hawaiian
Yankee Pot Roast
Maryland Broasted
   Cornish Hen
Broiled Red Snapper
   Filet, Lemon
Roast Prime Ribs of Beef, Au Jus
Lobster Thermodor, Mardi Gras
Roast Half Spring Chicken
Southern Fried Chicken
Chicken Cacciatore

Low Calorie Diet Specials

Chef Salad
Vegetable Platter du Jour
Broiled Red Snapper
   Filet, Lemon
Fruit Platter Deluxe

Cheese Platter
Western Broiled Chopped Steak
Poached Bahamian Grouper
   Filet
Reuben Platter (Sliced Turkey,
   Ham and American Cheese)

Vegetables

Black Beans & Rice
Brussel Sprouts
Yams & Pineapple
Potato Pancakes
Glazed Carrots
Kraut Wilma
Lyonnaise Potatoes
French Cut Beans, Almandine
Beets Vermiere
Yellow Rice
Spaghetti (Carbonara or Ad
   Aglio-E Olio Sauce)

Cauliflower Au Beurre
Baked Idaho Potato
Corn On The Cob
Mixed Garden Vegetables
Sauteed Tomatoes & Peppers
White Rice
Baked Squash
Garden Fresh Peas
Scalloped Tomato

Salads

Mixed Bean Salad Barbados
   (Herb Dressing)
Caesar Salad

Continental (Tomato, Cucumber,
   Cooked Egg, Lettuce)
Isle of Mallorca Salad (Crisp

Tossed Green   Romaine, Diced Egg &
Mandarin (Bean Sprouts, Diced   Tomato, Bacon Crumbles)
   Tomatoes, Toasted Cocoanut   Italian Mixed (Wedged
   Sprinkles)   Tomatoes, Celery, Olives,
Hearts of Lettuce   Carrots, Mixed Greens, Olive
                                   Oil, Vinegar & Garlic Dressing)
French   —   Russian   —   1000 Island   —   Blue Cheese   —   Oil & Wine Vinegar

Desserts
Freshly Baked Pies, Cakes and Pasteries from the Dessert Tray
French Ice Creams (Chocolate–Vanilla–Strawberry–Butter Pecan)
Fuit Sherbets (Raspberry–Lime–Orange–Pineapple)
Cheeses (Gouda–Swiss–Cheddar–Gruyere–Edam–Danish Blue–
   Cream Cheese)

Beverages
Coffee   Postum   Milk

Sample Cocktail and Wine Lists

	Aperitifs and Sherries	85¢
	International Cocktails	95¢

Bacardi Cocktail	Martini
Champagne Cocktail	Negroni
Collins	Old-Fashioned
Daiquiri	Orange Blossom
Dubonnet	Paradise
El Presidente	Ramos Fizz
Gin Fizz	Rob Roy
Gibson	Sazerac Sling
Gimlet	Side Car
Manhattan	

	Tropical Favorites	$1.00

Pina Colada	Yellow Bird
Mardi Gras	Carousel
Banana Daiquiri	Rum Punch
Singapore Sling	French 75 or 90
Planters Punch	Rum Swizzle

	After Dinner Drinks	$1.10

Creme de Menthe	Sombrero
Cacao Brown or White	Godfather
Cherry Brandy	White Spider
Brandy Alexander	Spanish Kiss
King Alfonso	Blackberry Brandy
Anisette	Grasshopper
Coffee Liqueur	Rusty Nail
Stinger	

LIFE ON BOARD

	Our Special Coffees $1.75
Cafe Pepe	Italian Coffee
Irish Coffee	Mardi Gras Coffee
Spanish Coffee	Jamaican Coffee

Scotches	Gins	Vodkas	Whiskeys
	Bourbons	Rums	85¢

Plus: Brandies, Liqueurs, Blends and other specialties

	Bottle		Bottle
Champagnes and Sparkling Wines		**White Bordeaux Wines**	
Cold Duck, Henri Marchant, New York	4.50	Baron De Luze, Graves Vintage	5.50
Rothschild Blanc de Blanc, France	5.50	Moutòn Cadet, Baron Philippe De Rothschild, Vintage	fifth 6.50 tenth 3.50
Asti Spumante, Martini & Rossi, Italy	6.00	**White Burgundy Wines**	
Great Western Extra Dry Champagne, New York	fifth 6.50 tenth 3.50	Chablis, Barton, Guestier, Vintage	7.50
Paul Masson Brut Champagne, California	7.00	Pouilly-Fuisse, Barton & Guestier, Vintage	9.50
Chauvenet Red Cap Champagne, France	7.50	Meursault Louis Latour, Vintage	10.50
Piper Heidsieck Extra Dry Champagne, France	14.00	**German Wines** Liebfraumilch, Crown of Crowns, Langenbach, Vintage	5.50
Mumm Cordon Rouge Burt Champagne, France	15.00	Bernkastler Riesling, Langenbach, Vintage	5.50
Red Bordeaux Wines		Zeller Schwartze Katz, Julius Kayser, Vintage	6.00
Medoc, De Luze, Vintage	5.75		
Baron De Luze St. Emilion, Vintage	fifth 6.00 tenth 3.25	**Wines of Italy** Lambrusco, Fratelli (Red) Vintage	4.25
Mounton Cadet, Baron Phillippe De Rothschild, Vintage	fifth 6.50 tenth 3.50	Soave, Ricasoli (White), Vintage	4.50
Chateau Cantenac-Brown, Margaux, Vintage	9.00	Chianti, Ricasoli (Red), Vintage	4.50
Red Burgundy Wines		**Imported Rose Wines**	
Beaujolais St. Louis, Barton & Guestier, Vintage	fifth 5.50 tenth 3.00	Rose D'Anjou, Nectarose, Vintage, France	4.00
Chateauneuf Du Pape, Barton & Guestier, Vintage	7.50	Mateus, Vintage, Portugal	4.50
Gevrey-Chambertin, Barton & Guestier, Vintage	9.00	Lancers, Vintage, Portugal	fifth 5.50 tenth 3.00
Pommard, Barton & Guestier, Vintage	10.50	**Kosher Wines** Mogen David Concord	4.00

Food... And More Food.

T.s.s. F A I R W I N D
Captain RODOLFO POTENZONI, Commanding

Welcome Dinner

Sunday, April 9, 1978

MELBA TOAST IRANIAN CAVIAR ON ICE THRONE
AMERICAN DRESSING
FLAKES CRAB MEAT COCKTAIL
FRESH TROPICAL FRUIT CUP WITH LIME SHERBET
CELERY AND VEGETABLE RELISH TRAY

JELLIED CONSOMME MADRILENA
HOT BEEF TEA PRINCE OF GALLES   CREAM VELOUTE, AGNES SOREL
HOME MADE RAVIOLINI THE BLUE COVE

OCEAN SOLE FILLETS IN CHAMPAGNE SAUCE, FLEURONS
ISLAND ROCK LOBSTER , CARDINALE, RICE PILAW

ROAST CORNISH HEN, MONTMORENCY GLAZED CALF'S SWEET BREAD, SOUVAROFF
PRIME BEEF TENDERLOIN, DUKE OF WELLINGTON

STEAMED BROCCOLI   BUTTERED GARDEN PEAS   CRETAN POTATOES

WALDORF SALAD

GRAND GATEAUX ST. HONORE   COUPE SULTANE   ITALIAN ASSORTED PASTRIES

WINE SUGGESTION

White   Pouilly-Fuissé
        Capri-Scala
        Riesling P. Masson

Red   Clos de Vougeot '71
        Medoc
        Rubion P. Masson
        Rose Antinori

T.s.s. F A I R W I N D
Captain RODOLFO POTENZONI, Commanding

Farewell Dinner

Thursday, April 13, 1978

BELUGA MALOSSOL CAVIAR ON ICE THRONE   MELBA TOAST
HOT BUTTERFLY DEEP FRIED SHRIMPS TARTAR SAUCE
AMERICAN DRESSING   ST. HUMBERT VENISON PATTY
PINEAPPLE RINGS   RELISH TRAY

JELLIED CONSOMME WITH CELERY
DOUBLE ESSENCE OF BEEF, SHERRY FLAVOURED
CHICKEN VELOUTE, QUEEN MARGOT   IMPERIAL OX-TAIL SOUP

COLD WATER BROILED FRESH STURGEON STEAK, LEMON SAUCE
ROCK LOBSTER, ARMORICAINE, PATNA RICE

MILK FED VEAL CHOP, LA BELLE EPOQUE   FRIED CHICKEN SUPREME A LA KIEV
ROAST PRIME RIBS OF BEEF NATURAL GRAVY, YORKSHIRE PUDDING

CORN ON THE COB   BAKED IDAHO POTATOES   STEAMED BROCCOLI

BELLE HELENE SALAD

FLAMING BAKED ALASKA   DELICATE PATISSERIE DES DAMES

SPARKLING WINE

COFFEE

LIFE ON BOARD

CRUISE LINE CUISINE

One of the most enjoyable activities at sea is eating, and it is for this reason that cruise lines attach great importance to their chefs. Some ships follow the ethnic and cultural personalities of the lines, e.g., if you sail a Greek vessel, expect Greek food. Most Caribbean cruise ships provide "international cuisine" which can mean anything from informal dishes from different countries to very dramatic preparations by gourmet chefs. Experienced ship travelers know that a cruise is an opportunity to eat well, not just a chance to see glamorous ports or relax.

Sailing in the Caribbean are cruise vessels flying the flags of Norway, Greece, Italy, France, Great Britain, Russia, Panama, Liberia, West Germany, and the Netherland Antilles, and this may determine the nationality of the crew serving as deck and engine room officers. Many cruise ships in the Caribbean have mixed crews serving the dining rooms and cabins.

If you want to speak French, and have complimentary wines with your meals, then sail on MERMOZ, CALYPSO or DOLPHIN of Paquet Cruise Line. Dutch cheeses and chocolates can be found on Holland America's ROTTERDAM, VEENDAM, and VOLENDAM. The Russian ships, like the ODESSA, offer the best vodka and caviar. Knowing what kind of food each cruise line serves or what specialties each line features, can complete your sailing plans: so that the listing follows logically.

Passengers aboard Bahama Cruise Line's VERACRUZ sailing from Montego Bay to Caribbean islands have a choice of fish, meat or fowl each evening prepared with a Continental flavor. Three meals are served daily with two seatings in the ship's forward dining room. Lunch is occasionally served buffet-style and features such delights as cherries jubilee. Mid-morning snack and afternoon tea are also included and special dietary or baby food requests can be arranged provided notice is given 60 days in advance of sailing.

Menus aboard Black Sea Shipping Company cruises like the

ODESSA sailing from New Orleans to Havana and other Caribbean ports, feature Continental and Russian specialties. Such delicacies as caviar and borscht comprise part of the evening menu along with Vodka, domestic and international wines and Soviet champagne reasonably priced from $6 a bottle. All tipping is included in the cruise rate. Three meals are served on board along with two mid-morning and afternoon snacks and a midnight buffet. Similar service is available on the ALEXANDER PUSHKIN, KAZAKHSTAN, and MIKHAIL LERMONTOV.

During Carnival Cruise Line's seven-day excursions on the CARNIVALE, FESTIVALE and MARDI GRAS, an international cuisine is offered on the line's three ships. Each night the menu features such dishes as veal Scallopini Marsala, roast ducking in wine sauce and Lobster Thermidor. Lobster Bisque soup is another popular favorite. Wine prices range from $5.50 for domestic vintages to $45.50 for French imported champagne. Two late-night buffets are served each evening aboard the "Fun Ships." Twenty-four-hour cabin service is available for passengers on board. Full breakfast in bed any day you wish! Special dietary requests can be arranged prior to departure. Free champagne at the Captain's Farewell Dinner.

On ships AMERIKANIS, BRITANIS, and VICTORIA the Greek, French and Italian menus are rotated daily during Chandris cruises' meals for each of two sittings. Seasonal menus change from December to April and May to November. French, Italian and Greek wines usually accompany corresponding menus. The line will fill Kosher food requirements if the request is made at the time of booking.

Commodore Cruises on the BOHEME and CARIBE offers an Oktoberfest cruise each fall featuring a German cuisine, and a Mayfest each spring with assorted French wines and cheeses served buffet-style. Other times the line offers a Continental menu with large buffet spreads and gourmet brunches featuring smoked salmon and hot and cold entrees served in the dining room or on deck. Most menus include a special listing for weight watchers but any other dietary request be it Kosher, baby food or vegetarian, should be given two weeks in advance to sailing. Three meals are included on board with snacks available throughout the day.

Costa Cruises features a Continental cuisine highlighting specialties prepared by the firm's Greek and Italian culinary staff. "Saltimbocca alla Romana"—a delicate veal entree served in white wine and topped with Copocolla—is just one of the staff's gourmet delights. Wine prices range from $3.50 for an inexpensive Verdicchio to $15

LIFE ON BOARD

A ship cruise offers passengers the fun of skeet shooting with the experts. For most landlubbers, it's a new sport, particularly well suited to the cruisin' life.

A "turn" around the deck used to mean a stroll. But if it's fitness you are after, 5 times around the deck of Costa's CARLA C equals one mile— which burns off 100 calories.

for a full bottle of Patriarche chablis. In addition to the basic Continental cuisine with Greek and Italian specialties, international nights offer passengers a taste of both eastern and western European dishes. Passengers on each of the 11 ships sailing the Mediterranean and Caribbean partake in six meals served on board. Full cabin service is available to guests from 6 a.m. to 10 p.m. daily.

The Cunard Line has a history of more than 140 years of passenger service and ships serving the Caribbean include CUNARD COUNTESS, CUNARD PRINCESS and QUEEN ELIZABETH 2. The QE2, for example, features an international cuisine in addition to a regular Continental menu. Approximately 1700 diners are accommodated within the ship's four dining areas with each offering passengers a choice of Parisian, Florentine, Londoner, or Oriental decor. Five-course meals at dinner include such delicacies as Beef Wellington and crepes suzette and souffles for dessert. A choice of over 20,000 bottles of international wines are available to passengers. Cabin service is available for breakfast, lunch and dinner. All special diet requests can be made two weeks prior to sailing by your travel agent.

The ROTTERDAM, PRINSEDAM, VEENDAM and VOLENDAM offer international nights which feature a variety of Dutch treats and Indonesian buffets, a part of Holland America Line's menu. Passengers have their choice of the Lido restaurant, the main dining room or the main deck for breakfast, lunch and snacks. Cabin service is available for Continental breakfast only. Holland America's ships fly the flag of the Netherland Antilles but have Dutch officers, and Indonesians serving in the dining rooms and cabins.

Menus aboard Hellenic Mediterranean Line's AQUARIUS sailing from San Juan to Caribbean islands list Continental dishes featuring a variety of Greek specialties. "Surf and Turf" is the ship's more popular main course but dietary dishes may also be ordered. Six meals are provided with three snacks served daily on deck and dinner and lunch served at two sittings in the ship's forward dining area.

On Karageorgis Line's 14-day cruise, a Continental cuisine is offered with a Greek emphasis. On the NAVARINO a variety of international wines and champagnes, (some relatively inexpensive) are served with lunch and dinner which is served in two seatings. Special dietary requests for Kosher, baby or vegetarian food may be made two weeks prior to sailing.

The SKYWARD, SOUTHWARD, STARWARD, SUNWARD II, and NORWAY of the Norwegian Caribbean Line, offer an American

LIFE ON BOARD

For outstanding cuisine, Costa's FLAVIA relies on the expertise of 15 chefs and assistants schooled in the culinary arts. During a typical 4 day cruise, Costa chefs handle an average of 8,200 pounds of meat, fish and poultry; 9,000 pounds of fruits and vegetables and 4,100 pounds of pasta.

and Continental cuisine with a Norwegian specialty dish at every meal. There are three main meals in the regular dining areas: breakfast, lunch, and dinner, and as many as six outdoor meals: coffee and danish, late breakfast, coffee/tea or boullion, outdoor lunch, snacks, and a midnight buffet. The wine list comprises American and Continental vintages and includes 48 different brands beginning at $6 a bottle. Regular seating assignments are computerized and done at the time of booking a reservation, i.e. first or second seating, table size, and smoking or non-smoking sections. Room service is available, although each ship posts different hours.

The SUN PRINCESS of Princess Cruises offers continental cuisine and a good wine selection of French, Italian and California vintage. There are usually, in addition to the three main meals, a morning snack, afternoon tea and midnight buffet. There are usually five entrees from which to choose (and always a pasta selection), plus extensive appetizer, dessert and cheese courses. Seating is requested at booking, and final arrangements are worked out by the maitre d' just before sailing. There is also a non-smoking section in the dining room.

The Royal Caribbean Cruise Line's NORDIC PRINCE, SUN VIKING, and SONG OF NORWAY specialize in continental cuisine (in addition to its theme nights). There are six appetizers each night, three soups, a choice of fish, fowl or beef, vegetables, desserts, cheeses and an extensive wine list. There is lunch, morning snack, lunch, afternoon snack, dinner and midnight buffet. In addition, in the night club, the waiter will pass trays of small sandwiches and 24-hour room service, with food available, is offered.

Aboard the STELLA MARIS, STELLA SOLARIS and the STELLA OCEANIS of the Sun Lines, an international cuisine is featured, along with Greek specialties. There are, in addition to the three main meals a day, a morning boullion snack around 11 a.m., an afternoon tea and a midnight snack. A typical luncheon would include a choice of omelette, a fowl, fish, meat or pasta selection and cold platter plus various vegetable salads. There is an extensive, moderately priced wine list, of Continental wines. Seats are selected at the time of booking.

LIFE ON BOARD

St. John, in the United States Virgin Islands, is three-quarters National Park; with many hiking trails and spectacular beaches. On the western end of the island is the famous resort, Caneel Bay Plantation, shown in the foreground.

CASINOS

For some individuals the opportunity to gamble at sea and at ports of call can be an exciting way to enjoy a cruise. Cruise lines offer shipboard casinos for entertainment and as an added attraction.

The following is a general listing by cruise lines of gambling facilities available aboard ships marketed in the U. S.

Carnival Cruise Lines — Roulette, blackjack, craps, slots and wheel of fortune on all three vessels.

Chandris Cruises — All Chandris vessels have mini-casinos with slots, joker seven and blackjack.

Commodore Cruise Lines — The Boheme offers blackjack and slots while the Caribe has blackjack, roulette and slots. No dice games on either ship.

LIFE ON BOARD

BLACKJACK / 21

It takes only minutes to learn to play Blackjack or "21" ...a card game favorite of millions.

You play against the dealer. The object is to draw cards totalling "21", or as close as possible without going over 21. Bets are placed, then the dealer gives two cards face up to each player and one card up and one down to herself. Aces count 1 or 11. Picture cards count 10. All other cards count their face value.

If you "Blackjack" (an ace with a picture card or 10), it beats any other combination except a dealer "Blackjack", and you win 3-2 for your bet.
........................If you do not "Blackjack", you decide from your hand to take more cards (draw) or not to take more cards (stand). You may take as many cards as you wish until you think you have a score closer to 21 than the dealer will have. The dealer must draw to 16 or under and must stand on 17 or over.

If your total is closer to 21 than the dealer, you win even money. If your total is lower than the dealer, you lose. If you tie with the dealer, it is a "stand-off". If you go over 21, you lose.

Down for double. If your first two cards total 11, you may double your original bet and draw only one more card.

Split bets. If your first two cards are a pair, you may split them into separate hands. You bet a like amount on the additional hand and receive extra cards on each hand. If you split two aces, you only receive one extra card on each ace. An ace and a 10 or picture card is not "Blackjack", but counts as 21 points.

Insurance bets. If the dealer's first card is an ace, a player may take insurance, i.e., he may bet half of his original bet. If the dealer has "Blackjack", player receives 2-1 for his insurance bet. If the dealer does not have "Blackjack", player loses his insurance money.

Gratuities: Should a player wish to reward a dealer for either courteous service or assisting with Lady Luck, gratuities may be handed directly to the dealer or a bet may be placed on the dealer's behalf in front of the respective player's box.

Costa Cruises — All ships have slots, joker seven and blackjack, no baccarat. According to a spokesman, the shorter the cruise the more active the casino, although it's not a Las Vegas-type crowd.

Cunard Line — The Queen Elizabeth 2 offers roulette, slots, blackjack and electronic gambling games, while the Cunard Princess and Countess have slots, blackjack and electronic roulette.

Eastern Steamship Company — Blackjack, roulette, wheel of fortune and slots. No craps.

Epirotiki Line — All ships have casinos with the larger vessels offering roulette, joker seven and slots, while the smaller ships only have joker seven and slots.

Holland America Cruises — The Volendam, Veendam, Rotterdam and Statendam have facilities for slots, blackjack and joker seven. The Prinsendam does not have gambling facilities.

Hellenic Mediterranean Lines — No casino facilities aboard.

Home Lines — The two vessels feature a separate room for slot machines and a casino with four to five tables for blackjack and joker seven.

Italian Line Cruises — No gambling facilities will be available until there's a licensing resolution from Italy which is not expected to take place before mid-February.

Karageorgis Lines — Slots are available as well as limited casino facilities.

K Lines-Hellenic Cruises — Slots but no casino gamblings.

March Shipping Passenger Services — The Kazakhstan offers slots and joker seven and the transatlantic vessels Alexander Pushkin and Mikhail Lermontov feature slots only.

Norwegian American Lines — The Caribbean cruises have slots, blackjack, roulette but no dice. Games available

LIFE ON BOARD

Now...
the M/S Caribe
is featuring the
ancient and exciting
game of Craps.
Craps is a game of chance where
the player can bet on every roll of the dice.

Some of the most common bets are as follows:

The Pass Line (sometimes called the win line): If the shooter throws a 7 or 11 on the first roll, you win even money. If he or she throws a 2, 3 or 12, you lose. Any other number becomes the shooter's point which must be thrown again before a 7 in order to win.

Place Bets: At any time while the game is in progress, you may bet the boxes 4, 5, 6, 8, 9 and 10.
Odds for place bets:
6 and 8 (Big Red)...Even money
5 and 9...7 to 5
4 and 10...9 to 5

Hard Ways: You win if the exact combination of the number you bet on comes up. You lose if the same total number is rolled any other way or if a 7 comes up.
Odds for hard ways:
2 deuces or 2 fives...7 to 1
2 threes or 2 fours...9 to 1

One-Roll Bets:

Any craps - A one-roll bet that pays 7 to 1 on a roll of 2, 3 or 12.

Craps 2 (2 aces) - A one-roll bet that wins with 2 only and pays 30 to 1.

Craps 3 (ace, deuce) - A one-roll bet that wins with three only and pays 15 to 1.

Craps 12 (2 sixes) - A one-roll bet that wins with 12 only and pays 30 to 1.

Eleven - A one-roll bet that wins with 11 only and pays 15 to 1.

The Field: A one-roll bet that wins even money on 2, 3, 4, 9, 10, 11 and 12.

Minimum and maximum bets are as advertised on the table.

in a separate room so as not to disturb non-gambling passengers. The longer cruises have the same gambling facilities, but they are not emphasized.

Norwegian Caribbean Lines — Like all ships of Norwegian registry, NCL is allowed to offer slots only.

Paquet Cruises — Slots only offered aboard the Mermoz.

Paquet-Ulysses Cruises — The casino aboard the Dolphin is being renovated to feature blackjack, slots, regular and electronic roulette.

Princess Cruises — On the Mexico and Caribbean cruises blackjack, roulette, craps and slots are available. On the longer cruises and Alaska sailings, slots only.

Royal Caribbean Cruise Lines — Again, of Norwegian registry, so slots only.

Royal Cruise Line — No casinos or slots.

Royal Viking Line — No casino or gambling whatever.

Sitmar Cruises — Slots only.

TAX AND DUTY FREE SHOPPING

The greatest privilege for an international traveler is the opportunity for Tax and Duty Free shopping.

A Tax and Duty Free shop is exactly what the name implies. This *specialty* shop carries a wide selection of quality merchandise free of all Federal, State, and Sales Taxes, and also free of all Federal import duties. Because of this, items are offered at substantial savings.

A Duty Free shop is a minature of Fifth Avenue, where you will find an assortment of gifts from many corners of the world but not at Fifth Avenue prices, but at tax and duty free savings. The outstanding gift shop selections range from Scandinavian crystal, such famous names as Kosta & Boda, to porcelain from Royal Copenhagen, designer jewelry from Sweden, Denmark, and Finland, and Scandinavian and Swiss chocolate for the most discriminating tastes. There are precision time pieces from Switzerland

LIFE ON BOARD

Hand in hand where shore meets sea.

and high quality electronics. For the children, there are toys from Europe.

For everyday needs our gift shop also represents the French fragrances from such famous couturiers as Chanel, Christian Dior, Madame Rochas, Jean Patou, and Nina Ricci, to name only a few.

An outstanding selection of the world's most famous beverages from only the best known labels such as Canadian Club, Ballantine's, Jim Beam, Bacardi, Beefeater, Smirnoff, Courvoisier Cognac, and a broad selection of liqueurs such as Kahlua, Drambuie, Tia Maria, and Cointreau. For that special occasion — Moet et Chandon champagne.

CARIBBEAN FLEET FEATURES

Many colorful brochures are available to help you in selecting your cruise ship. A cruise aboard a luxury ship is like no other vacation. Every passenger is on board to relax, make friends and have fun. Life aboard is special. On board activities are, of course, important features when considering a cruise vacation. The following listing of the Caribbean fleet features indicates: air conditioning, stabilized (improved stabilizers reduce seasickness), swimming pools available, "lounges" and "other features." Lounges refer to the number of public rooms, including bars but excluding special purpose rooms, such as theater, library which are listed in "other features." For more detailed information, consult the ship's deck plans or see your travel agent. Ford's *Deck Plans* as well as cruise line brochures provide the latest deck plans so you can see where the public rooms and cabins are located. This will help you to make your stateroom reservation. Try to familiarize yourself with the various locations of the lounges, elevators, and other facilities before you board

LIFE ON BOARD

CARIBBEAN SHIP FEATURES

Ship	Air Cond.	Sta-bilize.	Pools	Lounges	Other Features
Amerikanis	Yes	Yes	2	4	children's playdeck, beauty salon/barber shop, gym, sauna, cinema
Aquarius	Yes	Yes	1	4	hairdresser
Bohéme	Yes	Yes	1	5	beauty shop, sauna, cinema
Britanis	Yes	Yes	2	7	cinema, beauty salon/barber shop, gym, children's playroom, library
Caribe	Yes	Yes	1	5	beauty shop, cinema/conference room
Carla C	Yes	Yes	2	6	cinema, beauty/barber shops, library, sauna
Carnivale	Yes	Yes	5	7	library, children's playroom; gym, sauna, beauty salon/barber shop
Cunard Countess	Yes	Yes	1	6	library, cinema/conference room, hairdresser, sauna
Cunard Princess	Yes	Yes	1	6	library, cinema/conference room, hairdresser, sauna
Danae	Yes	Yes	1	4	cinema, playroom, library, gym, hairdresser
Doric	No	No	3	7	cinema, barber shop/beauty salon, library, gym, sauna

Ship	Air Cond.	Sta-bilize.	Pools	Lounges	Other Features
Fairsea	Yes	Yes	3	9	cinema, meeting rooms, children's center, sauna, beauty parlor/barber shop, library gym
Fairwind	Yes	Yes	3	9	cinema, meeting rooms, children's center, sauna, beauty salon/barber shop, library, gym
Festivale	Yes	Yes	3	8	library, children's room, barber shop/beauty salon, gym, sauna
Golden Odyssey	Yes	Yes	1	5	library, sauna, gym, beauty parlor
Island Princess	Yes	Yes	2	11	sauna, gym, beauty salon, barber shop, library
Kazakhstan	Yes	Yes	2	5	sauna, hairdresser, barber
Mardi Gras	Yes	Yes	3	7	cinema, sauna, gym, children's playroom
Mermoz	Yes	Yes	2	5	cinema, gym, sauna, library, barber shop/beauty salon
Nordic Prince	Yes	Yes	1	7	sauna, barber shop/beauty salon
Norway	Yes	Yes	3	9	cinema, library, children's playroom, chapel, beauty salon/barber shop

LIFE ON BOARD

Ship	Air Cond.	Stabilize.	Pools	Lounges	Other Features
Oceanic	Yes	Yes	2	11	children's playroom, gym, sauna, beauty salon, barber shop, library, cinema
Odessa	Yes	Yes	1	6	sauna, gym, barber shop, beauty salon, cinema
Pacific Princess	Yes	Yes	1	11	sauna, gym, beauty salon, barber shop, library
Queen Elizabeth 2	Yes	Yes	4	7	children's room, cinema, 2 libraries, hairdresser, barber shop, gym, sauna
Rotterdam	Yes	Yes	2	10	sauna, gym, beauty parlor, barber shop, cinema, library
Royal Viking Sea	Yes	Yes	1	6	library, sauna, gym, cinema, beauty parlor, barber shop
Royal Viking Sky	Yes	Yes	1	6	library, sauna, gym, cinema, beauty parlor, barber shop
Royal Viking Star	Yes	Yes	1	5	sauna, gym, beauty parlor/barber shop
Skyward	Yes	Yes	1	6	sauna, hairdresser, cinema
Song Of Norway	Yes	Yes	1	5	beauty parlor
Southward	Yes	Yes	2	6	cinema, beauty parlor, sauna, library
Starward	Yes	Yes	2	6	cinema, beauty parlor, conference room, sauna, planetarium

Ship	Air Cond.	Sta-bilize.	Pools	Lounges	Other Features
Statendam	Yes	Yes	2	7	cinema gym, Turkish bath, library, beauty parlor/barber shop
Stella Maris	Yes	Yes	1	3	hairdresser
Stella Oceanis	Yes	Yes	1	4	hairdresser
Stella Solaris	Yes	Yes	2	7	cinema, gym, sauna, children's room
Sun Princess	Yes	Yes	1	6	cinema, barber shop, beauty salon, gym, sauna
Sun Viking	Yes	Yes	1	6	sauna, barber shop, beauty parlor
Veendam	Yes	Yes	1	6	cinema, barber shop, beauty parlor/health center, gym, library
Veracruz	Yes	Yes	1	3	cinema, conference room, beauty parlor/barber shop
Victoria	Yes	No	2	7	gym, sauna, children's playroom, library, cinema, beauty salon
Vistafjord	Yes	Yes	2	7	cinema, gym, sauna, beauty parlor, barber shop, dance studio, library
Volendam	Yes	Yes	1	6	cinema, gym, barber shop, beauty parlor/health center, library
World Renaissance	No	No	2	4	cinema, library

Chapter 7

ALL ASHORE

After two or three days on the open sea, you may be ready to spend some time on land. Cruises are more than just ocean voyages. Shore excursions are more and more an integral part of most cruises and many passengers spend a significant amount of time ashore. Well-planned shore excursions for most cruise vacation ports are available.

Organized shore excursions are not included in the cruise package and the cost is variable. You can arrange your own sightseeing tours, which often means negotiating prices and itineraries on the dock, or sign up aboard ship for organized excursions at fixed prices in advance. You may also walk around the town on your own and enjoy the land under your feet.

ISLAND PRINCESS travels to Acapulco, Panama Canal, Cartagena, Aruba, Martinique, St. Thomas, San Juan.

SHORE PROGRAM NOTES

Try to be selective. Usually several tours are offered in each port. Learn something about the history of the ports-of-call from the lectures and films aboard ship. Talk to the shore excursion staff while at sea and read the brochures before deciding which holds the most interest for you. Find out what is included and what is not (meals, drinks, tips?).

Plan one tour a day, even if the one you do take is only a couple of hours long. Long bus trips can be exhausting especially if the weather is hot and the roads are bad. A night tour sometime might be a welcome change.

A couple on leave from their cruise ship visit Trinidad and Tobago beaches—dozens of white powder beaches.

ALL ASHORE

Respect local customs. Remember you are a guest in a foreign port. Don't expect everything to be like it is in the United States. Don't get upset if people, including the tour guide, do not speak perfect English

Take some extra money for tipping, as well as shopping. Tour guides and bus or taxi drivers expect a gratuity. A good guideline is at least $1 per person on a half-day or less tour, and a minimum of $2 each for anything longer, up to a full-day trip. It's a good idea, too, to carry a few $1 and $5 bills. In most cruise ports, US bills are as acceptable as the local currency and you won't get stuck with the money-of-the-land if larger denominations have to be changed.

Take plenty of film. The kind you need may not be available aboard ship or ashore. Ask permission to take closeups of people, their homes and family. Respect their rights to privacy.

Be careful of local food and drinks. Beer, bottled water and soft drinks usually are safe, and use a straw if drinking from a bottle, particularly in the Caribbean, Panama or Mexico. Don't drink the water and skip the ice cubes. Don't eat anything bought locally that cannot be peeled. If food is not included on the tour, ask the steward about a picnic lunch.

Dress comfortably. Veteran cruisers prefer conservative sport clothes for shore trips, with hats much in order when visiting churches and religious shrines. Since sightseeing involves a considerable amount of walking, low-heels, comfortable shoes are a "must." In hot weather ports, men can wear lightweight slacks, sport shirts and comfortable shoes, sandals or sneakers. Ties are rarely required during the day, even in the best restaurants. Slacks and blouses are fine for women. While ashore and at all times while in port, it is recommended that the ladies do not wear shorts and halters, for ladies' bare midriffs and other exposures are frowned upon in the localities you will visit. For an evening on the town in any port, a business suit will do although you'll be very much in style in a tuxedo as well. You will need protection against the sun, so dress sensibly, wear comfortable walking shoes, "cover-up" dresses and a straw hat. For a city tour, a good guideline for women is what they would wear in their hometown. On beach and boat tours, some kind of cover-up against the sun is essential as are sunglasses. A lightweight raincoat is always part of the wardrobe of the seasoned traveler, and many passengers bring along an umbrella or rain hat for inclement weather.

On seven day cruises to the Caribbean, Bahamas or Bermuda, you could spend between $25 and $60 on one or two shore excursions. An around-the-world voyage could have 99 different shore excursions from 30 ports-of-call.

Your customs inspection will be simplified if you retain your receipts for all purchases made while ashore.

The Counting House of Jamaica's Good Hope Estate is set amid flowering gardens. Its lower floor once imprisoned slaves.

ALL ASHORE

EXAMPLE OF SHORE TOURS

Shore excursions are offered at most ports of call on all cruises. These short trips are available for purchase aboard ship during the first full day at sea. On some longer cruises, a pre-packaged land tour can be purchased well in advance through your travel agent. In all cases, shore excursions are thorough, informative and popularly priced.

Prices of shore excursions generally include available local transportation, ranging from motor coaches, limousines, taxis, and boats. Meals and local taxes are included where specified in advance by your Cruise Director. Items of a personal nature are excluded.

Excursions are subject to cancellation or modification depending on the number of passengers participating. In some cases, the tours have a minimum booking requirement, or must be limited to a maximum number of participants.

Shore excursions are only available for reservations or purchase once you are aboard ship and en route to your destinations. This allows you to obtain a complete, up-to-date description of each excursion from your Cruise Director. Tickets will be sold at the Tour Office on board the ship.

All arrangements for shore tours are made by cruise line only as a convenience for the passenger. The services and facilities are furnished by the shore tour operators acting as independent contractors. The line is not liable for any loss, damage, injury, cost or delay arising from or in connection with such services. No refunds are made for failure to use all of the services included in the price. Cancellations must be made at a reasonable time in advance of the tour departure from the vessel. Passengers not wishing to avail themselves of any or all escorted shore excursions are reminded that the ship is their hotel for their entire stay in port and services continue on board.

The Cruise Staff, Pursers, and shore agents will gladly assist with information for independent sightseeing.

BRIDGETOWN, BARBADOS
Island Countryside Tour
A lovely ride through the Barbadian countryside starts from the pier and winds through Bridgetown's picturesque streets. Heading north along the Caribbean coastline, a stop at the monument to the island's first settlers is made before turning inland over Fortress hill. Heading east through the Scotland District, you will arrive on the Atlantic side of the island where a stop at St. John's Church affords a lovely view of the east coast. Turning south along the shore, your next stop is the Crane Hotel, a beautiful beach resort where a complimentary rum punch, beer of soft drink will refresh you. Heading back toward Bridgetown, the tour passes Seawell Airport and the town of Oistins where the Charter of Barbados was signed in 1652. A final point of interest, the house where George Washington allegedly visited for a brief period, is passed before your tour concludes at the harbor.
Approximately 3 hours $11.50

Jolly Roger Schooner Cruise
Relive the days of the Buccaneers! Set sail on the stately 70-foot schooner, Jolly Roger, for a 3-hour cruise through sparkling calm waters. Unlimited rum punch and soft drinks are available throughout the cruise. The boat is fully equipped with spacious decks, cabins for changing (although beach attire is recommended), head and safety gear. A brief stop for swimming will be made; however, this will be in deep water due to the size of the vessel. The tour includes a short taxi transfer to and from the ship. Truly a unique and colorful Caribbean adventure.
Approximately 3 hours. $13.00

Beach Party Tour
Sugar white sand, palm trees, a luxurious hotel and local drink favorites combine to create a festive beach party for your enjoyment. A short taxi ride to the Barbados Hilton is followed with a friendly greeting. A private area on the beach is reserved for ship's passengers complete with its own bar facility. The hotel will supply changing facilities. Relax in the shade or in the sun or take a stroll through the hotel's grounds, lobby and shops. Unlimited rum punch, beer and soft drinks are provided.
Approximately 2½ hours. $13.00

A diver is suspended amid a stream of curious and friendly tropical fish that abound in the crystal clear waters of Bonaire. This Dutch Caribbean island is famed for its beautiful coral reefs, and scores of varieties of gaily colored fish. Above its calm, almost currentless waters, Bonaire is equally noted as the largest flamingo sanctuary in the western hemisphere. It is also a haven for 130 other species of birds, and nature lovers and water lovers alike are enchanted with its tranquil loveliness, warm sunshine and creamy, white beaches.

CAP HAITIEN, HAITI
Citadelle Adventure Tour

This tour begins with a 30-minute scenic drive through the town of Cap Haitien and into the picturesque countryside. First stop is the village of Milot and the ruins of regal Sans Souci Palace, built by King Henri Christophe. You then proceed to the Citadelle, one of the greatest fortresses built in the Western Hemisphere. To get to the top of the 3,000-foot-high peak where the fortress is located, you can ride on horse/muleback from Milot or you can travel partway by station wagon or jeep and then finish the journey by horse or mule. The Citadelle is a fantastic feat of engineering. Built in the early 1800's at a cost of 20,000 lives, the fortress was Christophe's safeguard against an attack by Napoleon. The tour includes transportation, a picnic lunch and guide service. Participation limited.

Approximately 6 hours.   Mule/Horseback $17.00
                          Car/Mule/Horseback $25.00

Cormier Beach Tour

Colorful native "tap-tap" buses take you along a dirt road through the town of Cap Haitien and past typically Haitian landscape to Cormier Beach. Here on the secluded and unspoiled sand beach you can beachcomb, go for a swim or simply lie back and enjoy a boxed picnic lunch provided by the ship. A bar, set up on the beach, will serve complimentary rum punch and soft drinks. An interesting way to see the Haiti that the average tourist doesn't see. On the return trip to the ship, you can stop at the native market for shopping and browsing. Participation limited.

Approximately 3½ hours. $12.00

Sans Souci Palace Tour

This tour takes you on a delightful journey into the past. The first step is a drive past ruins of a French-built rampart, Pauline Bonaparte's castle and Fort Magny. Next is the Iron Market, the native "shopping center." Then a scenic drive to Milot, and the ruins of King Henri Christophe's Sans Souci Palace. The return route includes the Vertieres battlefield, where the French were finally ousted by the natives; Toussaint—Louverture Square; the College of Notre Dame, with its spectacular view of the city and harbor; and the Cathedral, built at the end of the 17th century and restored in 1942. The tour ends at the handicraft market place, near the wharf, for shopping.

Approximately 3½ hours. $10.50

ALL ASHORE 169

City Tour and Folkloric Show

Haitian architecture, landscapes, history and folkloric arts are all wrapped up in one neat package on this tour. The architecture, reflected in many of the town's buildings, is stamped with a distinct 18th century style. Landscapes are uniquely Haitian — ranging from tropical to high desert. History is everywhere. There are ruins of French ramparts, castles and forts, a battlefield monument at Vertieres, the Cathedral and the College of Notre Dame. You will be treated to the folkloric arts during a stop at Beck's Hotel for a luncheon buffet, spiced with rum punch. Here, you will see a typically Haitian floorshow. Participation limited.

Approximately 4 hours. $14.00

CHARLOTTE AMALIE, ST. THOMAS
City and Island Tour

Spectacular views highlight this tour through the bustling city of Charlotte Amalie, with a stop at Bluebeard's Castle Hotel. Then it's on to Drake's Seat overlooking Magen's Bay. Final destination is Mountain Top Hotel for an optional tropical drink and a panoramic view of Freebooter's Passage and the island below. Native paintings are on sale at the Hotel. There is ample time for duty-free shopping along the route and in Charlotte Amalie at the end of the tour.

Approximately 2 hours. $6.50

Island of St. John Land 'n' Sea Tour

This tour begins with a 20-minute surrey ride to Red Hook and then a ferry trip to the village of Cruz Bay, the main town on St. John. From there, you will be taken on a drive through the beautiful National Park, past Caneel Bay plantation to Trunk Bay, one of the ten most beautiful beaches in the world. The beach is an ideal setting for a walk, sunbathing, swimming or enjoying free snorkeling lessons, with all gear provided free. Weather and surf permitting, you can snorkel along a fantastic undersea trail above a coral reef harboring hundreds of exquisite, multi-colored fish. Included in the tour is a delicious rum punch. There is ample time at the conclusion of the tour for duty-free shopping in Charlotte Amalie.

Approximately 4 hours. $15.00

Scuba Adventure

One of the most exciting views of the "American Paradise" is from beneath the sparkling surface of the Caribbean. Expertly

City of Charlotte Amalie, St. Thomas, U.S.V.I.—For a "bird's-eye" view of Charlotte Amalie and the island—go to Drake's Seat or, to the top of Flag Hill. You won't be disappointed—the view from either point is spectacular.

While in the city, take time out of your shopping excursion to see some of the city's many attractions... the bustling waterfront, the second oldest synagogue in the Western Hemisphere, Government House, and the Orchidarium. Other notable monuments to the city's historic past include Bluebeard's Castle Tower, Ft. Christian (1666) now a museum and police headquarters, Crown House and the Nisky Moravian Mission.

ALL ASHORE 171

qualified staff members will pick up passengers at the ship and give one hour of classroom instruction. From there, it's off to one of the spectacular coral reefs, teeming with fish for a never-to-be-forgotten adventure. Close supervision at all times, small classes and diving groups and personal attention are part and parcel of this tour. The price includes round-trip transportation, instruction and all equipment.
Approximately 4½ hours. $25.00

Kon-Tiki Raft Tour

A delightful afternoon in the sun viewing Charlotte Amalie's picturesque harbor and beach areas. Come aboard the Kon-Tiki, a newly constructed raft, fully equipped with a bar, shade and a native steel band for your enjoyment. Cruise in the harbor and view a colorful panorama of marine life through glass-bottom panels in the Kon-Tiki. A brief stop at a nearby beach provides time for swimming, so dress casually for this excursion. Complimentary rum and fruit drinks are served aboard while the band plays Island music and adds gaiety and sparkle to this fascinating adventure.
Approximately 2½ hours $13.50

Whim Greathouse on St. Croix was the home of an 18-century plantation owner. Today Estate Whim is a museum, and is a favorite stop of visitors to the United States Virgin Islands. Fritz Henle Photo

FORT-DE-FRANCE, MARTINIQUE
Saint-Pierre Tour

A sightseer's and photographer's delight. In Fort-de-France, you will see Fort Saint-Louis XIV, completed in the 19th century; the Yacht Club; the statue of Empress Josephine; Government House; and Schoeler Library. Leaving the city, the tour route passes through Balata, noted for its miniature replica of Paris Sacre Coeur of Montmartre. Next is Absalon, a thermal resort, and Deux-Chous, highest point (1,943 feet) on the tour. Then the route drops down to the summer resort of Morne-Rouge and continues on the Saint-Pierre, a once-prosperous city that was completely destroyed in 1902 when Mt. Pelee erupted and killed 40,000 people. From Saint-Pierre, the tour proceeds to Carbet, said to be the spot Columbus landed on his second voyage to the New World. On the return to Fort-de-France, the tour follows the coast, passing fishing villages and black volcanic sand beaches. Participation limited. (Sequence of tour stops and itineraries may vary from the printed description.)
Approximately 2½ hours. $14.00

WILLEMSTAD, CURACAO
Curacao City Tour

This tour covers major points of interest in the fascinating city of Willemstad. There is the old residential section of Scharloo, with its Dutch colonial-style mansions and colorful floating market. There is a visit to the Chobolobo mansion where Curacao liqueur is distilled; as well as a visit to the Cas Cora Botanical Gardens. The tour also passes by Stuyvesant College and the Jewish cemetery, the oldest (1650) Caucasian burial ground in the Americas. You will also see the Shell Curacao plant, one of the largest oil refineries in the world, and a water distilling plant that daily converts 16,000 tons of sea water into pure drinking water. Next stop is the shopping center where you may disembark or remain aboard the bus and return to the ship. Participation limited.
Approximately 2½ hours. $7.50

Luncheon and Swimming Tour

A delightful and relaxing luncheon and beach outing. The tour begins with a short drive to the Curacao Hilton Hotel, where you will be welcomed with a pre-luncheon cocktail. Next, a delicious luncheon is served on the Hotel's beautiful Pisca Terrace. After lunch, you are invited to use the Hotel's beach and tennis facilities. Towels and chaise lounges are provided. Participation limited.
Approximately 4½ hours. $18.00

ALL ASHORE

With its neat Dutch houses and narrow seats, the capital city of Willemstad appears as though it were magically transported from Europe to Caribbean soil.

While on a walking tour of Willemstad, be sure to cross Queen Emma—one of the only floating pontoon bridges in the world. At one time, a penny "toll" was charged (free if no shoes were worn), but now, contrary to current trends, walks on the bridge are free with shoes on.

Stretching across St. Anna Bay, Emma links the Punda and Otrabanda areas of the city. You may have a temporary wait to walk across the bridge as Emma swings open several times per day for traffic to and from the modern Curacao harbor.

Located near Emma, is the colorful waterfront market with small crafts overflowing with fresh fruit, vegetables, and fish. Nearby is the Fort Amsterdam complex which includes the Governor's Palace, various Government buildings, the Protestant Church (built in 1769) and a charming 18th century square.

This VIKING CROWN Lounge rises 10 stories above the sea and offers passengers a breathtaking panorama of the Barbados Islands —nearly 12 miles in the distance.

Chapter 8

HEALTH AND SAFETY

Think back to the golden age of travel, when luxury cruises gave the word "luxury" a whole new meaning. Picture yourself on the deck of this majestic ship right now. Beneath you the quiet ocean slips softly and smoothly by. You're on a floating hotel that glistens with an elegance surpassing many of the finest hotels in the world. And the service is meticulously perfect. The kind of service so rarely found in the rushing, scrambling world of today. On a vacation like this, you recapture a tradition which has all but disappeared. The cruising lifts you to exhilarating new heights of dining pleasure. You meet fascinating people from all over the world, and new friendships blossom in the warmth of sunny days and moonlit nights. You learn what it's like to really relax. And to really live. These are the memories that make the golden age of travel so unforgettable. And these are the elegant traditions that make your Caribbean cruise a vacation you'll remember forever. Your holiday should be free of health and safety problems.

Recent years have been active and sparkling periods for the cruise industry. In 1978 nine new ships entered the North American steamship market. The most spectacular arrival as well as departure was the SS AMERICA. On its inaugural cruise to nowhere June 30, the vessel was heavily overbooked and about 250 passengers were ferried from the ship to Staten Island in the pre-dawn hours of July 1. The second cruise, July 3, encountered bad weather and

Shipboard dining is one of the genuine highlights of any good cruise and from the standpoint of health it must be properly prepared, cooked and served. As a cruise passenger you are entitled to all meals, and that includes a pre-breakfast coffee, juice and rolls; a regular breakfast, mid-morning bouillon; luncheon in the dining room or deck buffet (or both) then afternoon tea followed by a sumptuous dinner and to complete your day . . . a midnight buffet. If that isn't enough, on some ships you can order food at no extra cost via 24 hours a day room service. A modern cruise ship, no matter what size its galley, has an enormous task to serve a delicious, hot, multi-course, dinner to 600 passengers and 300 crew members.

massive breakdowns of the ship's plumbing system. The U.S. Customs Service fined the owners nearly $500,000 for irregularities in the two voyages; Public Health Service gave the ship a sanitation inspection score of six, New York State's attorney general launched an investigation and intervened to make sure passengers got refunds; more than a dozen suppliers slapped liens against the ship; and crew members charged that the line had left them without money or tickets to get home. The ship was sold at auction (August 1978) and was taken to Piraeus, Greece for

HEALTH AND SAFETY 177

refurbishing and cruises in the Mediterranean.

Several cruise ships based and/or regularly calling in Miami (and New York) have failed to pass U.S. Public Health Service inspections. Violations include: dirty dishes in storage compartments, infestations of roaches and weevils in food areas, and improperly treated drinking water. With more than one million vacationers on cruise ships this year from Miami and other ports, you certainly have the right to know the health and safety conditions aboard the ships on which you might be sailing.

Some cruise ships have health problems, from time to time, to be sure, just as such incidents break out on occasion in top restaurants and hotels ashore. Drinking the water and eating the food on modern passenger ships, however, with rare and usually temporary exceptions, is normally as safe as it is at home. Resort cities and areas in the Caribbean certainly pose far greater risks.

The U.S. Public Health Service regularly inspects cruise ships at least twice a year when they are in U.S. ports, rating them.

Each inspection involves a checklist of 42 items divided among six categories: water, refrigeration, food preparation, potential contamination of food, personal cleanliness of food handlers and general cleanliness and repair. Each of the first four categories counts 20 points, regardless of how many deficiencies are found in a category; put another way, it means that only one deficiency in any of those categories will cost the ship 20 points and mean failure to meet Health Service standards. Each of the 10 items in the other categories carries two points and is counted separately. The majority of the cruise lines serving the United States are routinely surpassing the required Federal standards. For example, a large cruise ship will use over 150,000 gallons of fresh water every day and U.S. Public Health rule requires two parts of chlorine, a

The 22,000-ton ROYAL VIKING SKY, second of the three Royal Viking Line sisterships to enter worldwide cruise service, sails resplendently in open waters. The vessel offers all-first-class accommodations for approximately 500 passengers, providing 94 per cent with an outside view from their staterooms. Royal Viking Line ships passed their most recent inspections (Public Health Standards 85-100 and 0-84) with high or perfect scores.

very effective disinfecting agent, per each one million parts of potable water. Even though a vessel may purchase 200,000 gallons of water from the port of Miami, already treated, the fresh water will be stored in the ship's holding tanks where a hypochlorinator adds the proper amount of chlorine before the water can be used in the ship's distribution system.

The Sanitation officer on your cruise ship is concerned with more than the water supply; he will see that the water is at least 150°F to wash the dishes and glasses; he will know that refrigerators and cold storage rooms are working correctly; and he will check all local food stuffs as delivered to the ship. The list of things seems endless when matters of health are of concern.

If you want to check on the sanitation rating of your cruise ship sailing from a U.S. port, write to the U.S. Public Health Service, Room 111, at 1015 N. America

HEALTH AND SAFETY

Monthly Summary of Vessel Sanitation Inspections Performed May 1979[†]

NAME OF VESSEL	DATE LAST INSPECTED	MEETS STANDARD (85-100)	DOES NOT MEET STANDARD (0-84)	NAME OF VESSEL	DATE LAST INSPECTED	MEETS STANDARD (85-100)	DOES NOT MEET STANDARD (0-84)
Amerikanis	04/20/79	X		Oceanic	03/05/79	X	
Aquarius	02/21/79		X	Odessa	10/17/78		X
Boheme	03/24/79	X		Oriana	05/06/79		X
Britanis	04/02/79		X	Pacific Princess	05/05/79		X
Canberra	01/14/79		X	Princess Patricia	07/28/78	X	
Caribe	04/17/79	X		Prinsendam	07/20/78	X	
Carla C	05/25/79		X	Queen Elizabeth II	04/21/79	X	
Carnivale	05/20/79		X	Rotterdam	05/05/79	X	
Cunard Countess	04/07/79	X		Royal Viking Sea	05/30/79	X	
Cunard Princess	01/31/79	X		Royal Viking Sky	04/05/79	X	
Dalmacija	12/30/78		X	Royal Viking Star	04/14/79	X	
Danae	03/27/79		X	Sagafjord	04/28/79	X	
Daphne	03/22/79		X	Santa Magdalena	01/20/79	X	
Dolphin	05/11/79		X	Santa Maria	05/20/79	X	
Doric	03/26/79	X		Santa Mariana	02/17/79	X	
Emerald Seas	05/25/79		X	Santa Mercedes	02/04/79	X	
Enna G	04/16/79		X	Skyward	03/07/79	X	
Eugenia C	11/24/78		X	Song of Norway	05/08/79	X	
Europa	12/29/78		X	Southward	04/21/79	X	
Fairsea	03/03/79	X		Starward	05/12/79	X	
Fairwind	03/31/79	X		Statendam	05/12/79	X	
Federico C	01/16/79	X		Stella Maris	12/19/78	X	
Festivale	05/15/79		X	Stella Oceanis	01/04/79	X	
Flavia	04/27/79		X	Stella Solaris	12/27/78	X	
Island Princess	02/03/79	X		Sun Princess	04/28/79	X	
Italia	12/17/78		X	Sun Viking	05/07/79	X	
Jupiter	12/16/78		X	Sunward II	03/16/79	X	
Kazakhstan	03/31/79		X	Tuhobic	08/01/78		X
Klek	04/11/78		X	Universe	02/15/79	X	
Kungsholm	08/10/78		X	Veendam	04/26/79	X	
Lindblad Explorer	05/26/78		X	Veracruz I	05/21/79		X
Marconi	05/18/79		X	Victoria	01/29/79		
Mardi Gras	05/23/79		X	Visevica	03/20/79		X
Maxim Gorki	05/07/79	X		Vistafjord	02/03/79	X	
Mermoz	02/16/79			Volendam	04/01/79	X	
Mikhail Lermontov	06/03/78		X	World Renaissance	02/23/79		X
Nordic Prince	05/19/79	X		Zvir	09/22/78		X

[†] Dept. of Health, Education & Welfare Public Health Service Center for Disease Control, Bureau of Epidemiology, Quarantine Division

Way, Miami, FL 33132.

Safety at sea is not a simple matter. Usually the first morning after leaving port or just prior to sailing, there is a lifeboat drill. The U.S. Coast Guard regulations require that ALL passengers participate in the life boat drill. You will receive instructions over the public address system regarding the actual drill. Please don your life jacket and proceed to your boat station. Printed instructions are in every stateroom giving your lifeboat station and diagramming how to don your lifejacket. If you are accompanied by a child, request a child's jacket from your room steward or through the Purser's Office. This is the one thing that anyone taking a cruise has to do. This compulsory exercise is announced by seven short signals on the ship's siren followed by one long signal and the sounding of alarm bells from bow to stern, the bridge to the lowest deck.

Safety in the Caribbean on all passenger ships is strict. Every cruise ship cabin, of all lines, contains a diagram and instructions for boat drill procedure, from where to find the life preservers to the fastest and best way to the spot on deck where passengers have to report in case of an emergency. The drills include practice lowering of the lifeboats and instructions on how to put on and use a life belt.

It is often the practice to exercise both fire and boat drills at the same time. The chance of having to abandon ship or fight a real fire is so small as to be practically negligible these days, but it is well to remember the signals and what you have to do when they are sounded just in case the real thing ever occurs. Your lifeboat station is posted inside your cabin in case you should forget it.

Fire Alarm Stations: Continuous and rapid ringing of the ship's bell for not less than ten seconds, supplemented by similar ringing of the ship's electrical general-alarm bells.

Dismissal from Fire Alarm Stations: General-alarm bells

HEALTH AND SAFETY

sounded three times supplemented by three short blasts of the whistle.

Lifeboat Stations: Seven or more short blasts on the whistle followed by one long blast, supplemented by similar signals on the general-alarm bells.

Dismissal from Lifeboat Stations: Three short blasts on the whistle.

Abandon Ship: Continuous blowing of the whistle supplemented by continuous ringing of the general-alarm bells and the order "Abandon ship" passed by word of mouth.

The SS ROTTERDAM, the 38,000-ton, 748 foot long world cruise line of the Holland America Cruises, has 11 decks, two motor-driven lifeboats, each holding 43 people, and 12 hand-propelled lifeboats each carrying 135 people. These can be loaded and lowered in an average of six minutes. Additionally, the ship has 23 inflatable life rafts holding 25 people, 1700 lifebelts on board, and four tenders each carrying 59 passengers.

Remember that the ship's lifeboats are extremely seaworthy and well-equipped with necessary food, water and sails. In some cases they carry a radio, and in all cases they carry the required equipment for facing any kind of weather and conditions.

All passenger ships of both U.S. and foreign registry that stop at U.S. ports are inspected by the U.S. Coast Guard to make sure they comply with the 1960 International Convention for Safety of Life at Sea. The required standards cover everything from emergency equipment, fire-safety regulations, drills for the crew and safety of the ship's hull and machinery. If a ship fails an inspection, the Coast Guard can either detain the vessel until the problem is fixed, or they will prohibit it from carrying any American passengers. This has happened in the past, but not in recent years.

SOME ADDITIONAL SAFETY PRECAUTIONS

For your own safety and that of the ship, the following precautions should be observed *at all times:*

1. Report any unsafe conditions which you may observe to the Master, Purser or Maitre d'Hotel.
2. Do not attempt to remove furniture which is secured.
3. Do not smoke in bed; extinguish cigarettes and matches only in ashtrays.
4. Be extremely careful in discarding matches and partly smoked cigars and cigarettes. Do not throw partly extinguished matches, cigars and cigarettes overboard as the indraught caused by the ship's speed may carry them back on board creating a fire hazard. Make sure they are completely out and use the ashtrays provided throughout the ship.
5. Do not attempt to enter or leave an upper bed without using a ladder; make sure the ladder is secure. Call

HEALTH AND SAFETY

your Room Steward if necessary.
6. Hook all doors in place when you wish them open. Swinging doors can be dangerous when the ship has motion, particularly when children are around.
7. Do not leave baggage unsecured in your room. Call your Room Steward to secure it and send baggage not required to the Baggage Room.
8. Use the handrails while in the shower or bathtub.
9. Use the handrails on all stairways.
10. Do not wear high heels when playing deck games. They are risky anywhere on board ship, particularly when the ship has motion. High heels should never be worn in unfavorable weather. Walk carefully on wet decks.
11. Use the lee deck doors. If weather doors are lashed shut, do not loosen them.
12. Remember your station number and location for all boat drills.
13. Be careful if vessel is rolling or pitching. In heavy seas, be especially sure to hold onto the hand rails.
14. Watch children carefully. Do not allow them to roam around the ship unattended, particularly during bad weather. The safest ship in the world may have hazards in bad weather which children cannot be expected to realize.
15. Due to necessity, the thresholds of doorways of bathrooms, public restrooms and the doors to the outside deck areas are raised. Because of this, you should use extreme caution to ensure against tripping over these raised thresholds.
16. Never enter a darkened cabin. There is always a light switch handy.
17. Do not run at any time in any section of the vessel and pay careful attention to any advice which may be given by the Master or the ship's Officers in the in-

terest of your personal safety. And remember that the orders of the Master govern at all times.

You will be safer in the Caribbean on your modern cruise ship than in some of the new, all glass, high-rise buildings.

VOLENDAM of the Holland America Cruises was rebuilt in 1973 and has a cruising speed of twenty-one knots.

Chapter 9

CUSTOMS AND OTHER MATTERS

INSURANCE

You may want "personal effects and baggage insurance," "trip cancellation insurance," and "air passenger insurance." Some people will have peace of mind and therefore make their trip more enjoyable with a vacation travel insurance. You can buy protection against air disaster and financial distress that would upset the most carefully organized vacation fly/sea cruise.

APPLICATION TO THE OMAHA INDEMNITY COMPANY — ONE COPY WILL BE YOUR POLICY SCHEDULE PLEASE COMPLETE WITH CARE — ONLY COVERAGES FOR WHICH PREMIUMS ARE SHOWN WILL BE IN EFFECT							
Do Not Write On This Line ▶	Signature of Licensed Resident Agent			Policy Date 12 APRIL	Policy Number	H 63298	
TRIP: From BOSTON	To TAHITI		Return Trip Destination LOS ANGELES		Carrier Tour PAN AM		
Family Members Covered Insured P.B. DUVAL Dependent JAMES O. Dependent THOMAS P. Dependent	Beneficiary STEPHEN F.	Relationship SON	Policy Form T16TPI Travel Accident Capital Sums are DOUBLE the Principal Sums.		Principal Sum $ 50,000. $ $ $	Premium $ 31.20 $ $ $	
			Snow Skiing Coverage (optional)			$	
Policy to be Effective 9:00 a.m. Date 30 APRIL Hour ⊠		Term of Coverage 27 Days	Policy Form PTB248 Baggage	Amount of Coverage		Premium	
PLEASE PRINT! BEAR DOWN	PAULINE B. DUVAL 231 S. PLYMOUTH AVENUE S. HADWICK, NH 03102		Subject to limitation and exclusion on certain items.	$ 1,000.		$ 26.50	
			Policy Form T16TCI Trip Cancellation	Benefit Amount $ 1,000.		Premium	
				No. of Insureds x premium per person		97.50	
			Snow Skiing Coverage (optional)			$	
5351 App	Signature of Insured Pauline B. Duval			Make Check Payable to Addressee▶ Total Premium $ 155.20 Place S. HADWICK, NH 03102 Date 26 APRIL 1979			

TRAVEL ACCIDENT INSURANCE

Sometimes "travel accident insurance" is called air passenger insurance and can be written at airport vending machines. Travel accident insurance pays the amount on the policy for (1) loss of *life, limb,* or *sight;* (2) *accident*

Travel Insurance Pac
A TIP For Your Trip

Complete Worldwide Coverage Featuring
Trip Cancellation Protection • Accident Benefits
Hospital Sickness Indemnity • Baggage Insurance

medical expenses; and (3) *in-hospital sickness* benefits; insurance covers injuries received while a passenger is on a scheduled "airline flight" or while a passenger is on any land or water carrier, i.e., train, ship, taxi, bus or other appropriate vehicle.

Vacation Travel Insurance

Accident • Trip Cancellation • Baggage
for Individuals or Entire Families

Benefits for Accidental Loss of Life, Limb or Sight
$10,000.00 to $100,000.00 (Capital Sum)

...pays the amount you select for injuries received while a passenger on a scheduled airline flight—or while a passenger on any land or water common carrier (train, ship, taxi, bus, etc.).

$5,000.00 to $50,000.00 (Principal Sum)

...pays the Principal Sum (50% of the Capital Sum) for injuries resulting from all other accidents, no matter when or where they occur, except as listed in the Exceptions and Limitations. Includes coverage for injuries received as a passenger on nonscheduled flights of any properly licensed United States aircraft (or its foreign equivalent) or aircraft (other than a single-engine jet) of the United States Department of Defense, United States Coast Guard, Army National Guard or Air National Guard used principally for transportation of passengers, including cargo.

Benefits under this policy are payable only for injuries received while the policy is in force and for loss occurring within 100 days of the accident.

Benefit amounts above are payable for loss of life, both hands or feet, sight or any two members. One-half the maximum benefit is payable for loss of one hand or one foot—and one-fourth the benefit amount for loss of one eye. Loss means severance of the limb and total and irrecoverable loss of sight. The maximum amount of insurance which you may have under all policies of this same type may not exceed $100,000.00.

Accident Medical Expense Benefits
$1,000.00 to $5,000.00 (maximum amount)

...pays up to 10% of the Principal Sum you select or $1,000.00, whichever is greater, for medical or surgical treatment by a physician, services of a registered graduate nurse or hospital care required because of accidental injuries received while the policy is in force (in Nevada, includes home health care and services as required by that state). Pays up to the maximum amount you select for as long as 52 weeks from the date of the accident.

In-hospital Sickness Benefits
$50.00 a day

Your coverage includes an In-hospital Sickness Benefit of $50.00 a day. This benefit is payable for as long as 60 days for hospital confinement beginning while the policy is in force as a result of sickness first manifesting itself while the policy is in force.

Dependents' Coverage

Dependents eligible for this coverage include the Insured's spouse and any unmarried dependent children under age 21 and living at home.

Exceptions and Limitations

This policy does not cover loss due to: suicide or attempted suicide; commission of or attempt to commit a felony or to which a contributing cause was engagement in an illegal occupation; an act of declared or undeclared war, invasion or civil war; participation in any armed service maneuvers or training exercises; snow skiing, unless additional premium is added; mountaineering, riding or driving in any kind of race, participation in any organized sporting competition as a team member, and, except in Washington, motor competition and participation in any body contact sport. In Washington, interscholastic sports are excluded.

BAGGAGE AND PERSONAL POSSESSIONS INSURANCE

Personal effects and baggage insurance covers baggage and personal possessions (not specifically or otherwise insured) for your entire trip, 24 hours a day, everywhere in the world, on land, sea or in the air. This includes clothing, luggage and recreation equipment. Not covered are animals, artificial teeth and limbs, contact lenses, credit cards, documents, furniture, rugs or carpets of any type or for any use, money, property pertaining to business or profession or occupation, securities, tickets, automobiles, auto equipment, boats, motors, motorcycles, campers, motor homes and any other conveyances or their appurtenances, except bicycles while checked as baggage with a common carrier.

The baggage and personal possessions policy insures against all risk of loss or damage except when caused by: normal wear and tear; hostile or warlike action; deterioration; vermin; insects; inherent vice; illegal act; insurrection; rebellion; revolution; radioactive or nuclear contamination; confiscation by order of authorities.

The policy requires immediate reporting of loss or damage in writing to the proper authorities (airlines, police, hotel management, etc.) and reporting as soon as possible to the Company. Failure to comply will invalidate any claim. All losses, damage and values shall be substantiated by the Insured.

A specified limit usually applies to loss of or damage to any one classification as follows: objects of art, antiques, books, cameras and equipment, china, collections or portions thereof, glass objects, furs, jewelry (including watches), paintings, or religious articles.

TRIP CANCELLATION INSURANCE

Trip cancellation insurance provides up to the maxi-

CUSTOMS AND OTHER MATTERS

mum amount you select for nonrefundable portions of travel expense (air fare, land and water common carriers such as trains, boats, etc., hotel and other land accommodations) specified and prearranged by your travel agency or other authority (airline, steamship company, rail, etc.).

For Travel Expense Loss Due to Illness or Injury

When you or a Covered Dependent require medical treatment and have to cancel or change your travel plans, this policy covers the nonrefundable expense incurred.

Prior to Departure for Entire Trip or Return Trip—If you must cancel your trip, you are covered for nonrefundable deposits paid for the trip.

During the Trip—If the trip is interrupted, benefits are provided for transportation to catch up to the trip, or transportation to the return trip destination. Transportation costs may not exceed economy class air fare, up to the amount of coverage selected.

The benefits described above apply equally if a member of your family is stricken, forcing you to cancel or interrupt your trip. Family members include spouse, children, brothers or sisters, parents, parents-in-law, grandparents or grandchildren, provided they reside in the United States or Canada.

Dependents' Coverage

Dependents eligible for this coverage include the Insured's spouse and any unmarried dependent children under age 21 and living at home.

Preexisting Conditions

Benefits are not payable for loss resulting from injuries or sickness for which the Insured or Covered Dependent received medical treatment, advice, or a prescribed medicine during the one-year period immediately prior to the date the policy application is received.

Exceptions and Limitations

Benefits are not payable for loss resulting from: an act of declared or undeclared war, invasion or civil war; accident or damage to the aircraft in which the Insured or Covered Dependent is traveling; the Insured or Covered Dependent's: suicide or attempted suicide; commission of or attempt to commit a felony or to which a contributing cause was engagement in an illegal occupation; snow skiing, unless additional premium is added; normal childbirth or normal pregnancy; participation in organized team sports, mountaineering, riding or driving in any kind of race, and except in Washington, motor competition. In Washington, interscholastic sports are excluded.

TRAVELER'S CHECKS AND FOREIGN CURRENCY

American Express Traveler's Cheques, Thomas Cook & Son, Bank of America, First National City Bank of New York, Barclay and other banks sell traveler's checks in denominations of $10, $20, $50, $100, and $500. When paying for service on board, you may use cash, traveler's checks, or credit cards. Remember, no personal checks are accepted. Banking services are available on board for cashing U.S. traveler's checks and exchanging U.S. currency, along with advice on using foreign money.

You may charge liquor, bar bills, sauna, laundry and ship-to-shore radio messages to your shipboard account, but all charges must be paid prior to disembarkation.

Many travel agents encourage their clients to obtain some foreign currency before leaving for foreign destination(s). "Pre-Packs" (prepackaged foreign money) is very popular with travelers; most major airports offer exchange. Foreign currency is not a significant problem in the Caribbean for the traveler.

DOCUMENTARY REQUIREMENTS

To assure ease of travel, it is necessary that you be in possession of credentials that will permit you to leave one country and enter another and, what is just as important, to return to the U.S. Regulations vary widely and depend upon the country, status of the traveller, purpose of the visit, length of stay and the discretionary authority of the custom officials. You should understand that these regulations are subject to change at any time.

The major documentary requirements are: passport, tourist card, visa, special papers, and health records (certificates). International travel requires that an individual be able to prove citizenship, prove identity, and have certain vaccination certificates. Any one of the following are Proof of Citizenship: Passport (valid or expired), Birth

CUSTOMS AND OTHER MATTERS

Certificate, Baptismal Certificate, Certificate of Naturalization or Citizenship, or any other official document issued by the government showing the person is a citizen or was born in that country. Proof of Identity is established with any document which contains signature and either a photograph or a physical description of the applicant. A driver's license, passport and identification card are some examples of Proof of Identity. Vaccination Certificate is a booklet in which records of vaccination(s) are shown. The booklet issued by the World Health Organization is accepted as the approved format by all members of the United Nations; you will not need a Vaccination Certificate for your Caribbean trip. If you were to travel to Central or South America, you should have the specified vaccinations.

The Immigration Forms enclosed with your ticket must be completed before arrival at the pier.

No tourist cards are necessary to visit any of the ports in the Caribbean as long as you don't plan to go inland or leave the ship for another destination. The only identification you need is proof of U.S. citizenship. A passport, birth certificate, or voter's registration receipt will do. However, a passport is required to visit South American ports. Passengers on cruises originating or terminating in Mexico must have a Mexican tourist card. This document will be provided in your ticket wallet. Generally, there are no special inoculations required, but a smallpox vaccination is recommended. Information regarding other special health requirements, if any, will generally accompany your ticket.

U.S. PASSPORTS

A passport is a formal document issued by a government to its citizens, subjects or nationals. It officially establishes the bearer's identity and nationality, and authorizes the bearer to travel outside of his own country.

A passport is required of U.S. citizens returning from outside of the Western Hemisphere or Guam. In addition, a passport is required for entry into some Western Hemisphere countries. See specific entry requirements of all countries to be visited and countries through which your client travels.

A U.S. passport may include: the spouse of the bearer; unmarried minor children less than age 13 (including stepchildren and adopted children) of the bearer; unmarried minor brothers and sisters of the bearer. A person included in a passport of another may not use the passport for travel unless he is accompanied by the bearer (signator). Application for passport must be made in person by anyone 13 years of age and older.

PASSPORT INFORMATION FORM

THIS FORM MUST BE COMPLETELY FILLED OUT AND RETURNED BEFORE TICKET CAN BE ISSUED

VESSEL: _____ SAILING FROM PORT OF: _____ DATE: _____

PASSENGER DISEMBARKING AT PORT OF: _____

						☐ MALE
1 NAME Mr./Mrs./Miss	LAST NAME	FIRST NAME	MIDDLE INITIAL	AGE	☐ FEMALE

2	PASSPORT NUMBER	COUNTRY	DATE OF ISSUE

3	PLACE OF BIRTH	DATE	COLOR OF EYES	HEIGHT

4 MANNER AND DATE OF ACQUIRING PRESENT NATIONALITY

5	LENGTH OF TIME PASSENGER INTENDS TO REMAIN ABROAD	PURPOSE OF VISIT

6	ADDRESS	AREA CODE TELEPHONE	OCCUPATION

7 FORWARDING ADDRESS ABROAD

8 IF A MEMBER OF YOUR COUNTRY'S MILITARY FORCE, OR THEIR RESERVES, STATE BRANCH AND RANK HELD

9 IF NOT A U.S. CITIZEN, PLEASE FILL IN A, B, C, D and E BELOW

(A) ALIEN REGISTRATION NUMBER AS PER FORM NUMBER 1-94

(B) DATE AND PLACE OF LAST ENTRY INTO U.S.A.

(C) WAS SUCH ENTRY AS A PERMANENT RESIDENT OR FOR TEMPORARY STAY?

(D) VIA WHICH AIRLINE DID YOU ENTER COUNTRY?
———— OR ————
(E) VIA WHICH STEAMSHIP LINE DID YOU ENTER COUNTRY?

CUSTOMS AND OTHER MATTERS

What is Needed to Obtain a U.S. Passport:

1. Proof of citizenship — An expired passport or birth certificate, (evidence of birth in the U.S. recorded soon after birth). If this is not obtainable, applicant should submit statement issued by appropriate authorities that no birth records exist and secondary evidence of birth in the U.S. such as baptismal certificate, certificate of circumcision or other documentary evidence created shortly but not more than 5 years after birth. Those born outside the U.S. require either a certificate of naturalization or certificate of citizenship (when citizenship is obtained through parent) or naturalization certificate of the parent.
2. Photographs — Two duplicates, 2 inches by 2 inches, taken within six months. Black and white or color photos are acceptable. In a joint passport, the bearer must have his or her own photo alone, and all inclusions must share space in a group photo.
3. Proof of identity — Any document, such as a passport or driver's license, which contains signature and either physical description or photograph of applicant. If document is not available, an identifying witness who has known the applicant for at least two years is acceptable.
4. Fee — $13.00 ($10.00 plus $3.00 execution fee) if obtained by personal appearance at passport agency, or Clerk of Court; $10.00 for mail applications. Check or money order should be payable to "Passport Office."
5. Application for passport must be made in person unless applicant meets requirements established for securing passport by mail (see item 6 below).
6. Application by mail is allowed under following conditions: (a) mail application may be used only in the United States; (b) applicant must have been issued in his own name a U.S. passport within 8 years of the cur-

rent application. Previous passport must have been issued when applicant was 13 years or over; (c) previous passport must accompany the mail application; (d) two photos, taken within 6 months, must accompany the application. Mail application may not be made for passport to include more than one person.

U.S. Passport Offices

John F. Kennedy Bldg.
Government Center
Boston, Mass. 02203

Medallion Tower Bldg.
344 Camp St.
New Orleans, La. 70130

Federal Bldg, Rm. 244-A
219 So. Dearborn St.
Chicago, Ill. 60604

International Building
630 Fifth Ave.
New York, N.Y. 10020

Federal Bldg., Rm. 304
Honolulu, Hawaii 96813

401 North Broad St.
Philadelphia, Pa. 19108

300 No. Los Angeles St.
Los Angeles, Calif. 90012

1410 Fifth Ave.
Seattle, Wash. 98101

Federal Bldg., Rm. 1201
11000 Wilshire Blvd.
Los Angeles, Calif. 90024
(Los Angeles annex)

Federal Bldg., Rm. 1405
450 Golden Gate Ave.
San Francisco, Calif. 94102

Federal Office Bldg.
Rm. 812, 51 SW First Ave.
Miami, Fla. 33130

Federal Bldg.,
Rm. G-102
17th & H Sts., N.W.
Washington, DC 20524

TOURIST CARD

A Tourist Card is a document issued to prospective tourists as a prerequisite for entry and departure. A tourist card is *usually* the only travel document required by the issuing country, i.e., no passport is required, but a passport without the card is insufficient.

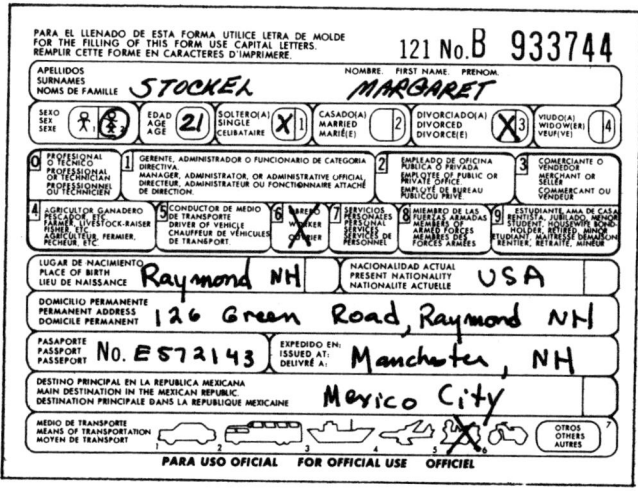

VISA

Most foreign countries require an American citizen to obtain a visa from one of their consular officials in the United States if he wishes to enter their territory. Americans who arrive abroad without the necessary visa may be refused entry into certain countries. It is the responsibility of the bearer of the Passport to obtain any necessary visas.

A visa is generally a stamped notation in a passport indicating that the bearer is to be permitted to enter the country involved for a certain purpose and length of time.

A number of foreign countries waive the visa requirement for certain kinds of travel, such as the brief visits of tourists. Most Caribbean countries do not require visas for temporary visits, the specific time depending on the individual country. Travelers should be careful to check the length of time for which the visa will be waived.

A visa is an endorsement placed in a passport or a document issued in lieu of passport by a consular or other government to indicate that the passport has been examined by such an official. A visa may be obtained from a consul representative or through a visa service agency in the country of residence prior to departure.

The visa application is an important part of preparing

```
                                                            Форма № 95
КОНСУЛЬСТВО (консульский отдел посольства) СССР в  США
     Дата начала действия визы:                    страна      Place for
     Дата окончания действия визы:                             photograph

                        Questionnaire
                    В И З О В А Я   А Н К Е Т А

Nationality    AMERICAN                  Национальность
Present citizenship / if you ever had USSR citizenship    Гражданство / если Вы имели гражданство СССР, то
               when and why did you lose it? /                       когда и в связи с чем его утеряли?
   U. S. A.
Surname
(in capital Letters)   DUVALSKY          Фамилия
First and middle names  BEATRICE ETHEL   Имя, отчество
                                         (имена)
Day, month,                              Дата рождения              Пол
year of birth  26 JAN 1940    Sex   F
Object of journey,                       Цель
to the USSR            TOURISM           поездки
                                         в СССР
USSR. department, / tourists mention "Intourist"/    В какое
organisations proposed    VISIT KREMLIN &             учреждение
to be visited          OTHER SCENIC AREAS
Route of journey                         Маршрут
(points of destination)                  следования
                                         (в пунктах)
Date of entry       | Date of departure  Дата въезда           Дата выезда

Profession    SECRETARY                  Профессия
Position      SECRETARY                  Должность
Place of birth / if born in the USSR, when    Место рождения / если Вы родились в СССР, то
             and where-to emigrated /                         куда и когда эмигрировали? /
   MANCHESTER, NEW HAMPSHIRE
Passport №  6832567  expiration date 1982    Паспорт №             действителен до
Maiden name     N/A                      Девичья фамилия
Husband's name                           Фамилия мужа
Index and name                           Индекс, наименование
of the tourist group                     туристской группы
Dates of previous
visits to the      FIRST TIME            Даты Ваших поездок в СССР
USSR
Place of work or study, its address                     office tel.
Место работы или учебы, адрес.                          рабочий тел
Permanent address                                       home tel.
Адрес постоянного места жительства                      домашний тел.
```

CUSTOMS AND OTHER MATTERS

for a trip; for example, an incorrect application is rejected by the Soviet Embassy and can cause delay, confusion and sometimes considerable extra expense. The Soviet visa shows the name and passport number, both of which must agree with the passport presented upon arrival in the USSR. The visa will indicate dates of travel and cities of entry and exit. Should any of this information change after applying for the visa, the visa may not be valid.

SPECIAL PAPERS

Additional requirements may take the form of a police certificate of good conduct, letter of recommendation or a ticket to leave the particular country.

HEALTH CERTIFICATES

Vaccination certificates are required under the regulations of the World Health Organization for quarantinable diseases. You should check the latest list of areas which are infected with cholera, smallpox, and/or yellow fever. These areas are subject to change at any time. Anyone traveling or leaving these areas must be vaccinated against the particular disease. Unless otherwise indicated, vaccinations are not required for transit passengers not leaving the airport. Validity of vaccination certificates and incubation periods are:

1. Upon initial vaccination
    a. Smallpox — not less than 8 days nor more than 3 years old. Incubation period — 14 days.
    b. Cholera — not less than 6 days nor more than 6 months. Incubation period — 5 days.
    c. Yellow Fever — not less than 10 days nor more than 10 years old. Incubation period — 6 days.
2. Upon revaccination
    a. For smallpox, the certificate becomes valid on date of revaccination. Cholera revaccination to be valid

immediately must be done within 6 months of previous vaccination. Yellow Fever vaccination to be valid immediately must be done within 10 day period.

Travelers are advised to contact their local health department, physician, or private or public agency that advises international travelers at least 2 weeks prior to departure to obtain current information on countries to be visited. You are advised to read HEALTH INFORMATION FOR INTERNATIONAL TRAVEL, DHEW—Center for Disease Control (CDC).

Because the situation with regard to the quarantinable diseases (cholera, plague, smallpox, and yellow fever) may change frequently, the Bureau of Epidemiology, CDC, distributes weekly "Blue Sheet" (Countries with Areas Infected with Quarantinable Diseases) that shows which countries are currently reporting these diseases. Some countries require vaccination against cholera, smallpox,

CUSTOMS AND OTHER MATTERS

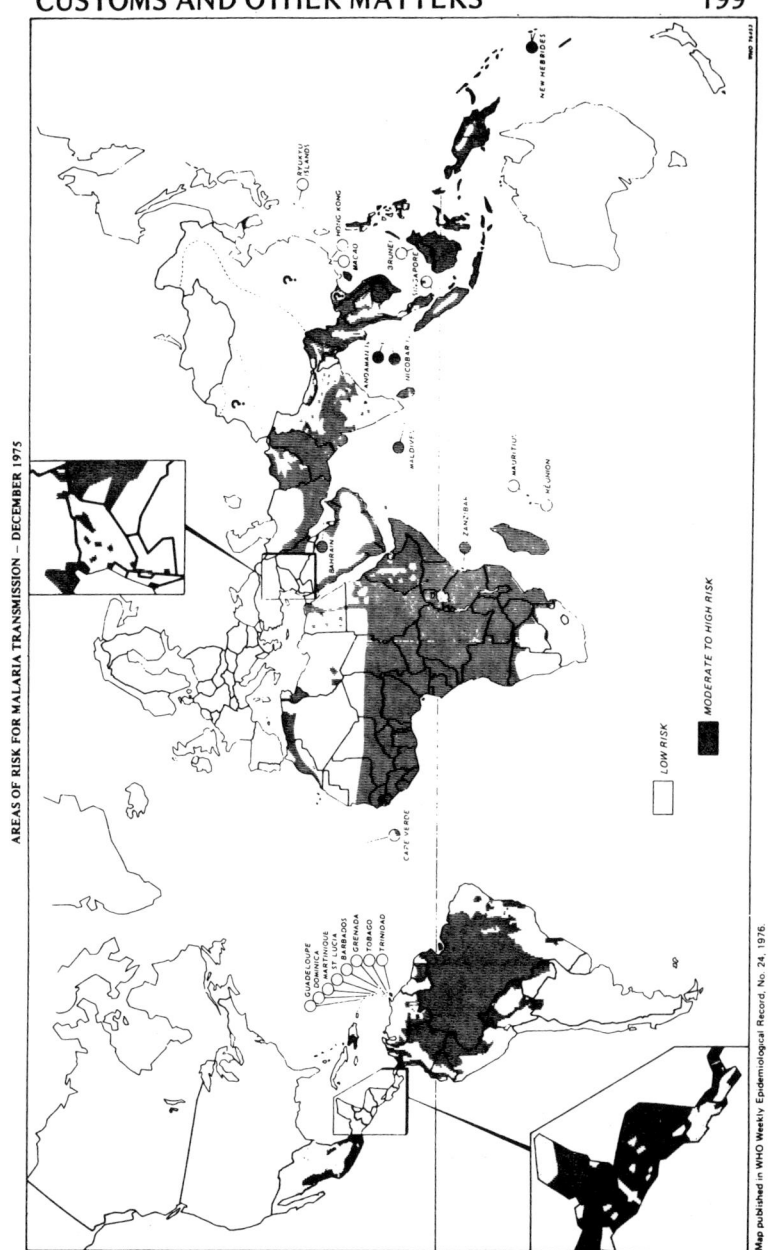

AREAS OF RISK FOR MALARIA TRANSMISSION — DECEMBER 1975

Map published in WHO Weekly Epidemiological Record, No. 24, 1976.

and yellow fever only if a traveler arrives from a country infected with these diseases; therefore, it is essential that infected areas be considered in determining whether vaccinations are required.

Official changes in vaccination requirements reported by the World Health Organization (WHO) are published in the "Blue Sheet" and also in the *Morbidity and Mortality Weekly Report* (CDC) under "International Notes — Quarantine Measures."

U.S. CUSTOMS AND IMMIGRATION

Upon returning to the U.S., all passengers must show their passports when clearing immigration. After immigration, everyone must clear customs, where their bags may or may not be opened. Articles acquired abroad and brought into the United States are subject to applicable duty and internal revenue tax, but as a returning resident you are allowed certain exemptions from paying duty on items obtained while in the Carribbean.

United States and Canadian citizens do not require passports or re-entry permits, but should carry documentary proof of citizenship such as birth certificate or voter's registration, or other similar document. Aliens who are permanent residents of the United States require only their alien registration receipt card, Form 1-151.

All other non-citizens of the United States must be in possession of passports and visas normally required for entry into the United States.

A U.S. Sailing Permit is not required of United States citizens or diplomats; or to visitors leaving the United States within 90 days and who are not required to have a visa; or to aliens who are in direct transit through the United States and who will not have been in the U.S.A. more than 5 days from the day of departure; or to visitors in possession of a B-2 Visa; or to visitors for business B-1

CUSTOMS AND OTHER MATTERS

and/or B-2 visas leaving the U.S.A. after not more than 90 days during the taxable year; or to aliens who will not have received any gross income from sources within the United States.

All other aliens, whether a temporary visitor or permanent resident of the U.S.A., should obtain from the Internal Revenue office of the district in which they reside or have been visiting, a "Certificate of Compliance" for presentation to the Government officer at the pier at the time of embarkation.

On Caribbean cruises, no Re-entry Permit is required. However, permanent resident aliens must be in possession of a Form 1-151 "Alien Registration Receipt Card."

No vaccinations are needed in the Caribbean.

Passengers bringing valuable jewelry should register such articles with the U.S. Customs inspector in Miami prior to sailing to avoid difficulty and unnecessary delay when returning to the United States. Alternatively, passengers may carry with them insurance policies covering such jewelry which, upon return to the United States, will be accepted as evidence that the articles were owned by the passengers before leaving the country.

Also, any items previously purchased abroad and of foreign manufacture such as cameras, musical instruments, phonographs, radios, typewriters, watches, and other articles, which, for any reason, may be subject to customs duty when brought into the United States, should be registered with U.S. customs in Miami before embarkation.

Duty-free Allowance

Clearing customs is simpler and often faster now, thanks to liberalized legislation passed by the Congress.

Under the new law, the amount of duty-free goods travelers can bring back to the United States has been raised from $100 to $300. The allowance for those returning from U.S. island possessions—e.g. Virgin Islands is $600.

With the increased exemptions and a streamlining of customs procedures, returning travelers will encounter shorter waits at U.S. international ports of entry. Under the former law, an inspector had to search through the rules to determine the exact duty rate for each item beyond the exempted $100. Now, a flat 10% rate is applied to amounts over the new allowance. Only when purchases exceed $900 will the time-consuming old procedure be used.

Travelers returning from the U.S. island possessions with more than the new $600 limit are now assessed a 5% duty. At the end of the cruise, the ship must be cleared by U.S. Customs and Public Health. All luggage must be placed on the pier before you can disembark. You will be notified in ample time of disembarkation arrangements.

YOUR CUSTOMS DECLARATION

All articles acquired abroad and in your possession at the time of your return must be declared. This includes:
- Gifts presented to you while abroad, such as wedding or birthday presents.
- Repairs or alterations made to any articles taken abroad and returned, whether or not repairs or alterations were free of charge.
- Items you have been requested to bring home for another person.
- Any articles you intend to sell or use in your business. The wearing or use of any article acquired abroad does not exempt it from duty. It must be declared at the price you paid for it. The customs officer will make an appropriate reduction in its value for wear and use.
- In addition, articles acquired in the U.S. Virgin

DEPARTMENT OF THE TREASURY
UNITED STATES CUSTOMS SERVICE

CUSTOMS DECLARATION

PRESENT TO THE IMMIGRATION AND CUSTOMS INSPECTORS

FORM APPROVED
OMB NO. 48-R0386

EACH ARRIVING TRAVELER OR HEAD OF A FAMILY MUST WRITE IN THE FOLLOWING INFORMATION. **PLEASE PRINT**

1. FAMILY NAME   GIVEN NAME   MIDDLE INITIAL

2. DATE OF BIRTH *(Mo./Day/Yr.)*   3. VESSEL, OR AIRLINE & FLT. NO.

4. CITIZEN OF *(Country)*   5. RESIDENT OF *(Country)*

6. PERMANENT ADDRESS

7. ADDRESS WHILE IN THE UNITED STATES

8. NAME AND RELATIONSHIP OF ACCOMPANYING FAMILY MEMBERS

9. Are you or anyone in your party carrying any fruits, plants, meats, other plant or animal products, birds, snails, or other live organisms of any kind? ☐ YES ☐ NO

10. Have you or anyone in your party been on a farm or ranch outside the U.S.A. in the last 30 days? ☐ YES ☐ NO

11. Are you or any family member carrying over $5000.00 (or the equivalent value in any currency) in monetary instruments such as coin, currency, traveler's checks, money orders, or negotiable instruments in bearer form? *(If yes, you must file a report on Form 4790, as required by law.)* Note: It is not illegal to transport over $5000 in monetary instruments; however, it must be reported. ☐ YES ☐ NO

12. *I certify that I have declared all items acquired abroad as required herein and that all oral and written statements which I have made are true, correct and complete.*
SIGNATURE:

NON-CITIZENS ONLY ▶   13. U.S. VISA ISSUED AT *(Place)*   14. VISA DATE *(Mo./Day/Yr.)*

The laws of the United States require that you **declare ALL articles acquired abroad** *(whether worn or used, whether dutiable or not, and whether obtained by purchase, as a gift, or otherwise)* which are in your or your family's possession at the time of arrival. **Repairs made abroad also must be declared.**

Nonresidents may make an oral declaration. **Returning Residents** may make an oral declaration if the total price of articles declared *(price actually paid or, if not purchased, fair retail price in country where obtained)* is not more than the sum of $300 per person. Otherwise **You Must List In Writing On The Reverse Of This Form All Articles And Repairs Acquired Abroad Which You Are Now Bringing Through Customs.** *(See additional instructions on reverse.)* If you are arriving *(directly or indirectly)* from American Samoa, Guam, or the U.S. Virgin Islands and are having articles sent from these possessions, you must list **ALL acquired articles** *(accompanied and unaccompanied)*.

All your baggage *(including handbags and hand-carried parcels)* may be examined. **False Statements Made To A Customs Officer Are Punishable By Law.** Consult "U.S. Customs Hints" and your inspector for full information.

Islands and not accompanying you must be declared at the time of your return.

The price actually paid for each article must be stated on your declaration in U.S. currency or its equivalent in country of acquisition. If the article was not purchased, obtain its fair retail value in the country in which it was acquired.

Oral Declaration

Customs declaration forms are distributed on vessels and planes and should be prepared in advance of arrival for presentation to the immigration and customs inspectors. Fill out the *identification* portion of the declaration form. You may declare orally to the customs inspector the articles you acquired abroad, if the articles are accompanying you and you have not exceeded the duty-free exemption allowed. A customs officer may, however, ask you to prepare a written list if it is necessary.

Written Declaration

A written declaration will be necessary when:

The total fair retail value of articles acquired abroad exceeds your personal exemption.

More than one quart of alcoholic beverages, 200 cigarettes (one carton), or 100 cigars are included.

Some of the items are not intended for your personal or household use, such as commercial samples, items for sale or use in your business, or articles you are bringing home for another person.

Articles acquired in the U.S. Virgin Islands, American Samoa, or Guam are being sent to the U.S.

A customs duty or internal revenue tax is collectible on any article in your possession.

CUSTOMS AND OTHER MATTERS

Family Declaration

The head of a family may make a joint declaration for all members residing in the same household and returning *together to the United States.* Example: A family of four may bring in articles free of duty valued up to $1,200 retail value on one declaration, even if the articles acquired by one member of the family exceeds the personal exemption allowed.

Infants and children returning to the United States are entitled to the same exemption as adults (except for alcoholic beverages). Children born abroad, who have never resided in the United States, are entitled to the customs exemptions granted nonresidents.

PROHIBITED AND RESTRICTED ARTICLES

Because customs inspectors are stationed at ports of entry and along our land and sea borders, they are often called upon to enforce laws and requirements of other Government agencies. For example, the Department of Agriculture is responsible for preventing the entry of injurious pest, plant, and animal diseases into the United States. The customs officer cannot ignore the Agriculture requirements—the risk of costly damage to our crops, poultry and livestock industry is too great.

Certain articles considered injurious or detrimental to the general welfare of the United States are prohibited entry by law. Among these are *absinthe, liquor-filled candy, lottery tickets, narcotics and dangerous drugs, obscene articles and publications, seditious and treasonable materials, hazardous articles (e.g., fireworks, dangerous toys, toxic or poisonous substances), products made by convicts or forced labor, and switchblade knives.*

Other items such as automobiles, food products and other things must meet special requirements before they can be released. You will be given a receipt for any articles retained by Customs.

Although there is no limitation in terms of total amount, if you transport or cause to be transported (including by mail or other means), more than $5,000 in monetary instruments on any occasion into or out of the United States, or if you receive more than that amount, you must file a report (Customs form 4790) with U.S. Customs. Ask a customs officer for the form at the time you arrive or depart with such amounts, or obtain the form from any Customs office. Monetary instruments include U.S. or foreign coin, currency, traveler's checks, money orders, and negotiable instruments or investment securities in bearer form.

CUSTOMS POINTERS
"Duty-Free Shops"

Articles bought in "duty-free" shops in foreign countries are subject to U.S. Customs exemptions and restrictions.

Duty-free cigars and cigarettes can be purchased on board, to be taken ashore at the end of your cruise.

Articles purchased in U.S. "duty-free" shops are subject to U.S. Customs duty if reentered into the U.S. Example: Liquor bought in a "duty-free" shop before entering Canada and brought back into the United States will be subject to duty and internal revenue tax.

Keep Your Sales Slips

You will find your sales slips, invoices, or other evidence of purchase not only helpful when making out your declaration but necessary if you have unaccompanied articles being sent from the U.S. Virgin Islands, American Samoa, or Guam.

CUSTOMS AND OTHER MATTERS

Packing Your Baggage

Pack your baggage in a manner that will make inspection easy. Do your best to pack separately the articles you have acquired abroad. When the customs officer asks you to open your luggage or the trunk of your car, do so without hesitation.

Photographic Film

All imported photographic films, which accompany a traveler, if not for commercial purpose, may be released without examination by Customs unless there is reason to believe they contain objectionable matter.

Films prohibited from entry are those that contain obscene matter, advocate treason or insurrection against the United States, advocate forcible resistance to any law of the United States, or those that threaten the life of or infliction of bodily harm upon any person in the United States.

Developed or undeveloped U.S. film exposed abroad (except motion-picture film to be used for commercial purposes) may enter free of duty and need not be included in your customs exemption.

Foreign film purchased abroad and prints made abroad are dutiable but may be included in your customs exemption.

Shipping Hints

Merchandise acquired abroad may be sent home by you or by the store where purchased. As these items do not accompany you on your return, they cannot be included in your customs exemption, and are subject to duty when received in the U.S. Duty cannot be prepaid. There are, however, special procedures to follow for merchandise acquired in and sent from the U.S. Virgin Islands.

Mail Shipments (including parcel post) have proven to

be more convenient and less costly for travelers. Parcels must meet the mail requirements of the exporting country as to weight, size, or measurement.

The U.S. Postal Service sends all incoming foreign mail shipments to Customs for examination. Packages free of customs duty are returned to the Postal Service for delivery to you by your home post office without additional postage, handling costs, or other fees.

For packages containing dutiable articles, the customs officer will attach a mail entry showing the amount of duty to be paid and return the parcel to the Postal Service. The duty and a postal handling fee will be collected when the package is delivered.

If you pay the duty on a package but feel that the duty was not correct, you may file a protest. This protest can be acted on only by the Customs office which issued the mail entry receipt—Customs form 3419—attached to your package. Send a copy of this form with your letter to the Customs office at the location and address shown on the left side of the form. That office will review the duty assessment based on the information furnished in your letter and, if appropriate, authorize the refund. If duty is refunded, the postal handling fee will also be refunded. If an adjustment is made with a partial refund of duty, the postal handling fee will not be refunded.

Another procedure would be not to accept the parcel. You would then have to provide, within 30 days, a written statement of your objections to the Postmaster where the parcel is being held. Your letter will be forwarded to the issuing Customs office. The shipment will be detained at the post office until a reply is received.

Unaccompanied tourist purchases, acquired in, and sent directly from the U.S. Virgin Islands may be entered, if properly declared and processed, as follows:

Up to $600 free of duty under your personal exemp-

CUSTOMS AND OTHER MATTERS

tion. Remember, that if up to $300 of this amount was acquired elsewhere than in these islands, those articles must accompany you at the time of your return for duty-free entry under your personal exemption.

An additional $600 worth of articles, dutiable at a flat 5% rate of duty.

Any amount over the above, dutiable at various rates of duty.

The procedure outlined below must be followed:

STEP 1.

You will:

a list all articles acquired abroad on your baggage declaration (Customs form 6059B) except those sent under the $40 bona fide gift provision to friends and relatives in the U.S.;

b) indicate which articles are unaccompanied;

c) fill out a Declaration of Unaccompanied Articles (Customs form 255) for each package or container to be sent. This form may be obtained when you clear Customs if it was not available where you made your purchase.

STEP 2.

Customs at the time of your return will:

a) collect duty and tax if owed on goods accompanying you;

b) verify your unaccompanied articles against sales slips, invoices, etc.;

c) validate form 255 as to whether goods are free of duty under your personal exemption or subject to a flat rate of duty. Two copies of the 3-part form will be returned to you.

STEP 3

You will return the yellow copy of the form to the

shopkeeper (or vendor) holding your purchase and keep the other copy for your records. You are responsible for advising the shopkeeper at the time you make your purchase that your package is not to be sent until this form is received.

STEP 4.

The shopkeeper will place the form in an envelope and attach the envelope securely to the outside of the package or container, which must be clearly marked *"Unaccompanied Tourist Purchase."* This is the most important step to be followed in order for you to receive the benefits allowed under this procedure.

STEP 5

The Postal Service will deliver the package, if sent by mail, to you after Customs clearance. Any duty owed will be collected by the Postal Service plus a postal handling fee.

U.S. CUSTOMS' WARNING

If you understate the value of an article you declare, or if you otherwise misrepresent an article in your declaration, you may have to pay a penalty in addition to payment of duty. Under certain circumstances, the article could be seized and forfeited if the penalty is not paid.

If you fail to declare an article acquired abroad, not only is the article subject to seizure and forfeiture, but you will be liable for a personal penalty in an amount equal to the value of the article in the United States. In addition, you may also be liable to criminal prosecution.

Don't rely on advice given by persons outside the Customs Service. It may be bad advice which could lead you to violate the customs laws and incur costly penalties.

If in doubt about whether an article should be de-

CUSTOMS AND OTHER MATTERS

clared, always declare it first and then direct your question to the customs inspector. If in doubt about the value of an article, declare the article and then ask the customs inspector for assistance in valuing it.

DESCRIPTION OF ARTICLES	PRICE
Attach Continuation Sheets If Necessary — **TOTAL PRICE**	

State price **ACTUALLY PAID**. If not purchased, state fair price in country where obtained. You may combine articles costing less than $5 each and list as **MISCELLANEOUS** up to a total of $50. List separately all other items regardless of cost.

Customs inspectors handle tourist items day after day and become acquainted with the normal foreign values. Moreover, current commercial prices of foreign items are available at all times and on-the-spot comparisons of these values can be made.

It is well known that some merchants abroad offer travelers invoices or bills of sale showing false or understated values. This practice not only delays your customs examination, but can prove very costly.

Beautiful, bright pink flamingoes fill the skies over Bonaire in the Dutch Caribbean. The island has one of the largest flamingo sanctuaries in the western hemisphere and is also a haven for hundreds of species of other birds. Bonaire's magnificient coral reefs and scores of friendly tropical fish have made it popular with scuba divers from all over the world. Its white, sandy beaches and crystal-clear, almost currentless waters are a delight to swimmers, snorkelers and sailing buffs.

Chapter 10

CARIBBEAN PORTS

The Caribbean is a region that is broad not only geographically, but also in various other ways. It has independent nations—some large, some small, some new, some old; colonies of major European nations; and former colonies that are now self-governing. Here a variety of languages will reach your ears. The main ones are French, English, Dutch, Spanish, and Papiamento—a language form of four others.

More than ten different national flags are flown by the places discussed in this chapter. About the only things they have in common are geography and climate. In almost all other matters there is much variety: size, political and economic structure, history, ethnic background, customs, and so on. Information on these subjects is provided, as well as more specific descriptions of the countries or islands where U.S. tourists are likely to visit, and also descriptions of the major groupings, such as the Greater Antilles, Windward Islands, and the Bahamas.

The turbulent history of this area has resulted in its being a patchwork of separate cultures, nations, languages, and races. During the course of 400 years the original West Indians (the Carib and Arawak Indians) have been joined by people from Spain, England, Holland, Denmark, France, Africa, India, and oddly enough—the East Indies.

Dark-skinned people form the overwhelming majority of the population. Within the various islands there is, however, a surprising variation. It runs from about 98 percent dark-skinned on some of the British Caribbean islands to about 30 percent in the Dominican Republic and about 50 percent in Puerto Rico. Panama runs about 15 percent Negro, 12 percent white, and 70 percent mixed.

It has been said that the "overtone of all the islands is African." Visitors feel it in the warmth of the people and their philosophy. They see it in the colorful customs and costumes, and in the native dances, and they hear it in the music.

You could study a detailed map of the area all day long and still find new things about it. Though it is a bit confusing at first glance, the Caribbean area can be brought into better focus by getting a few geographic terms straight in your mind.

Islands and the Sea

The Caribbean Sea is bounded on the north and east by the islands known collectively as the West Indies. These are an archipelago, and break down into two groups. The first, the Greater Antilles, takes in the western portion, while the Lesser Antilles takes in the eastern. The Greater Antilles has the larger islands—Cuba, Jamaica, Hispaniola, and Puerto Rico—plus a small number of subsidiary islands and rocks. The Lesser Antilles has many more islands, although they are smaller.

The Lesser Antilles are divided into the Leeward Islands and Windward Islands. The "Leewards" were so named, supposedly, because they are farther from the direct route of the northeasterly trade winds than the "Windwards," which lie to the south of them.

Lying to the north of Cuba and Hispaniola are the Bahama Islands. These are not considered as Caribbean islands.

Curving to the southwestward, the Lesser Antilles also take in certain small islands just off northern Venezuela. Among these are the "Dutch Islands": Aruba, Bonaire, and Curacao. In the far southeast corner sit Trinidad and Tobago.

CARIBBEAN PORTS

Gold and Other Treasures

Stories about undiscovered pirates' gold are bound to reach your ears. Some say that treasure still lies buried on lonely beaches or in the jungle in Panama. This may be true, and your chances of finding a treasure chest are probably as good as the next man's. Still, it may be more profitable to enjoy the free and obvious treasures of the Caribbean than to spend your time hunting for pirates' gold.

Here is a rundown on some of the other treasures:

• Dazzling sand beaches rimmed with palm trees and bathed by clear turquoise seas. Inland roads for exploration of jungle and plantation country, up the sides of extinct volcanoes and down into lush valleys. Vividly colored fish in the waters, tropical birds in the trees, foliage along every lane.

• Nearly ideal climate all year around (except in Panama where it is often hot and humid), with temperatures generally between 80 and 90 degrees. Trade winds to blow away the day's heat. Even in the rainy season (there are two: May-June and September-November) showers are intermittent. Between showers, the sun shines brightly to dry you off quickly.

• Unexcelled facilities for relaxation, indoor-outdoor living, and every kind of water sport. The Caribbean is a mecca for fishermen from all over the world.

• Variety of cultures jostling each other amiably; cheerful and hospitable people; free ports where goods from all parts of the world can be bought at bargain prices.

However, you must take precautions against sunburn and heatstroke, as well as skin and fungus diseases, prevalent in places where high heat and humidity combine.

You can freely drink water and milk, and eat raw fruits and vegetables served in hotels and major restaurants. In some of the places off the beaten track, however, it would be advisable to stick to bottled water, canned milk, and cooked fruits and vegetables.

Never swim alone (except in pools or on guarded beaches) so that someone is nearby in case you run into trouble. Coral can cut deeply, so you must be careful when exploring a reef or coral beach.

Free ports, a feature of this region, are those at which the merchants pay no customs duty on imported merchandise, with the savings being passed on to the buyer. They are found in the U. S. Virgin Islands, Panama, and the Dutch islands. At some other locations—Jamaica, Barbados, Martinique, and Guadeloupe, for example—similar low prices prevail under a different system.

The islands and Panama are a shopper's paradise. Your eyes will be dazzled by the arrays of merchandise from all over the world, not to mention intriguing local products. In most cases, the best buys are items made locally or made in the country with closest national ties to the island.

Island-hopping planes will get you over a lot of territory fast, but sailing gives you a much closer view of the islands. Traveling on an island calls for the use of facilities at hand. In most places, taxi or jitney service is available. All of Puerto Rico's main routes are covered by fast, clean buses. But on some islands the buses date back to the early 1930's. There are places where you'll have to travel by jeep, horse, or donkey.

United States currency is accepted just about everywhere in the area. Sometimes, though, you can get a better bargain by paying in local currency. Prices at many places are listed only in the local currency, so you should know the official exchange rate.

CARIBBEAN PORTS

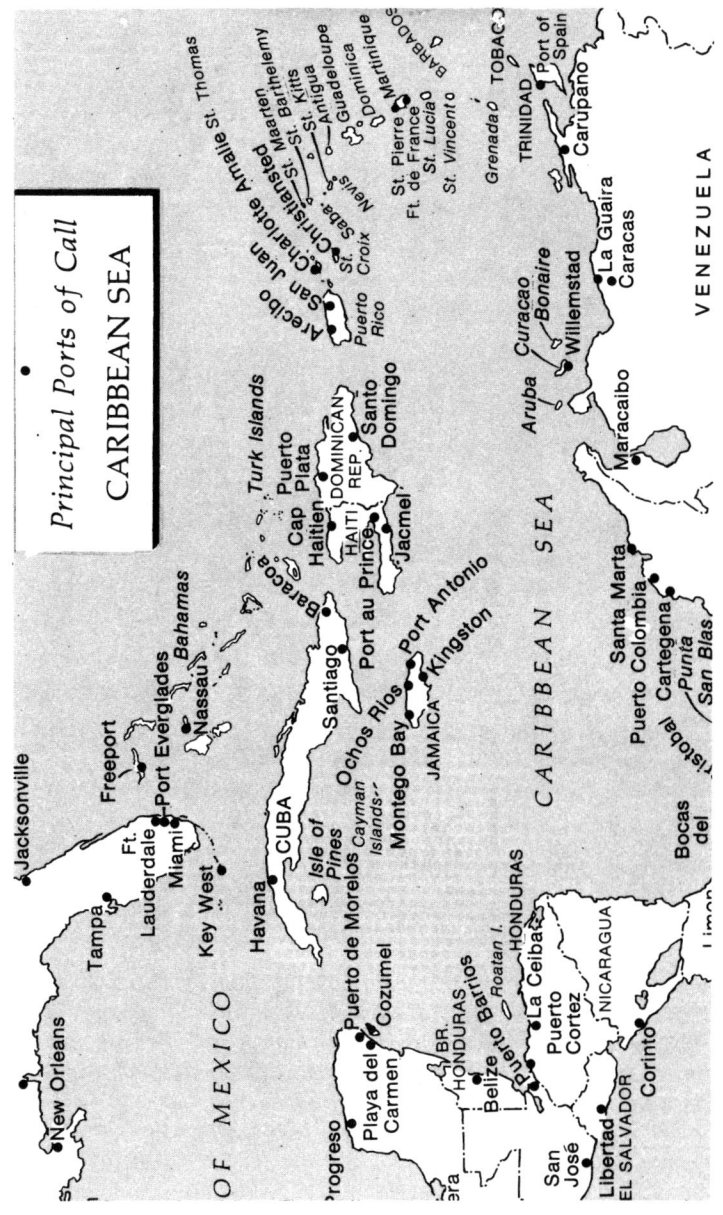

A land rich in history—you will find a never-ending list of "firsts" in Santo Domingo. A few of these firsts include the Chapel of the Rosary built in 1496, the Tower of Homage—a building completed in 1502 and the ruins of San Nicholas de Bari Hospital. Still overflowing with the riches of colonial Spain is the majestic Cathedral of St. Maria la Menor. Other notable historic attractions include the Tomb of Christopher Columbus and the Alcazar Castle, built in the early 16th century for Diego, the son of Columbus.

A SHORT HISTORY

It all began with Christopher Columbus. The history of America as we know it began on 12 October 1492 when Christopher Columbus first set foot in the Caribbean area. The island of his first landfall, which he called San Salvador, held a few Arawak Indians. They traded him parrots and crude cotton thread for glass beads and little bells. Pretty small pickin's for what he had in mind, and in short order he was off for further exploring.

Fifteen days later he discovered Cuba, which he believed to be Japan, or a peninsula of China—or perhaps the *East* Indies.

Sailing eastward across the Windward Passage some 50 miles, Columbus next discovered the island of Hispaniola, which served for a few years as the headquarters of Spain's New World Empire. By 1515, however, it had been replaced in importance by Havana, Cuba, which lay much closer to the gold-carrying route from the coast of the mainland (the original "Spanish Main") to Spain.

From Cuba there was a general pattern of exploration and military expeditions westward and southward toward Central America, Colombia, Venezuela, and Mexico. There was a smaller movement eastward, and it ended at Puerto Rico. Perhaps the smaller islands beyond Puerto Rico, the Lesser Antilles, were too small to rate notice; perhaps the Caribs were too fierce.

Thus it was that the three larger islands (along with the nations of the mainland) acquired a strong Spanish or Spanish-African flavor, while the smaller islands to the eastward have a flavor that is tempered by other European countries.

Ponce de León was Puerto Rico's first explorer, settler, and governor. He conquered the native population during a two-year period. In 1514, acting on a rumor of a wonderful Fountain of Youth on an island called Bimini, he sailed to the north-northeast, and although he didn't find the fountain, he did discover several islands of the Bahamas, as well as what he thought was a much larger island, which he named *Florida*. Seven years later he tried to conquer and colonize Florida, but his efforts and life were brought to an end by an Indian's arrow.

On the mainland, other conquistadors were moving at a faster pace—for it was there that supposedly lay *El Dorado*, the legendary city of gold; and beyond that, Asia proper. In 1509, an expedition was on the move in the Isthmus of Panama. Another was in northern Columbia. Both were routed by Indians. Others followed. In 1510, following two earlier Spanish expeditions into Mexico, Cortez struck out with 11 vessels and 550 men on the conquest of Mexico. In 1513 Balboa marched west from his base at Darien, Panama, and sighted the Pacific.

But whether overrunning an island or marching toward a mainland treasure-trove, the conquistadors enslaved most of those with whom they came in contact. Many of the natives died at the hands of their captors or from disease, such as smallpox brought from Europe. As a result, very few pure or nearly pure Indians have survived anywhere in the West Indies. Only a single settlement of the hardier Caribs survives on Dominica, in addition to a few families on St. Vincent.

As time went on, what little gold there was in the islands was pretty much worked out. Settlers began looking for other sources of riches—and sugar, followed by tobacco, cocoa, and coffee, proved to be the answer. Working these crops called for laborers. Since about 1502, slaves from West Africa had worked with the Indians in the gold mines. So in a few short years the slave trade multiplied. It is estimated that by the mid-1800's, when that evil practice died out, some 20 million slaves had been brought to the West Indies.

As time went on, the slaves began to outnumber their owners on most of the islands. That spelled trouble. The first rebellion took place in 1649, on Barbados. There was an uprising on Jamaica in 1831. The world's first Negro republic, Haiti, developed from the overthrow of the French owners and rulers—an uprising by slaves that Napoleon's troops were unable to put down.

Today the dark-skinned people of the West Indies look upon the sufferings and humiliations of their ancestors as historical fact... something past and done with and not something to be carried around as a "big hurt." During your travels in this area, you will become aware that the culture and way of life here is "West Indian," and that the people who live here are, regardless of their ancestry, "West Indians."

TRADE, TOURISTS, AND PROGRESS

On world economic charts this region is largely shown as being *tropical*. Its economy is based mainly on agriculture. Farmers are of two types. First is the plantation owner, with his spread of from 100 up to several thousand acres. The other type is the small cultivator working a few acres of land. Medium-size farms are rare. Truck farming is done near some of the cities. Some regions have mostly subsistance farming, in which families just manage to get by on what they grow.

As in the early days, sugar is the main product. Other export crops are cacao, tobacco, coffee, bananas, citrus fruits, and spices. From the West Indies also come oil, asphalt, chrome ores, and many forest products. Jamaica's bauxite (aluminum ore) reserves are the world's largest. Oil comes from Trinidad, Aruba, and Curaçao. But for many of the smaller islands, sugar is just about the only export.

Rum, which is distilled from sugar cane, is not to be disregarded. The world's best comes from this area. Local varieties run from the light rums of Puerto Rico to the heavier, darker rums of Barbados and Jamaica. In Curaçao, the well-known liquor of that name is made from rinds of a special locally-grown orange.

Ever since America's colonial days the Caribbean islands have been favorite places to visit. Since World War II tourism has expanded at an amazing rate. Not only do great numbers of people go there, but the islands have done much to accommodate the visitors . . . built hotels, developed harbors and airfields, improved beaches, expanded sea and air routes, and so on.

As in any other part of the world, this area has its differences in standards of living. Those who have money live well indeed. Those at the other extreme, and they far outnumber the wealthy, live in various stages of poverty.

You will find people of means living graciously in cool, Spanish-type houses or modern homes and apartments. Their servants might include a cook, a maid, and a nurse for the children.

Most of the people are quite poor, with annual incomes of only a few hundred dollars, or even less. In the towns they live crowded together in rows of tiny houses—painted in attractive colors when they can afford paint. In the countryside, the poor live mainly in shacks or lean-tos, put together in imaginative ways, or in the thatched-roof huts so symbolic of the tropics. Luxuriant growth of trees and flowering shrubs sometimes add an exotic backdrop. Children dress according to age. That is, the youngest often wear no clothing.

Rice and beans are the staple diet of the average family, varied with fish and local fruits. The midday meal is usually the main one. When economically possible, it begins with a light soup, followed by rice and fish or meat and beans, or some variation. There may be vegetables such as plantains, and for dessert, oranges, bananas, mangoes, or some other native fruit.

There are big differences among the islands, however; and some—Puerto Rico, Jamaica, Trinidad, and the Dutch islands—are relatively well off when compared to several of the much smaller islands.

Panama, the Dominican Republic, and Haiti—plus Puerto Rico, as a commonwealth with the United States— are all members of the Organization of American States (OAS). They, thus, join with most of the other nations of the Americas in an organization designed to further the cause of peace, freedom, security, and welfare. Founded on the principles of mutual cooperation and assistance, the OAS is thoroughly democratic. Each of the member states, regardless of size or power, has equal voice and vote. The OAS and its General Secretariat, the Pan American Union in Washington, D.C., are supported by the member nations. The OAS is a regional agency within the United Nations.

In 1961 at Punta del Este, Uruguay, the United States and 19 of the 20 Latin American countries (the exception: Cuba) established the Alliance for Progress. By that action they launched an enterprise to solve problems threatening the social, economic, and political stability of Latin America in particular and the Western Hemisphere as a whole.

Self-help is the keynote of the Alliance program in each country. This calls for the mobilization of manpower and economic resources to the fullest extent and the formulation of a national development program, by means of which each country will realize its maximum potential in the next decade or two.

The OAS plays a major role in implementing the program by means of basic studies, technicians, and evaluation of the long-term development plans submitted by Latin American governments.

SPORTS ON LAND AND SEA

About the only sports you won't find in the Caribbean area are winter sports. Almost anything else you can think of is available on a year-round basis: golf, tennis, horseback riding and horseracing, hiking, baseball, soccer, cricket and, of course, all kinds of water sports.

You can see a bullfight in Panama or a polo match in Antigua. Barbados stages exciting cricket matches; and Grenada, cricket and soccer. Nassau in the Bahamas, El Commandante in Puerto Rico, and St. Thomas in the U. S. Virgin Islands are three of the places where you can enjoy horseracing. Cockfighting is a popular spectator sport, and is legal throughout the Caribbean.

The Caribbean area is second to none when it comes both to variety and excellence in water sports... whether wading at a sandy beach or skin diving near a coral reef. Sailing, surfcasting, and deep sea fishing are also popular water sports.

YOUR LEGAL STATUS

Criminal law in the Caribbean region is generally similar to our own. Although court procedures may differ from ours and may not include all the rights guaranteed by our Constitution, this doesn't mean that trials will be unfair. Usually an offense will be committed through lack of knowledge, or from misunderstanding; perhaps, through failure to learn local currency regulations or customs provisions, or failure to show the respect to which public officials are entitled under local law. So, as soon as you arrive at a location, try to find out your individual legal status and any local variations in laws you may need to know.

CARIBBEAN PORTS

Local fishing boats in a sheltered inlet in the Caribbean.

Lower Antilles, yacht haven and cruising center.

THE CARIBBEAN NATIONS

PANAMA

The Isthmus of Panama, colonized by the Spanish in the early 1500's, became the crossroads of Spanish America with the conquest in 1533 of the Incan Empire by Francisco Pizzaro. Gold, silver, and other treasures from Peru and elsewhere on the Pacific coast of Central and South America were brought each year to what is now the "old city" of Panama on the Pacific side of the isthmus. Then it was transported by horse and mule over the *Camino Real* (Royal Road) to Portobelo on the Atlantic coast, where it was loaded aboard galleons on Spain's treasure fleet. Storms and pirates took a heavy toll on ships and treasure between Panama and Spain.

PANAMA CANAL

Nearly four centuries later, Panama became the crossroads of the world with the opening of the Panama Canal in 1914. The 50-mile-long waterway across the Isthmus eliminated the need for thousands of miles of travel around Cape Horn for sea traffic between the Atlantic and Pacific Oceans.

The canal and zone bisect not only the isthmus but the Republic of Panama as well. The zone, which is about 65 miles long and 10 miles wide, is administered by the Republic of Panama.

Because of the curved shape of the isthmus, the Pacific entrance of the canal is 27 miles *east*, not west, of the Atlantic entrance.

Ships of all nations use the canal and transits through the waterway number about 11,000 annually. The canal's strategic importance to the United States is underlined by the fact that our Navy's fleet units as well as ships carrying defense cargoes can be quickly shifted between the Atlantic and Pacific Oceans. For example, the canal reduces the voyage from New York to San Francisco by 7,873 miles, which translates into a savings of three weeks' sailing time by a 15-knot ship.

The U. S. Government began construction on the canal in 1904, after buying the rights and property of a French company that had made a valiant but unsuccessful campaign against malaria and yellow fever conducted in the jungle and swamp of the isthmus. This campaign was as important to the success of the canal-building venture as the complex engineering feats performed.

REPUBLIC OF PANAMA

No border guards or barricades separate the Canal Zone from the Republic of Panama. As a matter of fact, the border between Panama City, capital of the republic, and the zonal city of Balboa runs along 4th of July Avenue. One sidewalk and the street are in the zone and the other sidewalk is in the republic.

As countries go, Panama is small. It is larger than West Virginia, but smaller than South Carolina. Its population of 1,250,000 is less than that of any other Latin American country. Its most important exports are petroleum products, bananas, and shrimp.

Columbus visited Panama on his fourth voyage in 1502 and claimed it for Spain. Panama was a Spanish colony until 1819, then became part of the Republic of Colombia. In 1903, Panama declared itself independent of Colombia. It was promptly recognized as such by the United States, which then negotiated a treaty with the

CARIBBEAN PORTS

new republic for the construction and operation of the Panama Canal.

THE LIVELY COASTAL CITIES

Panama City, on the Pacific side, the republic's capital and largest city (population: 273,000 in 1960), was founded in 1519. Today it is a blend of Spanish culture and North American progress. Adjacent to it is Balboa, site of the zone headquarters, and Ancón, a residential city in the zone.

Among the many things to see in Panama City is the *National Museum,* with its collection of ceremonial relics from ancient Indian mounds. Another is the impressive *Presidential Palace.* Onetime home of Spanish governors, it is now the home and office of the President of the Republic of Panama.

Several blocks from the palace is the public market with its display of tropical fruits and vegetables, live monkeys and birds, and native products.

Of historic interest is the old *Convent of San Francisco,* where delegates from a number of American republics came together in the Congress of Panama, convoked in 1826 by Simón Bolívar, "Father of Pan Americanism." This was the first step toward creation of a league of American nations.

Las Bóvedas (the Vaults) is an old fortification named for its dungeons in which political prisoners once languished. It stands at the extreme tip of land jutting into Panama Bay. Twelve miles from Panama City is Taboga, "Isle of Flowers," whose palm-fringed beach and gentle waters make it a favorite resort.

Just seven miles east of Panama City are the ruins of *Panama Viejo* (old Panama City), for 150 years one of the most important and prosperous cities of the Spanish colonial empire. Along the wide crescent bay you will find the stone docks where Spanish ships unloaded their cargos of treasure for the trans-isthmian trek to the Atlantic side.

It is said that Francis Drake, the English pirate who became a knight, held up a treasure train on this road in 1552 and took so much loot that his followers could not carry it all. Part is still supposed to be buried along the roadside where they left it.

ACROSS THE ISTHMUS

On the Atlantic side lie Cristóbal, in the Canal Zone, and Colón, in the republic. Colón was part of Panama's "Gold Coast"—not just because of Spanish gold, but because, in 1849, there was a rush through there of adventurous North Americans on their way to the gold fields of California.

For an unusual excursion offshore, visit the emerald green islands of San Blas. The Indians who live here do not mingle with people of the white race, and live according to traditional ways. The women wear rings in their noses and may not leave the islands. They use coconuts as currency among themselves, but they will exchange trinkets and hand-crafted articles for silver money from tourists.

LOCAL COLOR

One of the gayest times in Panama is *carnaval,* the four days before Ash Wednesday. *King Momo* and the elected *Queen of the carnaval* rule over the general merrymaking. You will have ample opportunity to see the spirited national dance, the *tamborito,* and sample the Panamanian foods.

Fish and shellfish are great local specialties. Among the Spanish and Creole dishes you may enjoy are a fish pie called *pastel de pescado,* and *ceviche,* which is raw fish marinated in lime juice and hot peppers. When you try ceviche avoid eating the bits of pepper served with the fish unless you're used to very hot food.

For certain types of hunting, Panama offers an almost unparalleled opportunity. About 175 miles due west of the Canal Zone are the *Chiriqui Highlands,* a place where wild game abounds, including wild pigs, game birds, deer —and jaguar, ocelots, tigrillo, and puma. Local guides are available and the facilities are good. A weekend spent in Chiriquí can be a real experience for the sportsman.

Living in Panama is an experience most families enjoy very much. Indoor-outdoor living all year around is one of the advantages. Another is the opportunity for getting acquainted with the Spanish culture of the coastal cities.

The hot and humid climate requires some adjustment. Many houses are built on stilts with a breezeway or carport underneath to keep them as dry and cool as possible. Instead of window panes, the houses have louvers, which keep out the rain but let in the air.

PUERTO RICO

Puerto Rico is neither a state, colony, nor territory— though it was the latter for many years. Since July 1952, it has had the status of a free commonwealth; or, to translate the official Spanish-language term, a "free associated state" of the United States. Puerto Ricans enjoy a representative form of government. The Commonwealth Government's legislative branch consists of a Senate and House of Representatives, while the executive branch is headed by the elected governor, assisted by a cabinet. It also has its own judiciary system.

The flavor of Puerto Rico is Spanish, for the island was a Spanish colony from 1508 to 1898—when it was ceded to the United States as a result of the Spanish-American War.

ISLAND ON THE MOVE

A land reform program started about 25 years ago has given small plots to thousands of squatter families. Annual profits of plantations controlled by the Land Authority, a government agency, are distributed among all employees. Redevelopment projects have transformed San Juan. Waterfront shacks and slum neighborhoods have given way to neat housing projects and the latest word in resort hotels complete with pools, beaches, and shops.

Along with economic advances, a cultural revival program has been carried on under government supervision. This is aimed at preserving relics of Puerto Rico's cultural heritage and developing contemporary arts and culture. As a result of this program, you can examine treasures in 16th and 17th century churches and museums, and attend fiestas and ceremonies in which the old customs and costumes have been revived.

Elementary education has been free and compulsory since 1899. The literacy rate is high—about 88 percent for those 10 and older. There are four institutions of higher learning on the island.

English is taught in the schools, though the instruction is in Spanish below the senior high school level. In San Juan, English is about as common as Spanish. Elsewhere you may meet people who speak Spanish with only a minimum understanding of English. Try any Spanish you may know on them, and see what rewarding gestures of friendship you get in return.

EXPLORING SAN JUAN

San Juan is Puerto Rico's modern capital and home of nearly 500,000 people. It is built around the port, the busiest in the West Indies. The port and the large modern airport make San Juan the crossroads of North and South American traffic.

The "old city" of San Juan—now only six blocks square—was built and fortified nearly 500 years ago. Handsome bridges connect it to the main island. *Plaza Colón* is the center of the old city and the location of the bus terminal.

Balconies protected by wrought iron and grill-work overhang the narrow streets of the old city. Strolling down these streets can give you the impression of being transported back into old Spain. The shops sell a wide variety of merchandise, including high fashion resort-wear created in Puerto Rico.

El Morro is the high point of any tour. With the landside fort of *San Cristobal,* El Morro defended the early Spanish settlement against raids by French, Dutch, and English freebooters and pirates.

Other interesting things to see in old San Juan are the 16th century *Cathedral de San Juan Bautista,* where Ponce de León's remains rest; tiny *Cristo Chapel* and *San José Church* built in 1522; and *La Fortaleza,* official residence of the Governor.

Beyond the walls of the old city, modern San Juan has boomed out to the community of *Santurce,* to the university town of *San Piedras,* and to suburban areas where the tourist hotels, restaurants, beaches, and lagoons abound.

"OUT ON THE ISLAND"

That's the local way of referring to any part of Puerto Rico not in the San Juan area. Since the island is only 100 miles long and 35 wide, all of its varied beauty and places of interest are within easy reach of San Juan.

Less than 50 miles from the capital are such attractions as palm-shaded *Luquillo* public beach and *El Yunque,* a 3,500-foot mountain crowned with a beautiful rain forest. El Yunque is a U. S. National Park with good roads and inviting forest trails. Facilities are there for buying food, picnicking, and overnight stays.

On the Caribbean side of the island you can visit *Ponce,* "Pearl of the South," Puerto Rico's second largest city and an active port. In *San German,* an inland town, you can see what is probably the oldest church in this hemisphere; though not the oldest still in use. This well-preserved building overlooks the town's sleepy, flower-filled plaza.

La Parġuera, a picturesque fishing village on the Caribbean, is a favorite resort spot. From here you can make a short boat trip at night through *Phosphorescent Bay,* where the water takes on a bluish glow when disturbed. Puerto Rico's largest sugar mill is near *Guánica,* on the southeast coast. It was at Guánica that U. S. troops made their first landing on the island during the Spanish-American War.

When you order coffee in restaurants and hotels, specify *Puerto Rican* instead of *American* now and then to try the local blends. They are strong and distinctive and a new treat. As to the food—the best of the Spanish-Caribbean dishes are part of the island's cuisine, including *flan,* a favorite custard dessert. Turtle steak is a specialty at some restaurants, and most of the hotels occasionally stage a fiesta at which a barbecued pig is served with all the traditional trimmings.

HISPANIOLA

To the west of Puerto Rico, across Mona Passage, lies the much larger island of Hispaniola. The island, slightly smaller than South Dakota, is quite interesting in its own right. The city of Santo Domingo, founded in 1496, is the oldest settlement in the western hemisphere. The remains of Christopher Columbus are said to be buried there. Further, it is the only island in the world where two republics exist side by side.

Haiti occupies the western third of the island. It is the world's oldest Negro republic. French is its official language. It shares the island with the Dominican Republic, whose traditions and language are Spanish.

HAITI

The Arawak Indians called the entire island Haiti, meaning "highlands." Today the name applies only to the Republic of Haiti, which is almost entire mountainous.

By the time Haiti passed from Spanish to French control in 1697, the original Indian inhabitants had died out, and had been replaced by slaves from Africa. The French brought in even more slaves. The slaves rebelled during the French Revolution, and Toussaint L'Ouverture, a Haitian Negro leader, ruled the island during 1801-1802. Napoleon sent an expedition to Haiti which overthrew Toussaint.

Another Haitian Negro leader, Dessalines, finally drove the French from Haiti in 1803, and declared the island's independence in 1804. He proclaimed himself Emperor the same year. Haiti became a republic in 1820, but its history continued to be turbulent and its internal affairs unstable.

A common bond between the United States and Haiti was established during our Revolutionary War, when 800 Haitian volunteers fought alongside the Continentals during the siege of British-held Savannah, Georgia.

Between 1908 and 1915, Haiti became burdened with debts and torn by internal disorders. To prevent international complications, the United States sent Marines into the country. They remained there until 1934, when the country's affairs were in order again.

Since the turn of the century the country has made some advances in sanitation and education and improved the roads. Over the centuries the soil has been depleted by overcultivation, and there are few natural resources. Haiti's gross national product in 1961 was about $75 per person.

Almost 95 percent of the Haitians are of African descent. The rest of the population is mostly of mixed African-Caucasian ancestry (mulattoes). A small number of Haitians are of European or Levantine stock, Haiti is the only republic in the Western Hemisphere in which French is the official language, but it is spoken only by about 10 percent of the people. The remainder speak Creole.

The Republic of Haiti occupies the western one-third of the island of Hispaniola in the Caribbean Sea between Puerto Rico and Cuba (The Dominican Republic occupies the eastern two-thirds of the island.). Although it is in the tropics, the country is generally semiarid because the mountains that divide Haiti and the Dominican Republic cut off the moist trade winds. About two-thirds of the country is rough, mountainous terrain unsuitable for cultivation.

A colorful and mysterious country, Haiti's mainland is covered with densely wooded mountains. Peaks rise as high as 10,300 feet and in many places right from the sea. In between the mountain ranges are fertile plains, rivers and lakes. The coastline of cliffs is broken by indented coves and harbors.

Average temperature in Furcy at 5,000 feet is 66 degrees while in Port-au-Prince on the coast it is 80 degrees. There are two rainy seasons, April to June and August to October. May and September have the most rain.

Forests contain fine woods—mahogany, cedar, oak, pine, lignum, vitae, satinwood, rosewood. Cacti and dwarfed thorn trees grow in the arid areas. *La Gonave* on the bay is headquarters for sport fishermen. Pine Forest near *Jacmel,* is an area that covers 150,000 acres and contains rare birds and tropical plants. *Lake Etang Saumatre* is a hunter's paradise for wild goat, wild boar, crocodile,

CARIBBEAN PORTS

duck, guinea hen and pigeon. For the butterfly collector, summer is the best time.

Haiti was the first independent Negro republic in the world. Its president is elected for a six-year term. Haitian people are proud and sensitive and have an Old World dignity. The "elite" minority is well educated and formal. The peasant is lighthearted and friendly. Although Roman Catholicism is the state religion, voodoo is the cherished religion of the larger peasant class.

Exports are coffee, sisal fiber, raw sugar, molasses, cocoa, oils, mahogany ware, cotton and bananas. Some copper is mined.

Cap Haitien, the most historic city, was the French capital in 1670 and French influence can be seen in the Notre Dame Church, La Citadelle de la Ferriere—a mountain fortress built as a defense against Napoleon by slave labor at a claimed loss of over 10,000 workers, and multi-hued French colonial homes with wrought-iron balconies.

Port-au-Prince, the capital, has a mixture of architecture ranging from old but elegant wooden French colonial homes, thatched roof huts to ultra modern buildings. There's a boulevard named for Harry Truman, museums containing collections of Columbian, Indian and African relics and voodoo ritual items, the three-domed National Palace—a replica of the Petit Palais in Paris and the National Museum which has the iron anchor of the Santa Maria, flagship of Columbus.

Swimming is popular at hotel and club pools in Port-au-Prince and at Kyona Beach. There is also water skiing, spearfishing and snorkeling at Sand Cay. Glass-bottomed boats are available for charter. Other sports include golf, tennis, horseback riding, soccer, baseball and cockfighting. The meringue is danced at hotels and nightclubs and the International Casino is popular.

Food specialties include pain patate—sweet potato

pudding, mango pie, homard flambu—flaming rock lobster. Haiti is known for its fine Barbancourt Rum.

There are free-port prices on German cameras, Swiss watches, French perfume, English cashmeres, woolens and leather goods, Danish silver, Swedish crystal and China. Local items include fine mahogany, paintings, sculpture, hand-loomed textiles, hand-woven and hand-dyed rugs, embroidered dresses and blouses, ceramics, tortise shell jewelry, voodoo drums, sisal hats, bags and place mats, dolls and native recordings.

If you visit Port-au-Prince, you'll particularly enjoy the nearby resort suburb of *Pétionville*. Farther on, in the Haitian "Alps," the resorts of *La Boule, Kenscoff,* and *Furcy* all afford superb climate and scenery. On the northern peninsula, visit *Port-de-Paix,* the republic's oldest city—founded in 1664 by French buccaneers. The seat of the first French garrison, it was briefly the capital of the colony. At *Cap-Haitien,* you can see the ruins of the sumptuous palace of Pauline Bonaparte, Napoleon's sister. She held sway in a lavish court while her husband, General Leclerc, lost France's prize colony and his own life. Don't miss the ruins of King Henri Christophe's fabulous *Sans-Souci* Palace and his *Citadel,* whose history is stanger than fiction.

In many "back country" places, voodoo rites are still practiced by many people, though the country's official religion is Roman Catholic. Voodoo is a folk religion evolved from African ceremonies. It traditionally includes an animal sacrifice. As a visitor, you will have an opportunity to see modified ceremonies, complete with drumming and chanting, but without the sacrifice.

DOMINICAN REPUBLIC

Occupying the greater part of Hispaniola, this country was once called *Santo Domingo.* Its early history, like

Haiti's, is one of European domination—first Spanish and later French. In the 1800's, Haiti extended its control over the entire island and ruled Santo Domingo for about 20 years. The Dominicans, under Juan Pablo Duarte, revolted, and in 1844 they established an independent republic.

Haitians form the largest foreign minority group, while Spanish and West Indian colonies comprise other important foreign groups. About 9,000 U. S. citizens reside in the Dominican Republic. The Dominican Republic occupies the eastern two-thirds of the island of Hispaniola in the Caribbean Sea between Puerto Rico and Cuba. Haiti occupies the western third. The country has a coastline of more than 1,000 miles and its common border with Haiti is 193 miles long. The principal mountain range and primary watershed is the Cordillera Central, which crosses the middle of the country.

Like Haiti, this country has had its troubles. Threats of invasion and internal instability once led the new Dominican Republic to ask the United States to annex it. A treaty to accomplish this was negotiated shortly after the Civil War, but the U. S. Senate rejected it. In 1905, with growing financial difficulties, the country asked the United States to take over control of its customs. This our government did. Local affairs were so unsettled that the U.S. Marines were landed in 1916 and took over the country's administration. In 1924 the Marines withdrew, and in 1941 the customs receivership ended.

In the spring of 1965, U. S. troops were landed to save the lives of U. S. citizens and citizens of 30 other countries and to prevent the establishment of another Communist state like Cuba in the Americas. Some of the troops were withdrawn after a few weeks. The others were assigned to an inter-American peacekeeping force under the Organization of American States, removed in 1966.

Dominicans claim that theirs is the purest Spanish culture in the New World and make strong efforts to preserve it. They have retained much of the old, formal manners of the Spaniards. Dominican art, literature, and even fiestas, are almost completely in the traditions of Spain.

In the capital, venerable *Santo Domingo,* you'll find the *Tower of Homage,* oldest stone fortress in the hemisphere, and the ruins of the first hospital, *San Nicolás as de Bari,* built in 1503. Other aspects of the city are quite modern. *Boca Chica,* a delightful beach resort, is about 20 miles from the capital.

Temperatures in the coastal cities average about 78 degrees. Average rainfall is about 55-60 inches. Clothing suitable for Washington, DC summers is appropriate in Santo Domingo year round.

A valid passport or tourist card is required for visitors. The tourist card, valid for 15 days, can be extended for 45 days. Charge for the card at airline offices is $1; proof of citizenship is required. Visa; no charge. No immunization requirements for tourists.

Santo Domingo has many American-trained dentists and doctors who speak English. City water is not potable. Santo Domingo's *Cathedral Santa Maria La Menor,* oldest in the world, holds the remains of Christopher Columbus in this marble sarcophagus in the nave of the church.

Telephone service links all major points in the country. Long-distance connections can be made to the U. S. and other countries without difficulty or undue delay.

Flights are available from the U. S. to Santo Domingo's International Airport, with or without stopovers in Haiti or Puerto Rico. Some companies in Santo Domingo arrange special chartered, air-conditioned bus tours for groups. A group of five persons can charter a car at reasonable cost. Taxies are available in the capital, and improved bus service is anticipated.

VIRGIN ISLANDS

U. S. VIRGIN ISLANDS

When Columbus sighted the cluster of islands to the east of Puerto Rico, he named them *Las Vírgenes*—for their large number put him in mind of the legendary 11,000 virgins of Colonge, who were martyred around 400 A.D. About 50 of these islands have been under the American flag since 1917. The others form a British colony. The present U. S. Virgin Islands were a Danish possession until 1917, when the United States bought them ($25 million) for their strategic value.

As a leading pirate base, trading region, and wholesale slave market in the early days, the islands prospered. About the middle of the last century a rapid decline set in, continuing until recent years.

St. Thomas, St. Croix, and St. John are the main islands; the others are largely uninhabited. More than 85 percent of the islands' 33,000 inhabitants are Negro. Small groups of the islanders are of European ancestry. In recent years, Americans from the U. S. mainland and Puerto Rico have been settling in the islands in growing numbers.

The U. S. Virgin Islands are under the Department of the Interior, but the President appoints the Governor, key officials, and judges. The legislature has 11 senators, elected for 2-year terms. U. S. citizenship was conferred on the islanders in 1927. There are U. S. air and naval bases on the islands, though they are mostly in a caretaker status at present.

English is the language of the islands. Virgin Islanders staff most of the stores, offices, and government agencies. The islands produce raw sugar and rum, but there is very little industry. The people engage in truck farming and cattle raising to a limited degree. Tourism is the major business.

The islands' capital and chief port is Charlotte Amalie (population about 13,000). Located on St. Thomas, it is a cosmopolitan town, with fine hotels, shops, and restaurants. One noted landmarks is *Bluebeard's Tower,* another is 17th-century *Fort Christian. Cha-cha Town,* the old French quarter, is now largely inhabited by newly-arrived Puerto Ricans.

St. Croix and St. John have no particular landmarks, but are scenically beautiful and ideal spots for a quiet, restful vacation. Most of St. John, in fact, has been made a National Park because of its natural beauty.

BRITISH VIRGIN ISLANDS

The British Caribbean islands over a wide span, extending from the Cayman Islands on the northwest to Trinidad on the southeast, comprise the British Virgin Islands.

Jamaica, about the size of Connecticut, is the largest of the islands, and Trinidad is the second largest. The rest range in size down to rock-size islets. Most of the islands are in the Lesser Antilles group.

This group, in turn, breaks down into the Leeward Islands (starting with Dominica, and going north) and the Windward Islands. The Leewards consist of four territories: Antigua (with Barbuda and Redonda); St. Kitts-Nevis-Anguilla; Montserrat; and the Britsh Virgin Islands. The make-up of the British Virgin Islands will give some idea of just how "islandy" this area is, for they themselves are formed of 36 islands (plus numerous reefs and rocks) of which 11 are inhabited.

Lying some 60 miles east of Puerto Rico, the British Virgin Islands are chiefly volcanic in origin, with the exception of Anegada, a coral and limestone atoll. There are over 50 islands, rocks and cays, sixteen of them inhabited. They are favoured by yachtsmen, divers and nature lovers. One of the islands is Treasure Island, after which Robert

Government House, located in the heart of Christiansted, the principal city of St. Croix, largest of the three major U. S. Virgin Islands, is perhaps the loveliest of all colonial structures in the West Indies. Among its treasures is an exquisite period ballroom complete with 18th century chandeliers and rare imported furnishings. Truly an antique lovers delight.   *Fritz Henle Photo*

Louis Stevenson named his famous novel and still believed by some to be the hiding place of buried treasure. The islands cover 59 square miles and have a population of 10,500. The capital is *Road Town* on Tortola Island. The main religion is Protestant and the U. S. dollar is the currency.

Because the islands are positioned within the Trade Wind belt, the climate is balmy and sub-tropical. Temperatures usually stay within the range of 77-85 degrees both in winter and summer. The best time to visit is December through April.

U. S., Canadian and British citizens enter on proof of identity or round trip ticket. Other nations require onward ticket, passport, and in some cases, visa. Smallpox vaccination certificate is required except for U. S. citizens arriving directly from the States.

There are flights from the U. S. to San Juan, St. Croix, or St. Thomas where one can get a connecting flight to Beef Island, Tortola Airport or to Virgin Gorda. There are taxies available at the airport. Cars, preferably 4-wheel drive type, can be rented; driving is on the left. Roads are narrow and many are unsurfaced. There is regular ferry service between the islands.

The sun and sea are the main attractions, however, exploring the islands by rented car is a rewarding experience. On Tortola, visit the *Sage Mountain National Park*, a new mahogany plantation, the ruins of forts and many distilleries. There are many spectacular views, and in Road Town, there are many shops. On Virgin Gorda, visit *"The Baths,"* the superb beaches and the remains of a copper mine. There are many, sandy white beaches on the islands as well as a tropical beach at *Little Bay*. There are yacht clubs where arrangements can be made for boat rentals. These clubs also have hotels, bars, and restaurants. There are also sightseeing tours which are arranged through the hotels, surfing, tennis and horseback riding.

Virgin Gorda is well known for 'The Baths', a unique rock formation with dimly lighted ethereal pools. A trip to the abandoned copper mine in the southeast tip of the island to see the remains of the chimney and a boiler is an interesting experience. The photo is beach at Biras Creek, Virgin Gorda, British Virgin Islands.

Nestled under towering, cloud-shrouded Mt. Pelée on the island of Martinique is the town of St. Pierre, once called the "Paris of the West Indies." It was a gay, cultivated city of 30,000 until May 8, 1902 when the mountain suddenly erupted in a terrifying avalanche of fire, gas and lava, obliterating town and townspeople. Today Mt. Pelée is one of the major sightseeing attractions on this French Caribbean island.

THE LEEWARD ISLANDS

Superb beaches and excellent fishing and boating facilities make the Leewards perfect for those who like outdoor activities at the seaside. Sugar, cotton, and molasses are the main exports. Chief places of interest include:

ANTIGUA

Antigua is truly a holiday island with many beaches, luxurious hotels (the centers of social life), sailing, swimming and all water sports. Antigua was once an important British naval base and the key to the Caribbean. Today, the forts are in ruins and Admiral Nelson's dockyard is a fine yachting harbor. The island is 108 square miles with a population of 70,000 (25,000 of whom live in St. John's, the capital). The climate is dry and pleasant all year round, the hottest months being September and October. English is the language most widely spoken and the country is primarily a Protestant community.

A passport is not required for citizens of the U. S. and Canada; only proof of identity. A visa is not required for entry for holiday purposes. You need confirmed onward reservations and proof of sufficient funds. Smallpox vaccination certificates are not required for U. S. or Canadian citizens arriving directly from the U. S. or Canada. Cholera and yellow fever inoculation certificates are required if arriving from an infected area. There are many English speaking doctors. One should drink only boiled water.

A rural bus service is the only form of public transportation. Taxis are available at a fixed rate or for rent. There are rental cars available. Traffic moves on the left.

ST. KITTS AND NEVIS

St. Kitts is the oldest British settlement in the West

Indies. (Also known as *St. Christopher.*) Chief town is Basse-Terre. Most interesting sight is *Brimstone Hill,* a fort that once caused the island to be called the "Gilbraltar of the West Indies." Growing sugar cane and catering to tourists are the main businesses there. Nevis, just two miles across the Narrows, was the most fashionable resort in the West Indies in the 18th century. Admiral Nelson married a rich young widow there and it was the birthplace of Alexander Hamilton, the first U. S. Secretary of the Treasury. St. Kitts is 65 square miles and Nevis is 36 square miles and the capital is Besse-Terre on St. Kitts. Charlestown is Nevis' only town. The combined population of the two islands is about 46,000. The primary language is English and the islands are mainly Protestant.

The islands are located in the path of the North East Trades so cooling breezes keep the temperature between 73 and 84 degrees.

No passports are needed for United Kingdom, United States and Canadian citizens. Only proof of citizenship and a round trip ticket are needed. No smallpox certificate is required of U. S. citizens.

The best hotels are on St. Kitts. During the summer there are reduced rates. Inexpensive guest house accommdations are also available.

St. Kitts is the shopping center of the islands and the best buys are English imports, perfume, china, linens, clothing cosmetics and island handicrafts. There is a nine hole golf course on St. Kitts and there are tennis clubs on both islands. There is good fishing from the shore and deep-sea fishing trips can be arranged. The highlight on St. Kitts is the *Brimstone Hill Fortress,* built in 1694 and still impressive. There is also *Mt. Misery,* densely forested, and the home of many small black-faced grey monkeys. Nevis rises from the sea to a perfect cone at *Nevis Peak.* This volcano is live and the sulphuric springs on the island are what made it a fashionable resort in the 18th century. One mile north of Charlestown is *Pinney's Beach,* probably the prettiest beach in the Caribbean. The coral reefs make for fascinating snorkeling and skin diving.

Another island, *Anguilla,* originally federated with St. Kitts and Nevis, is some 70 miles from St. Kitts. It broke away in the 1960's and since 1971 it has been under direct British control. It is small, flat and ringed with sandy beaches. The waters are clear and excellent for water sports, but you must bring your own equipment.

DOMINICA

Lies between two French islands. You're more likely to hear French spoken than English. It is the location of the world's only Carib Indian reserve. Politically, it is considered to be a Windward Island.

Dominica today is almost exactly as Columbus saw it in 1493, as it is the largest and least developed of the windward islands. It is a mountainous, tropical jungle with many rivers and banana and lime plantations. Dominica was the last retreat of the Carib Indians as the rest of the West Indies were colonized. The English and French battled over the island until 1805 when the English bought it from the French for 12,000 pounds. The island is 290 square miles with a population of 74,000. The capital is Roseau. The language is English and the religion is almost totally Roman Catholic.

The temperature varies relative to altitude. Rainfall is 60-70 inches on the coast and as much as 300 inches in the mountainous interior. The driest, and best, time for visiting is November to June.

U. S., Canadian and United Kingdom citizens need only proof of citizenship and a round trip ticket. Other countries require a passport. A smallpox certificate is recommended. Firearms must be declared and there are restrictions on taking wild life and plants out of the country.

The island is served by the small, but modern, *Melville Hall Airport* which is 30 miles across the island from the capital and the hotels. Taxis meet all flights and one buys a seat in one for up to $10 for the journey, which takes well over an hour. Charges for accommodations are considerably reduced in April to December. The East Caribbean dollar is at a par with the U. S. dollar.

THE WINDWARD ISLANDS

These consist of St. Lucia, St. Vincent, Grenada, and the small patchwork of islands known as *The Grenadines.*

GRENADA

Most important island of the group. Known as the "Spice Island," it exports nutmeg, cloves, cinnamon, ginger. Of special interest are the *Falls of Annadale* and *Grand Etang,* a lake in a volcano's crater.

Most of the population is of African descent; there is now little trace of Grenada's early Indian population—the Arawaks and the Caribs. About 30 percent of the island's population is concentrated around the capital. The rest is distributed evenly throughout Grenada, mostly on small farms. About 6,000 people live in the Grenadines.

English is the official language of Grenada and is the only one in general use. A French patois can still be heard, but it is rare. A more significant reminder of Grenada's historical link with France is the strength of the Roman Catholic Church. Most Grenadians are Catholic.

Grenada, the most southerly of the Windward Islands, is located about 150 miles southwest of Barbados and 90 miles northwest of Trinidad. The State of Grenada also includes the southernmost Grenadines, an arc of small islands extending from Grenada to north St. Vincent. The islands north of Carriacou, the largest of the Grenadines (13 square miles), are dependencies of St. Vincent. Like the other Antilles islands, the island of Grenada is volcanic in origin. Its rich, dark soil and high annual rainfall make it well suited for tropical agriculture.

Pearls International Airport has an asphalt runway 5,000 feet long and is served twice daily by Leeward Islands Air Transport. Flying time from Barbados to Grenada is approximately 45 minutes.

Long-distance telephone and telegraph services are available.

Grenada belongs to the Eastern Caribbean Currency Authority. One EC$ dollar is worth approximately U. S. $0.37. Grenada has several major hotels, including the Holiday Inn. Chase Manhattan Bank and First National City Bank of New York both have branch offices in St. George's, Grenada.

ST. LUCIA

Typical of the many "saint islands," it was named by its discovers who sighted it on its namesake's day. Largest of the British Windwards, it was once ruled by France.

The beauty of St. Lucia is so great that Hollywood made it the setting for *Dr. Doolittle*, the Rex Harrison masterpiece. It has lovely harbor towns; white sandy beaches and clear blue sky; orchids, fruit trees and vast banana plantations and volcanic peaks. The island is 238 square miles with a population of 101,000. The capital is *Castries;* the language is English and the religion is Roman Catholic. The temperature range is 70 to 90 degrees; the winter is dry, sunny and not too hot. July is the wettest month.

A passport (for U. S. citizens only proof of citizenship), with a round trip or onward ticket is needed. A smallpox vaccination certificate is required.

There is an irregular bus service to outlying districts, but an overnight stay is involved as buses do not return until the following day. There are taxis and rental cars available; driving is on the left. There are also boats and planes linking the islands.

The outstanding local dish is lobster, prepared Creole style, and rum is the local drink. There are movie houses, nightclubs where the popular dance is the Calypso, and in the high season all hotels have a busy night life. St. Lucia is a free port so shopping is good and inexpensive. Best buys are crystal, jewelry, cameras, watches, perfumes and liquor. All main stores are downtown and easy to find. Golf and tennis can be arranged through the hotels. Deep-sea fishing equipment can be rented or, to see the island, you can charter a Carib Cruise for just a day or for a week or two.

ST. VINCENT

St. Vincent, and its surrounding islets, known as the *St. Vincent Grenadines,* make up one of the healthiest and most relaxing tourist spots in the Caribbean. Originally claimed by the French, the islands were ceded to Britain in the 18th century. St. Vincent is 133 square miles, and the population is 89,632. The capital is Kingstown. Kingstown, a trim little place very English in tone and character, is the largest town, particularly famous for its *Botanical Gardens,* oldest in the Americas.

Collectively the Leewards and Windwards are made up of seven territories presided over by two British-appointed administrators. They have a ministerial form of government, with strong local representation. English is spoken everywhere and the main religion is Roman Catholic.

It is sunny and warm with an average temperature of 78 degrees and rainy spells in the summer and fall. Though the dry period runs from December to April, the island has no real seasons, making it a year round resort.

U. S. citizens need only proof of identity if the stay is less than 6 months. Visitors from U. S. and Canada may take out up to U. S.$100 of duty-free goods.

Kingstown has an island-wide bus service. Taxis are available by phone. They charge fixed rates. There are also rental cars, and chauffeur-driven cars. Driving is on the left; a local license is needed and it is obtainable on presentation of your own license and a payment of EC$2.50.

Restaurants in hotels offer American and European food with local specialties, especially fish dishes. Rum is the local drink. There are movie theaters, but most of the night life is put on by the local hotels. Good buys for the shopper are local handicrafts, batik and tie-dye materials, cameras, perfumes, and other duty-free merchandise. Swimmers, snorkelers and fishermen will enjoy superb sport in the islands. Spear fishing and deep-sea fishing expeditions can be arranged by the hotels.

Kingstown's two cathedrals are example of colonial architecture at its best. There is also *Fort Charlotte*, the Botanic Gardens and the exquisite *Marriaqua Valley* with banana, nutmeg, cocoa, coconut and breadfruit plantations. The most spectacular excursion is to the top of *Mount Soufrere* which rises to cover 4,000 feet. It last erupted in 1902 and began to show signs of life again in 1971. Its crater lake and desolate slopes are unforgettable.

BARBADOS

Barbados is the easternmost of the West Indies islands. The English took possession in 1625 and have been there since. Frequently called "Little England," the island has retained virtually intact its English atmosphere. Bridgetown is the capital and only city. The harbor police still wear uniforms like those of Nelson's sailors. Sugar, molasses, and rum are the main exports.

British sailors landed on Barbados at the site of present-day *Holetown* in 1624 or 1625. It was uninhabited at the time of their arrival, but it is believed the original Arawak Indians were destroyed by the fiercer Carib Indians, who then abandoned the island. From the arrival of the first British settlers in 1627-28 until independence, Barbados was under uninterrupted British control. Its House of Assembly, which began meeting in 1639, is the third oldest legislative body in the Western Hemisphere preceded only by Bermuda's legislature and the Virginia House of Burgesses.

Barbados is a 20 by 14 mile island located 100 miles east of the general arc of the Caribbean islands. It lacks the lush tropical growth of other nearby islands. In the south it has soft, rolling fertile countryside and to the north it has hills of virgin forest. The climate is the best and healthiest in the West Indies. Though tropical, almost constant trade winds keep it comfortable except from July to September when there are some hot and humid days.

Barbados' 250,000 people make it one of the most densely populated islands in the world with more than 1,400 people to a square mile. Some 95 percent are Barbadians of African descent with some whites of British descent and some from other countries. The colorful native people call themselves "Bajans" and include boys with gleaming purple black bodies diving for coins thrown from ships in the harbor and women in multicolored cotton dresses with enormous loads on their heads. The language is English but the native dialect is a fascinating mixture of pure English, Cockney, Irish and Scotch plus local "Bajan Talk." The religion is mainly Anglican.

Main crops are sugar cane, cotton and arrowroot. The

main industry is sugar refining. Fishing and pottery are also important. Principal exports are rum, cotton lint and "fancy molasses" syrup.

Bridgetown is a picturesque, colorful town, it has busy wharfs, narrow winding streets, pastel-colored homes and charming gardens. Points of interest include Gothic-type public buildings, *St. Michael's Cathedral*, the *Broad Street* shopping area, the *Rum Distillery* and interesting museums and great houses such as *Farley Hall*.

Both deep sea and spear fishing are good all year round, but best between December and May. Sailboats and motorboats are available for hire. There are many fine beaches including the lovely *Bathsheba* area, and fine motels, clubs, and guest houses. Sports include horse racing, cricket, football, basketball, hockey, polo matches, swimming competitions and boat regattas.

The great food specialty is flying fish—baked, broiled, boiled or fried or as a flying fish pie with hard boiled eggs, tomatoes, onions, yams, butter, Worcestershire sauce and sherry. Mawby juice—mawby bark steeped with sugar and spices—is the native drink. Green swizzles, gin slings, and scotch are also popular.

Shoppers can choose from native handicrafts in pottery, basketware, tortoise shell and sea shell costume jewelry, needlework, wearing apparel, sea-island cottons and mahogany novelties. There's a wide range of free port shopping for British items such as china, cashmere sweaters, gloves, sport jackets, top coats, woolen materials, tweeds, silks, Irish linens. And excellent light Barbados rum is very inexpensive.

Two regularly scheduled U. S. airlines fly to Barbados. A pleasant climate has made the island a popular tourist resort, and a wide variety of luxury and budget-class hotels and guest houses are available. Health and sanitation facilities are adequate to meet the needs of visitors; common medicines are available. No visas are needed at this time, but a U. S. passport is recommended. Good telephone and telegraph communications operate throughout the island and abroad, as well as daily radio and television. The monetary unit is the Barbadian dollar which is equivalent to U. S.$.50. Bridgetown has seven commercial banks, of which four are U. S. owned, that can handle financial and foreign exchange matters.

TRINIDAD AND TOBAGO

These islands lie off the coast of Venezuela. Trinidad dwarfs Tobago. Though 20 miles apart, they are a single political unit. Since 1962 they have been an independent member state of the British Commonwealth. Economically, they are the wealthiest unit of the British Caribbean islands. Oil from local wells plus the refining of imported crude oil are major factors in the strong economy.

Trinidad has several cultures, as shown by the fact that in addition to churches and synagogues, you'll see Moslem mosques and Chinese and East Indian temples. East Indians on Trinidad number more than 300,000, by far the largest concentration of them in the Caribbean. Calypso and steel bands, popular throughout the islands, are in their native element there, both having originated in Trinidad.

Port-of-Spain, the capital, has a polyglot population of about 95,000. Eight miles to the northwest is Chaguaramas Bay, site of a U. S. naval base.

Tobago, a "coral island," has excellent beaches and scenery. Less than a mile from it is tiny *Little Tobago*, a 750-acre sanctuary for the rare bird of paradise, introduced in 1909 from New Guinea.

Trinidad and Tobago are the southernmost islands of the Lesser Antilles chain in the Caribbean. Trinidad, the

CARIBBEAN PORTS

largest island of the chain, has an area of 1,864 square miles. It is separated from Venezuela by the 7-mile wide straits of the *Gulf of Paria*. Geologically it is an extension of the South American continent. Trinidad has a cosmopolitan English-speaking society with Negro (43 percent), East Indian (40 percent), Syrian, Chinese and European elements. Tobagans are mostly Negro, who live in urban and industrial areas. The East Indians, who arrived in the last century as indentured agricultural laborers, have for the most part stayed on the land as independent farmers, although some are also prominent in business and professions.

The island of Trinidad is one of the most picturesque and different of the Caribbean islands. The Carib Indians who once lived there called it the "Land of the Hummingbird," for which the island is famous. And the countless varieties of birds can be seen at *Caroni Swamp Bird Sanctuary* which covers 10 acres. There are many other forms of wildlife, however, including alligator, armadillo, agouti, lappe, wild pig, oppossum and many types of fish.

Trinidad's variety of natural resources gives it one of the most stable economies in the West Indies and makes it the wealthiest and most important of the East Caribbean islands.

Although Port-of-Spain has a comparatively fast-paced business district for a tropical town, there is a relaxed old world atmosphere in its residential area with wide tree-lined streets and a wide variety of 18th century Spanish and 19th century French architecture. There are many beautiful beaches for swimming, and all kinds of boats are available for charter for excellent deep-sea and spear fishing.

Trinidad is where steel bands originated during World War II and this fast-moving sensual sound is heard everywhere in the island especially during festivals and street parades of costumed dancers.

There is wide variety in food including specialties such as a river fish called cascador; callaloo soup; pastettes—meats wrapped in a corn meal mixture, and stuffed crab backs. The local drink is rum though a green swizzle is equally popular.

Good buys can be found in silver filigree, gold bracelets, ceramics, straw, fiber and wood articles as well as imported china, crystal, French perfumes, Oriental curios, ivories, brasses, Indian saris, native Calypso and steel band recordings, cameras, watches, china silk, woolens and linens.

Though a tropical climate, Trinidad has an average temperature of 85 degrees—but nights are at least 10 degrees cooler.

Observe the usual precautions when eating fruits and vegetables and when drinking water from an unknown source.

Radio-telephone and cable services are available.

Port-of-Spain's *Piarco International Airport* is served by a number of airlines. Internal air service is limited; there is no rail service. Taxis and rental cars are available on both islands.

JAMAICA

Jamaica has been an independent nation and Commonwealth member since 1962. The name is Indian and means "land of wood and water." Spain took the island from the native Caribs and Arawaks and held it until Admiral Penn (father of the founder of Pennsylvania) captured it for England in 1655. In a few years Port Royal, at the tip of a peninsula that helps form Kingston Harbor, became the headquarters for buccaneers and pirates and was known as the "richest and wickedest city in the Caribbean." However, a severe earthquake in 1692 caused much of the city to slip into the sea. As time went on, Kingston took the

CARIBBEAN PORTS

old port's place as the island's governmental and commercial center.

Jamaica well illustrates the Caribbean area's amalgamation of people. There is a small percentage of Europeans, plus some East Indians and Chinese. Over three-fourths of the population is Negro, descended from slaves imported from Africa in past centuries.

The island's gross national product per person is about $440—almost six times that of neighboring Haiti. Economic mainstays are tourism, light industry, agriculture, and bauxite (aluminum) ore.

Some 130 miles to the northwest of Jamaica lies a 3-island group: the Cayman Islands. They have less than 100 square miles of land, have fewer than 10,000 residents, and are a British colony.

Traditionally, Jamaica has enjoyed harmonious racial and cultural relations. Jamaica's national motto, "Out of Many, One People," suggests their desire for harmony. Class distinctions which have lingered from the colonial period are being reduced as social mobility through education and greater opportunities for property ownership is increasing.

Jamaica covers an area of 150 by 50 miles and is very picturesque with its white beaches and mountains rising to heights of 7,400 feet. There is almost perpetual sunshine in Jamaica with greatly varying temperatures in different localities. The year-round average in the lowlands is 77 to 82 degrees though it's somewhat cooler on the North Shore. Rainfall ranges from 22 to as much as 200 inches a year in the mountainous northeast. Interlaced with the fascinating scenery of Jamaica are the tales by some of the native peasants who are highly superstitious and still hold firm beliefs in their ghosts.

Columbus landed on Jamaica during his second voyage in May, 1494 at *Discovery Bay* on the north coast which

New Ocho Rios Craft Park offers a welter of Jamaica-made goods including straw and cloth items as well as jewelry and wood carvings. Only a two-minute walk from the Intercontinental Hotel and Mallards Beach-Hyatt, the Park is open six days a week between 9 a.m. and 5 p.m.

he called *Santa Gloria*. Nine years later, he returned and was stranded for a whole year before being rescued. He and his men lived in their two battered ships which they fastened together and roofed over on the beach and fought illness and the Indians until help arrived. Later in 1655, England captured Jamaica and today, the population is very mixed—predominantly the descendants of slaves brought from Africa by the Spanish and British; also other British, Irish, Scottish, Portuguese, many Jews who migrated here in the late 16th century, East Indians and Chinese who came as indentured laborers from 1845 to 1885; Syrians from Venezuela, and also some Italians and Germans. In recent years, many persons from the United States have made their homes in Jamaica.

Of Jamaica's 1.8 million inhabitants, more than 400,000 live in Kingston and its suburbs. The language is English and a dialect is used by the native peasants.

Most Jamaicans live by farming and half the land is under cultivation. Leading crops include bananas, cacao, coconuts, coffee, sugar cane and a variety of fruits. Jamaica has over 2,000 types of flowering plants—450 species of fern—one growing to 20 feet, and fine timber. The matine pimento trees supply practically the entire world market.

Famous for its rum, more than 20 sugar factories produce over 350,000 tons of sugar annually, while distilleries turn out two million gallons of rum each year. Besides rum and sugar, Jamaica also exports liqueurs, bananas, citrus fruits, pimento, spices and bauxite—Jamaica leads the world in bauxite mining. Jamaica's industries include cement, textiles, matches, cigarettes, cigars and perfumes.

For sports fans, Jamaica's warm water, which averages 72 degrees throughout the year, makes swimming and water sports ideal. Also hunters can choose from pigeon, snipe, dove and migrating birds permitted from mid-August to February, teal duck in December or Jamaica's number one sport—crocodile hunting at night.

The peak tourist season is from November to April and visitors will feel comfortable in summer wear in this island of fascinating scenery and legend. The ever popular *Dunns River Falls* provides some welcome relief from the tropical sun for tourists of Jamaica. Walking up the natural steps and playing in the cascading waters are a not-to-be-missed experience on this lovely Caribbean island.

Summer clothes are suitable year round. The evenings, especially in the winter months, can be chilly, however, and light wraps or sweaters are recommended.

International telephone and telegraph services are good.

Local buses are over-crowded but provide fairly regular service. Taxis are available. Trunk roads are nearly all paved, but as Jamaica is largely mountainous, they are often narrow and winding, with uneven surfaces. Jamaica has a thriving rental car business.

Municipal water supplies are safe as are fruits and vegetables. Doctors are available 24 hours in Kingston and the principal resort areas.

A passport or other proof of U. S. birth or citizenship is required. Inoculations—none.

FRENCH ANTILLES

About 98 percent of the people of Martinique are of Afro-European or Afro-European-Indian descent. The rest are the old planter families and a sizable number of Metropolitan French (i.e., born in France). Most of the labor force is employed in agriculture or food processing and associated industries.

Most of the permanent residents of Guadeloupe are of mixed Afro-Caucasian descent. A few thousand Metropolitan French reside there; most are civil servants, members of the French military and police, and their dependents. *Iles-des-Saintes* and *St. Barthelemy* are still inhabited by descendents of the Normans and Bretons who arrived 300 years ago. St. Martin was occupied simultaneously by the French and the Dutch in 1648. An agreement dated March 23, 1648, gave France about two-thirds of the island, the capital of which is Marigot, a free port.

From the political standpoint, there is no logic to the geographic placement of the islands of the Lesser Antilles. French, British, and Dutch islands almost seem to leapfrog one another. For example, between the two main French islands of Guadeloupe and Martinique lies British Dominica. And well to the north, up among some British and Dutch islands, are two smaller French islands: St. Barthélemy and St. Martin.

MARTINIQUE

Martinique is the northernmost of the Windward Islands, which are part of the chain of the Lesser Antilles in the Caribbean Sea southeast of Puerto Rico. This volcanic island is characterized by an indented coastline and mountainous terrain. The highest point is Mt. Pelée with an altitude of 4,650 feet. It is the most exotic of the West Indian Islands. Martinique is 425 square miles and the capital is Fort-de-France, where 110,000 of the country's 340,000 population live. The climate is warm year round, but the rainy season is from July-November and it is rather hot at this time.

This is the largest of the Lesser Antilles. The French have been here since 1635. Ford-de-France has one of the finest harbors in the islands. Part of the French fleet sailed here after the fall of France in 1940 and later joined Allied units. Mount Pelée, the local volcano, erupted suddenly in 1902 destroying the nearby town of St. Pierre in three minutes and killing all but one of the town's

Shore excursions give you the opportunity to get away from organized ship activities. Visit Caribbean Islands and see natural scenic wonders where there are tranquil lagoons, hidden limestone caves, and cascading waterfalls. This gentle waterfall presents a challenging walk over tiers of smooth but not slippery rock. Notice the profusion of ferns and plants which are generally found in tropical rain forests.

nearly 30,000 inhabitants. Only the fact that he was in the dungeon-like prison saved him from death by the super-heated ash and steam.

Napoleon's first wife, the beautiful Josephine, was born on Martinique in 1763. At *Trois Ilets,* across the bay from Fort-de-France, you can visit her birthplace and a small memorial museum.

GUADELOUPE

Guadeloupe is one of the Leeward Islands, which are also part of the chain of the Lesser Antilles. Actually it is two islands: volcanic Basse-Terre to the west and the flatter limestone formation of Grande-Terre to the east. The two are separated by a narrow salt water stream called *Riviere Salee.* Although *Pointe-a-Pitre* is the principal city and commercial center of the island, the *Prefecture* is located in Basse-Terre. The climate varies greatly but is generally warm. Hurricanes occur in the rainy season from July-November. The best time to visit is November-May.

Like so many other Caribbean islands, butterfly-shaped Guadeloupe was made wealthy by sugar centuries ago. Later the one-crop economy nearly impoverished it. Now, bananas, rum, cacao, vanilla, coffee—and sugar and tourists—support the island's economy. Five smaller islands are dependencies of Guadeloupe.

Both Gaudeloupe and Martinique are *departments* of France, and their inhabitants are French citizens. Together the islands send six deputies and four senators to the French National Assembly and Senate.

Clothing should be the same type as what is worn in Washington, DC in summer. At beach resorts, dress is more informal than in the U. S.

U. S. citizens should carry a passport but do not need visas.

BON VOYAGE

A must for visitors to Jamaica is feeding time at Lisa Salmon's Bird Sanctuary, the Rockland's Feeding Station, in the town of Anchovy, near Montego Bay. There they can enjoy the unique experience of feeding the national bird, the doctor bird, from a feeder while the bird perches on a finger. The station plays host to many varieties of tropical birds.

Local doctors, dentists, and pharmacists are available for normal needs. Most visitors drink the tap water; however, check with local authorities.

International telephone and telegraph service is available. French Antilles are one standard time zone ahead of the Eastern U. S.

Adequate, generally reliable taxi service is available. Cars can be rented.

NETHERLAND ANTILLES

The *Netherlands Antilleans* are of widely varied origins; no less than 40 nationalities are represented. The population of Curacao and Bonaire is primarily African or Negro-Caucasian; most Arubans are American Indian-Caucasian; and the people of the Windward Islands are primarily of African descent and include an old, small settlement of Dutch, Scottish, and Irish. The prosperity of the oil industry has attracted Chinese, Europeans, Arabs, and North and South Americans.

Dutch is the official language, although Spanish and English are spoken widely. The Papiamento dialect has evolved from Portuguese, Spanish, Dutch, and some other languages and is spoken in the Leeward Islands Antilleans pride themselves on their linguistic diversity.

The Netherlands Antilles consists of two groups of three islands each, situated in the Caribbean Sea about 550 miles apart. The "Leeward Islands" group, composed of Curacao, Bonaire, and Aruba, are 15-38 miles off the northwestern coast of Venezuela, while the "Windward Islands" group of Sint Maarten, Sint Eustatius, and Saba are about 220 miles east of Puerto Rico. Curacao is the largest of the six islands. Most of its population of 156,200 is centered around Willemstad, capital city of the country and the island.

The Bottom is the name of the town on tiny (13 sq. miles) Saba. You climb up to The Bottom, for it is inside the crater of Saba's extinct volcano.

St. Eustatius has a special place in American history, for it was here that the flag of the new nation was first saluted by a foreign power—formal recognition for the struggling Thirteen Colonies. On 16 November 1776, the visiting Continental brig, *Andrew Doria,* received an 11-gun salute from the local fort's gun battery. Two months later the friendly Dutch governor who had ordered the salute was removed from his post—and his government withdrew the recognition. But still, a first is a first.

Aruba, Bonaire, and Curaçao are the three islands of the southern Dutch group, forming the "ABC Islands." The flavor of the islands is definitely Dutch. It is here that you'll hear *Papiamento* spoken, the language made up of Spanish-Portuguese-English-Dutch.

The story is that the three islands were so barren and isolated that no other European power really wanted to bother with them. But the practical Dutch held on to them—since 1634—and after a long spell of poverty the islands took on great economic importance in World War I. Oil was the reason... the refining of crude oil from nearby Venezuela on Curaçao and Aruba. Since rain is so scanty on these islands, fresh water is distilled.

CURAÇAO

Largest of the three islands, Curaçao has drawn its population of about 130,000 from all over the world. Willemstad, capital of the ABC group, is located there. It is a neat city of well planned design with many brightly colored houses.

ARUBA

The American-controlled Lago refinery on Aruba is

one of the world's largest. Oranjestad, its main city and a free port, is distinguished for its quaintness. There are probably more American civilians living on Aruba than on any other non-U. S. island in the West Indies.

BONAIRE

Arid like its two sister islands, Bonaire has no industry, but is much esteemed as a restful place. It is famous for its numerous varieties of birds, flamingoes in particular. These breed along the salt pans at the island's southern end.

Previously colonies, the Netherlands Antilles are now equal partners of the Netherlands, and have self rule in all internal matters.

Visas are not required for Curaçao. A valid passport or birth certificate showing birth in the U. S. is sufficient for entry for a temporary visit, provided a ticket indicating intent of onward transportation is also presented.

The effect of heat and humidity is lessened by the almost constant northeast trade winds. Rainfall averages only 22 inches annually, causing the islands to be dusty. August, September and October are the warmest months; December, January, and February, the coolest. Summer clothes are worn all year.

Curaçao has three types of public transportation: buses, privately owned automobiles operating as buses, and taxis. Roads are fair.

Because of the unavailability of natural water, sea water is distilled. The resulting product is so pure that it is passed through a lime filter to give it taste. Local water does not need to be chlorinated. Sewage disposal systems are adequate. Food is mostly imported. Food handling controls are adequate.

Carnival time in February brings a street procession with colorful costumes, floats, and street dancing. Each

Forget everything you've ever heard about the Caribbean. It's more fabulous than can be told or even dreamed.
A string of unspoiled little islands with picturesque ports, sparkling coral reefs and soaring peaks. An ever-changing kaleidoscope of unrivaled scenic beauty. You'll be surrounded by brilliant tropical blossoms and graceful palm trees. You'll swim in crystal waters, and sunbathe on clean-white beaches. Cayman Island Photo.

April, the Curaçao Water Festival has water sports, boating events, and the arrival of "King Neptune" from the sea. New Year's is a colorful week-long celebration.

CAYMAN ISLANDS

The Cayman Islands, islands of the turtles, were first sighted by Columbus in 1503. Today, turtle soup and turtle steaks are specialties of the islands' chefs. The islands, and their lovely beaches and jagged coastlines, are surrounded by a ring of coral reefs which have meant the end to over 300 ships. The hulls of old sailing ships and sunken vessels are now an attraction for tourists and underwater divers. Tales of buried treasure form a romantic history to the Cayman Islands.

The main island, Grand Cayman, is 22 by 8 miles and the capital is *George Town.* Of the 10,700 population, 4,000 live in the capital. The temperatures are very mild throughout the year; the winter averages 75 degrees and the summer, 80 degrees. Rainfall is rare.

The Caymans are a self governing member of the British Commonwealth; English is the major language; the island is predominantly Protestant.

The Cayman Island dollar is at par with the U. S. dollar.

No passport or visa is required for citizens of the U. S. and Canada. You need proof of citizenship and a round-trip ticket. Smallpox vaccination certificate is not needed if arriving from the U. S. or Canada. There are no currency regulations. Duty-free allowances are 200 cigarettes or 50 cigars or ½ pound of tobacco; one pint of spirits; one quart of wine. There is a departure tax of $2.50 by air and $1.50 by sea.

Hotels are comfortable and you can rent villas and cottages or stay in lodges. Rates vary considerably between the winter and summer season.

Divi-divi trees on the sun-basked Dutch Caribbean island of Bonaire all point to the west, thanks to the constant, cooling trade winds blowing in from the east. These winds, combined with Bonaire's crazy boomerang shape, afford near-ideal sailing conditions on the island's sheltered side. And below the sparkling emerald waters is a scuba diver's delight—marvelous coral reefs and scores of gaily colored tropical fish, friendly and unafraid (spearfishing is prohibited).

CUBA

The population of Cuba is composed largely of people of Spanish and African origins. Some observers estimate that 30-40 percent of the population is black, with whites and persons of mixed ancestry making up the rest. The capital, *Havana,* located on the northwest coast, is the principal port and city. Other large cities include *Santiago de Cuba, Camaguey, Santa Clara, Holguin, Matanzas, Cienfuegos,* and *Pinar del Rio.*

Cuba is the largest island in the West Indies and lies on the northern boundary of the Caribbean Sea about 90 miles south of Key West, Florida. Including the *Isle of Pines* and some 1,600 adjacent keys and isles, Cuba accounts for more than one-half of the West Indian land area. Three main groups of mountains are located in the eastern, central, and western sections of the island. The most rugged of these is the Sierra Maestra range in the eastern section, where peaks rise to almost 6,000 feet above sea level.

A dialogue with Cuba has begun, and some progress toward improved relations has been made, but difficult issues and hard negotiations remain. However, for travelers, a passport and a visa are required; also a smallpox vaccination.

THE BAHAMAS

The name Bahamas may derive from the Spanish word bajamar for "shallow sea." The islands are a coral formation, the highest about 400 feet above sea level. The group consists of some 700 islands, 40 of them inhabited, and more than 2,000 cays and dry rocks. The oolitic limestone islands that make up the Bahama group are the summits of a submerged mountain range. They form a 760 mile arc from 50 miles off the east coast of Florida down to about the same distance from Haiti and Cuba. High plateaus form the "Bahama Banks" covering thousands of yellow sandy square miles underwater. And due to the effect of the sun shining through the crystal clear water on this sand and on the coral formations, the gold and purple and blues and greens to be seen make these waters breathtakingly beautiful.

The Bahamas have a climate that is practically perfect all year round, claiming 360 days of sunshine a year. The temperatures range from the winter average of 72 degrees to the summer average of 82 degrees. There are brief rains throughout the year, slightly heavier from mid-August to October, averaging 49 inches of rainfall a year.

The language is English. Bahamains are chiefly descendents of the English settlers, the American Loyalists and confederates who came in the late 17th and 18th centuries and the slaves from Africa who now account for around 80 percent of the population. Many Britains, Americans and Canadians have chosen to establish residence here. And some 28 religious denominations are represented. The Bahamians consider Christopher Columbus, who arrived on October 12, 1492, to be their first tourist, the generally accepted spot being the island of San Salvador. The original inhabitants called themselves "Ceboynas" or "Siboney." It was Columbus who first called them Indians, thinking he had arrived in India. The Spaniards did not consider the Bahamas worth colonizing but they did use the Lucayan Tribe of Arawak Indian inhabitants of San Salvador. Within an eight-year period, the Spanish had rounded them up and either killed or transported them to work in the mines of Cuba and Haiti.

The population of all the islands totals over 140,000 with approximately 81,000 living in Nassau. The best known out islands are: the Island of New Providence

CARIBBEAN PORTS 275

where *Nassau* the Capital City is located; Abaco, Andros—the largest; Turtle Cay; Berry Islands; the Biminis; Cat Island; Eleuthera; Exuma Islands; Grand Bahama; Great Inagua Island; Harbour Island; Long Island; St. George's Cay; San Salvador and Walker Cay.

Waters teem with fish and turtle. There is a riot of color in the oleanders, the hibiscus, the bougainvillaea, royal poincianas and a myriad of other flora. There is a great variety of birds, flamingos, hummingbirds, parrots, wild geese and duck. Fruits and vegetables are grown on the islands. Some livestock is raised and the combined poultry and dairy farm on Eleuthera is one of the largest in the world. Among the important exports are crawfish, salt, lumber, tomatoes and cascarilla bark.

Tourism is the major industry of the Bahamas. The fine straw work, baskets, bags, and hats amount to a large part of tourist exports. And rum, liqueur, paper, lentils, cement products, plastics, chem-bleaches and rubber goods are a few of the small industries being encouraged. And once again, the sponge beds are being worked.

In January, 1964, Great Britain handed over the reins of international self government to the Bahamas. Government costs are mostly paid for by customs revenue. There is no tax on income, inheritances or unimproved property and the tax on improved property is small.

Summer clothes are perfect for this year-round land of sunshine. And though in late summer and early autumn, days can be hot and humid, sweaters are needed in the nights which are always cool. Peak tourist season is from December to April.

You may know them as a "key," such as those of southern Florida. "Cay" has the same meaning: a low islet or reef.

These islands relate closely to U. S. history. It was on San Salvador that Columbus made his epic first landfall in the New World. George Washington visited the Bahamas as a young man. This country's first amphibious operation, in March 1776, saw a landing party capture vitally needed cannons and gunpowder from two forts on New Providence. During the Civil War, they were trans-shipment points for war goods bound from Europe to the Confederate forces. Today, some of them serve as missle tracking sites.

Spain had the first claim on the islands. Since the islands held little promise, they were pretty much ignored until the mid-1600's, when the English began settling them.

No restriction is placed on the amount of U. S. money that can be brought into the islands. U. S. dollars may be used where prices are shown in both Bahamian and U. S. dollars.

No visa or special permission is required to enter the Bahamas. However, it is advisable to have proof of American citizenship when departing the islands for the U. S. or other destinations. A passenger departure tax is levied on both visitors and residents.

No inoculation or vaccination is required. It is not necessary to boil water or sterilize raw foods that are purchased in reputable stores. The saline content of local water is so high, however, that many people use bottled water. Mosquitoes, sandflies, and termites are ever-present pests. Poisonous insects include the ground spider, scorpion, centipede, and the black widow spider. The Bahamas are rabies-free, and the government is presently considering a ban on the importation of pets.

Both New Providence and Grand Bahama have international airports. Both have local bus service; however the vehicles are small, unscheduled and usually crowded. Taxis are plentiful, but rates are high. Traffic moves on the left. New Providence has more than 260 miles of paved roads; Grand Bahama and the other islands have 340. Other

CARIBBEAN PORTS

major islands also have motorable roads. There are no railroads. Transportation between the islands is by air and sea.

Nassau can be explored in about a week's time. Trips to adjacent beaches such as Paradise Island can be made by boat or bridge. Popular Out Islands are Eleuthera, Exuma, and Bimini, which offers fine fishing. Other Out Islands are accessible by air or by boat, but tourist accommodations on the more remote ones may be primitive. The most colorful events are the native Junkanoo parades on Boxing Day (December 26) and New Year's Day, comparable on a small scale to Mardi Gras or Carnival celebrations elsewhere.

This, then, is the Caribbean ... an oceanic region vital to the defense of the Americas. It is the region where America's history began, and it is a playground for carefree tourists. For all-around color and points of interests, few parts of the world can begin to compare with it. This brief guide has attempted to give you some idea of what you might expect there.

If your curiosity has been whetted, you'll probably wish to learn more about people, places, and things to see and do in the Caribbean by traveling there yourself.

CARIBBEAN FACTS AND FIGURES

Country or Region	Area in Sq. Mi.	Population	Currency	Products and Industries
BAHAMA ISLANDS	4,404	110,000: 73 percent Negro, 14 percent mixed, mainly white and Asiatic.	British system Pound = $2.00	Salt, crawfish, pulpwood, and sponges; tourism is chief source of income.
BRITISH LEEWARD ISLANDS	422	140,000: 88 percent Negro, 11 percent white.	British West Indies (BWI) Dollar = 58¢. BWI dollars (called "bee wees") may not be used in other currency areas.	Sugar, coconuts, tropical fruits, coffee, and cotton; tourism is a major industry.
BRITISH WINDWARD ISLANDS	810	224,000: 60 percent Negro, 35 percent mixed, others mainly white and East Indian.	See British Leeward Islands.	Cacao, sugar, spices, limes, and rum.

CARIBBEAN FACTS AND FIGURES

CANAL ZONE	648 (land and water)	60,000, of whom 42,000 are civilians. About half the latter are U. S. citizens (employees of the Panama Canal Co. or Zone Government and their families).	U. S. currency.	Operation and support of Canal Zone functions.
DUTCH CARIBBEAN ISLANDS (3 main islands)				
Curaçao	172	130,000: Negro, European, and East Indian.	Guilder (sometimes called florin) = 28¢	Oil refining, ship-servicing and repair.
Aruba	70	58,000: 60 percent Indian, 40 percent of Dutch origin and U. S. citizens.	Same	See Curaçao.
Bonaire	112	6,000: mostly Indian, small number of Dutch.	Same	None

Country or Region	Area in Sq. Mi.	Population	Currency	Products and Industries
GUADELOUPE	657	285,000: mostly Negro or mixed, small number of French	Franc = 20¢ (about).	Sugar, bananas, rum, coffee, cacao, and vanilla.
HAITI	10,714	4,000,000: 90 percent Negro, remainder mostly French-Negro.	Gourde = 20¢.	Coffee, sisal, sugar, bauxite, and copper.
DOMINICAN REPUBLIC	19,333	3,334,000: 61 percent mulatto, 28 percent white, 10 percent Negro.	Peso = $1.	Sugar, coffee, tobacco, cacao, and bananas.
JAMAICA	4,411	1,685,000: 75 percent Negro, 18 percent mixed, remainder European or East Indian origin.	Pound = $2.80.	Sugar, rum, molasses, tropical fruits, and mining and processing bauxite.

MARTINIQUE	420	292,000. See Gaudeloupe.	See Gaudeloupe.	Bananas, sugar, rum, cacao, and pineapples.
PANAMA	28,576	1,250,000: 72 percent mixed, 14.5 percent Negro, 12 percent white, 1.5 percent others.	Balboa = $1	Petroleum products, bananas, shrimp, cacao, and refining sugar.
PUERTO RICO	3,427	2,513,000: mostly of mixed Negro and Spanish ancestry.	U. S. currency.	Sugar, tobacco, rum, light industry, and textiles; tourism is a major industry.
TRINIDAD AND TOBAGO	1,864	800,000: 47 percent Negro, 35 percent East Indian, 14 percent mixed, others mainly white and Chinese.	See British Leeward Islands	Sugar, cacao, copra, and citrus fruits. Oil refining is island's main industry.
U. S. VIRGIN ISLANDS	133	33,000: 68 percent Negro, 19 percent mixed, others mainly white.	U. S. currency.	Sugar and rum. Tourism and servicing of ships are major industries.

SPANISH LANGUAGE GUIDE

Some knowledge of Spanish will be quite helpful while you're in the Caribbean area. Spanish is an easy language to learn. You can learn a lot by ear if you practice the language and listen to people speak.

POINTS ABOUT PRONUNCIATION

Pronounce AY as in *may, say, play* but don't drawl it as we do in English. Since it is not drawled, it sounds a little like the *e* in *let*. Example: ka-FAY meaning "coffee."

Pronounce EH exactly like the *e* in *let*. Example: ko-MEHR.

Pronounce O or OH as in *go, so, oh, note* but don't drawl it. Since it is not drawled it sounds a little like the *aw* in *saw*. Example: NO meaning "no."

Pronounce H as in *house, hat, hall* but stronger. Example: free-HO-less meaning "beans."

RR stands for a strongly rolled r-sound, like the telephone operator's "thuh-r r-ee" for "three." This double *rr* differs from the single *r*, which is made by a quick tap of the tongue against the gums back of the teeth. Example of *rr:* see-gah-RREE-yohss meaning "cigarettes." Example of *r:* ah la deh-RAY-chah meaning "to the right."

You will often hear Spanish speakers pronounce the *d* very much like our *th*-sound in "breathe" and "then," the *b* very much like our *v*, and the *v* at the beginning of a word like *b*. Thus, *guisado* meaning "stew" may sound like ghee-SAH-tho (*th* as in *then*); *sábado* meaning "Saturday" like SAH-va-do; and *veinte* meaning "twenty"

SPANISH LANGUAGE GUIDE

like BAYN-tay. (If you pronounce a *d* or *v* or *b* according to what you see written you will be understood, but it is of course best to try to imitate the sound you hear.)

In this guide you will find the words and phrases written in a spelling which you read like English. Each letter or combination of letters is used for the sound it usually stands for in English and it *always* stands for that sound. Thus, *oo* is always pronounced as in *too, boot, tooth,* never as anything else. If you should use some other sound—for example, the sound of *oo* in *blood*—you might be misunderstood.

Syllables that are accented, that is, pronounced louder than others, are written in capital letters. Unaccented syllables are not skipped over quickly, as they are in English. Hyphens are used to divide words into syllables to make them easier to read.

REGIONAL DIFFERENCES

You will find that spoken Spanish, like English in the States, varies among countries and regions.

In the Caribbean area the tendency is to emphasize the vowel sounds and to slur, or even eliminate, some of the consonants—particularly the final *s* (*tre* instead of *tres*) and the intermediate and final *d* (*naa* instead of *nada* and *ciudá* instead of *ciudad*).

Other peculiarities are the substitution of *l* for *r* (*gualdar* instead of *guardar*); the use of the guttural *r* (similar to the French *r*), and the slurring of the *r* (*impohta* instead of *importa*). While the softening of the *d* and the *s* is not serious, the other variations mentioned should be avoided. Actually they are difficult for an English-speaking person to imitate, and by trying to imitate them, you are likely to make worse errors of speech. Remember, it's better to speak Spanish clearly and correctly with an American accent, than to adopt the wrong pronunciation and not be understood.

You may find that people speak too fast to be understood by a foreigner. Of course, they don't do this purposely to confuse you; it's merely their exuberant nature. Just say: *"Más despacio, por favor; no entiendo bien el español"* Mahs dess-PAH-syoh, por fah-VOR; noh en-tee-EN-do bee-EN el ess-pahn-YOL. (More slowly, please; I don't understand Spanish well).

GREETINGS AND GENERAL PHRASES

English	Pronunciation	Spanish
Hello!	OH-lah!	¡Hola!
Good Morning *or* Good day	BWEN-ohz DEE-ahss	Buenos días
Good afternoon	BWEN-ahss TAR-dess	Buenas tardes
Good evening *or* Good night	BWEN-ahss NO-chess	Buenas noches
How are you?	KOH-moh ess-TAH oo-STED?	¿Como está usted?
I am well	ess-TOY bee-EN	Estoy bien
Sir *or* Mister	sen-YOR	Señor
Madam *or* Mrs.	sen-YO-rah	Señora
Miss	sen-yo-REE-tah	Señorita

Spaniards have several ways to say "please" and they use them often.

Please	SEER-vah-say— *or* por fah-VOR *or* TEN-gah lah bohn-DAHD day—	Sírvase — *or* Por favor *or* Tenga la bondad de—
Excuse me	dees-PEN-say-may	Dispénseme
Thank you	GRAHSS-yahss	Gracias
You're welcome	NOH AH-ee day KAY *or* day NAH-dah	No hay de qué *or* De nada

SPANISH LANGUAGE GUIDE

Other Useful Phrases

English	Pronunciation	Spanish
What is your name?	KOH-moh say YAH-mah oo-STED?	¿Cómo se llama usted?
My name is ____	may YAH-moh ____	Me llamo ____
How do you say *table* (or anything else) in Spanish?	KOH-moh say DEE-say *table* en ess-pahn-YOHL?	¿Cómo se dice *table* en español?

There are many ways of saying "Good-by" in Spanish. The most usual is: ahd-YOHSS (Adiós).

For "So long" or "See you soon," you say in Spanish: ah-stah LWEH-goh (Hasta luego).

For "I'll see you later" you say in Spanish: ah-stah lah VEESS-tah (Hasta la vista).

For "Until tomorrow" you say in Spanish: ah-stah mahn-YAH-nah (Hasta mañana).

For "Until tonight" you say in Spanish: ah-stah lah NO-chay (Hasta la noche).

Directions

The answer to your question "Where is such and such?" may be "To the right" or "To the left" or "Straight ahead."

To the right	ah lah deh-RAY-chah	a la derecha
To the left	ah las eess-kee-EHR-dah	a la izquierda
Straight ahead	ah-day-LAHN-tay	adelante
Where is ____ ?	DON-day ess-TAH?	¿Donde está ____ ?

"What's This?"

When you want to know the name of something you can say "What's this?" and point to the thing you mean.

English	Pronunciation	Spanish
What is this?	KAY ess ESS-toh?	¿Qué es esto?

Asking for Things

When you want something you say "I want" and add the name of the thing wanted. Always be sure to say "please"—por fah-VOR.

I want	kee-EH-ro	Quiero
cigarettes	see-gah-RREE-yohss	cigarrillos
I want cigarettes	kee-EH-ro see-GAH-RREE-yohss	Quiero cigarillos
to eat	ko-MEHR	comer
I want to eat	kee-EH-ro ko-MEHR	Quiero comer

Here are the words for some of the things you may require, all of which you can ask for by using *kee-EH-ro* and the word for the thing you want.

beer	sehr-VEH-sah	cerveza
fruit	FROO-tah	fruta
ice cream	ay-LAH-doh	helado
a match	oon FOHS-foh-roh	un fósforo
pepper	peem-YEN-tah	pimienta
salt	SAHL	sal
sugar	ah-SOO-kar	azúcar
tea	TAY	té
water	AH-gwah	agua
wine	VEE-noh	vino

Money

To find out how much things cost you say:

English	*Pronunciation*	*Spanish*
How much	KWAHN-toh	Cuánto
costs	KWESS-tah	cuesta
this	ESS-toh	esto
How much does this cost?	KWAHN-toh KWESS-tah ESS-toh?	¿Cuánto cuesta esto?

Days of the Week

Sunday	doh-MEEN-go	domingo
Monday	LOO-ness	lunes
Tuesday	MAR-tess	martes
Wednesday	mee-EHR-koh-less	miércoles
Thursday	HWEH-vess	jueves

SPANISH LANGUAGE GUIDE

Friday	vee-EHR-ness	viernes
Saturday	SAH-bah-doh	sábado

Numbers

One	OO-no	uno
Two	DOHSS	dos
Three	TRESS	tres
Four	KWAH-troh	cuatro
Five	SEEN-koh	cinco
Six	SAY-eess	seis
Seven	sée-EH-tay	siete
Eight	OH-choh	ocho
Nine	NWEV-ay	nueve
Ten	dee-EHSS	diez
Eleven	OHN-say	once
Twelve	DOH-say	doce
Thirteen	TRESS-ay	trece
Fourteen	ka-TOR-say	catorce
Fifteen	KEEN-say	quince

For the numbers "sixteen" through "nineteen" you put the words d-yess-ee (dies y) "ten and ____" and then add the words for "six" through "nine."

Sixteen	dee-EHSS-ee-SAY-eess	dieciséis
Seventeen	dee-EHSS-ee-see-EH-tay	diecisiete
Eighteen	dee-EHSS-ee-OH-cho	dieciocho
Nineteen	dee-EHSS-ee-NWEH-vay	diecinueve
Twenty	BAY-een-tay	veinte
Twenty-one	vaynt-YOO-no	veintiuno
Twenty-two	vayn-tee-DOHSS	veintidós
Thirty	TRAY-een-tah	treinta
Forty	kwah-REN-tah	cuarenta
Fifty	seen-KWEN-tah	cincuenta
Sixty	say-SEN-tah	sesenta
Seventy	say-TEN-tah	setenta
Eighty	oh-CHEN-tah	ochenta
Ninety	no-VEN-tah	noventa
A (one) hundred	see-EN (see-EN-toh)	cien (ciento)
One thousand	MEEL	mil

Appendix A

CARIBBEAN CRUISE SHIPS

BALTIC SHIPPING COMPANY
MS ALEXANDER PUSHKIN

Sails from New York, Leningrad, Bremerhaven, London, LeHavre and Montreal. Built/Rebuilt 1965/1975. Registry: U. S. S. R. Capacity: 700 Passengers; Normal Crew Size: 340 (U. S. S. R.).

Specifics: Gross Tonnage 19,860; Length—580 ft., Width—77 ft.; stabilizers; fully air conditioned; 3 elevators; inside and outside swimming pools; 9 passenger decks; gymnasium/sauna; gambling (slot machines); outside staterooms; inside staterooms, 350 dining room capacity; 125 theatre capacity.

Itinerary: Spring and Fall trans-Atlantic sailings from Montreal and New York to Europe. Summer cruising from Canada to Caribbean including Havana. Winter cruising in Europe (Mediterranean). Tenders some ports. Docks at most.

MS MIKHAIL LERMONTOV

From Leningrad, New York, Bremerhaven, London (Tilbury), LeHavre trans-Atlantic, Baltic countries and to Caribbean from New York and Montreal. Built 1971. Registry: U. S. S. R. Capacity: 700 Passengers; Normal Crew Size: 340 (U. S. S. R.).

Specifics: Gross Tonnage 19,860; Length—580 ft.; Width—77 ft.; stabilizers; fully air conditioned; 3 elevators; inside and outside swimming pools, 9 passenger decks;

CARIBBEAN CRUISE SHIPS

gymnasium/sauna; gambling (slot machines); outside staterooms; inside staterooms; 340 dining room capacity; 130 theatre capacity.

Itinerary: Trans-Atlantic from New York and Montreal to Leningrad, Bremerhaven, etc. during Summer and Fall. Winters from Montreal to Caribbean and West Indies, which include Havana.

BLACK SEA SHIPPING COMPANY

Services: Trans-Atlantic sailings from New York to Azores, Portugal, Greece and USSR; from Tampa to Las Palmas, Cartagena and Naples; from Montreal to French Canada and Bermuda; from New York-Boston to French Canada. Winter cruises from New Orleans to Mexico, Honduras, Jamaica, Curacao, Venezuela, Colombia, Grand Cayman Island. Summer cruises, New York/Philadelphia/Baltimore to Bermuda. (For main U. S. and branch office personnel, see Baltic Shipping Co.)

MV ODESSA

Built 1974. Capacity 470.

Specifics: Gross tonnage 14,000; air conditioned; 1 outside swimming pool; 6 lounges; gymnasium; barber shop, beauty salon; cinema.

MS KAZAKHSTAN

Built 1976.

Specifics: Gross tonnage 16,600; air conditioned; 2 outside swimming pools; 5 lounges; sauna; hairdresser, barber.

CARNIVAL CRUISE LINES

Services: Weekly Miami to San Juan, St. Thomas and St. Maarten (tss Festivale); and Miami to Nassau, San Juan and St. Thomas (tss Mardi Gras). Miami to San Juan, St.

Thomas and St. Maarten (tss Festival). Miami to Samana, San Juan and St. Croix (tss Carnivale); Miami to Santo Domingo, St. Thomas and Nassau (tss Mardi Gras).

TSS CARNIVALE

Sails Miami to Caribbean. Built/Rebuilt 1956/1976. Registry: Panama. Capacity: 950 Passengers; Normal Crew Size: 510 (Italian Officers with a mixed crew).

Specifics: Gross Tonnage 27,250; Length—640 ft.; Width—87 ft.; stabilizers; fully air conditioned; 4 elevators; 4 outside swimming pools and 1 inside pool; 9 passenger decks; gymnasium/sauna; gambling (full casinos: blackjack, craps, roulette); 575 dining room capacity; 180 theatre capacity.

Itinerary: Seven day cruises, leaving on Sunday and returning on Sunday. Stops Samana, San Juan (2 days), St. Croix. At sea three days. Air/Sea packages from most cities.

TSS FESTIVALE

From Miami to Caribbean. Built/Rebuilt 1961/1978. Registry: Panama. Capacity: 1,148 Passengers; Normal Crew Size: 570 (Italian Officers with a mixed crew).

Specifics: Gross Tonnage 38,175; Length—760 ft. Width—90 ft., Stabilizers; fully air conditioned; 4 elevators; 3 outside pools; 9 passengers decks; gymnasium/sauna; gambling (full casinos: blackjack, craps, roulette); 700 dining room capacity; 202 theatre capacity.

Itinerary: Cruises for seven days; leaving on Saturdays. Ports visited—San Juan (2 days), St. Thomas, St. Maarten. At see for 3 days. Air/Sea packages from most cities.

TSS MARDI GRAS

7-day Caribbean cruises from Miami. Built/Rebuilt 1961/1973. Registry Panama. Capacity: 906 Passengers;

Normal Crew Size: 510 (Italian Officers with a mixed crew).

Specifics: Gross Tonnage 27,250; Length—650 ft.; Width—87 ft.; Stabilizers; fully air conditioned; 2 outside swimming pools, 1 inside pool; 9 passengers decks; 4 elevators; gymnasium/sauna; gambling (full casino: blackjack, craps. roulette); 550 dining room capacity; 200 theatre capacity.

Itinerary: Sunday departures to Nassau, San Juan and St. Thomas. Air/Sea package from most cities.

CHANDRIS, INC.

Services: Caribbean Cruises, Greek Island & Turkey Cruises, Eastern Mediterranean, Black Sea and Holy Land Cruises, Western Mediterranean Cruises, Cruise & Hotel Stay Programs, Baltic & North Cape Cruises.

SS BRITANIS

From Amsterdam or Genoa. Built/Rebuilt 1932/1970. Registry: Greece. Capacity: 1,600 Passengers on Trans-Atlantic cruise; Normal Crew Size: 420 (Greek).

Specifics: Gross Tonnage 24,351; Length—642 ft.; Width—79 ft.; fully air conditioned; 3 elevators, 1 outside swimming pool; gymnasium/sauna; gambling (small casino); outside staterooms; inside staterooms; 732 (2) dining room capacity; 155 theatre capacity; 9 passenger decks.

Itinerary: 14-Day cruise from Amsterdam to Northern Capitals—Holland, Sweden, Finland, etc., or to North Cape & Norwegian Fjords.

MS VICTORIA

From Venice, Built/Rebuilt 1939/1959. Registry: Greece. Capacity: 450 Passengers; Normal Crew Size: 300 (Greek).

Specifics: Gross Tonnage 20.000; Length—575 ft.;

Width—72 ft.; fully air conditioned; 3 elevators; 2 outside swimming pools; gymnasium/sauna; gambling (small casino); 5 passenger decks; outside staterooms; inside staterooms; 250 dining room capacity; 250 theatre capacity.

Itinerary: 4 different cruises of 14 nights each. All depart from Venice on Saturdays. April through September is the Eastern Mediterranean-Egypt Israel cruise; May is the Ecumenical Cruise-Eastern Mediterranean including Katakolon, Heraklion, Haifa, etc.; June and September offer the Black Sea & Russia Cruise; and the final cruise is offered in October to Greece, Turkey, Israel and Egypt.

COMMODORE CRUISE LINE, LTD.

Services: Miami to Puerto Plata, San Juan, St. Thomas, Cap Haitien, Freeport.

MS BOHEME

Sails from Miami to the Caribbean. Built/Rebuilt 1968/1977. Registry: West Germany. Capacity: 500 Passengers; Normal Crew Size: 220 (International).

Specifics: Gross Tonnage 11,000; Length—450 ft.; Width—65 ft.; stabilizers; 2 elevators; 1 outside swimming pool; 7 passenger decks; gymnasium/sauna; gambling (blackjack, slot machines); outside staterooms; inside staterooms; 250 dining room capacity; 100 theatre capacity.

Itinerary: Departs every Saturday from Miami docking at Puerto Plata, St. Thomas, San Juan, Cape Haitien.

CARIBE

From Miami, Built/Rebuilt 1968/1976. Registry: West Germany. Capacity: 480 Passengers; Normal Crew Size: 200 (Mixed).

Specifics: Gross Tonnage 11,000; Length—441 ft.; Width—70 ft.; stabilizers; fully air conditioned; 1 outside swimming pool; 3 elevators; 7 passenger decks; gambling (blackjack, slot machines, roulette); outside staterooms; inside staterooms; 250 dining room capacity; 150 theatre capacity.

Itinerary: Saturday departures from Miami throughout the entire year. Docks at Freeport, St. Thomas, San Juan, Puerto Rico, Puerto Plata.

COSTA CRUISES

Services: Cruises every Saturday from San Juan to the Caribbean and South America. Year-round cruises (three and four days) from Miami to Nassau, Bahamas, Mediterranean cruises from Genoa and Venice, 7 to 12 days, Caribbean, Panama, 10 to 11 days.

SS AMERIKANIS

Charter from Chandris, Inc. Sails from Charleston and San Juan. Built/Rebuilt 1951/1971. Registry: Greece. Capacity: 650 Passengers; Normal Crew Size: 250 (Greek).

Specifics: Gross Tonnage 19,377; Length—576 ft.; Width—74 ft.; air conditioning throughout; 2 elevators; gymnasium/sauna; gambling (small casino); outside staterooms; inside staterooms; 350 dining room capacity; 115 theatre capacity; 8 passenger decks.

Itinerary: 7-Day Caribbean Cruises. Sailing Saturdays to St. Maarten, St. Lucia, Martinique, Antigua, Barbados, St. Thomas.

MS ANDREA C.

Leaves Venice. Built/Rebuilt 1942/1976. Registry: Italy. Capacity: 400 Passengers; Normal Crew Size: 180 (Italian).

Specifics: Gross Tonnage 8,600; Length—467 ft.; Width—57 ft.; fully air conditioned; 5 passenger decks; 2 outside swimming pools; 242 dining room capacity; 120 theatre capacity; outside staterooms; inside staterooms.

Itinerary: 12-Day cruises from Venice stopping at Piraeus, Delos, Mykonos, Istanbul, Corfu, etc.

MS CARLA C.

Sails from San Juan. Built/Rebuilt 1951/1976. Registry: Italy. Capacity: 748 Passengers; Normal Crew Size: 370 (Italian).

Specifics: Gross Tonnage 20,477; Length—600 ft.; Width—80 ft.; stabilizers; fully air conditioned; 8 passenger decks; 2 outside swimming pools; 5 elevators; gambling; outside staterooms; inside staterooms; 244 & 384 dining room capacity; 145 theatre capacity.

Itinerary: 7-Day Caribbean and South American Cruises, sailing Saturdays to Curacao, Caracas, Trinidad, Martinique, St. Thomas.

MTS DANAE

Sails from New Orleans; Villefrance and Genoa or Piraeus. Built/Rebuilt 1956/1976. Registry: Greece. Capacity: 465 Passengers; Normal Crew Size: 250 (Greek).

Specifics: Gross Tonnage 15,560; Length—532 ft.; Width—74 ft.; stabilizers; individually controlled air conditioning; 2 elevators; 2 outside swimming pools; 5 passenger decks; gymnasium/sauna (sauna massage room); outside staterooms; inside staterooms, 468 dining room capacity; 245 theatre capacity.

Itinerary: Winters and Spring from New Orleans to Mexico and Aegean. From Villefrance, Genoa and Piraeus to Mediterranean and Red Sea; From June-September to Mediterranean and Black Sea.

SS FEDERICO C.

From Genoa and Miami. Built/Rebuilt 1958/1976. Registry: Italy. Capacity: 800 Passengers; Normal Crew Size: 350 (Italian).

CARIBBEAN CRUISE SHIPS

Specifics: Gross Tonnage 20,416; Length—606 ft.; Width—74 ft.; stabilizers; 4 elevators; 3 outside swimming pools; fully air conditioned; 8 passenger decks; gym; gambling (when in Caribbean); outside staterooms; inside staterooms; 380, 218 & 135 dining room capacity; 170 theatre capacity.

Itinerary: 10-Day cruise from Miami to Caribbean and South America. Ports of call are Montego Bay, Aruba, Cozumel, etc.

MS WORLD RENAISSANCE

From Miami. Built 1966. Registry: Greece. Capacity: 528 Passengers; Greek Crew.

Specifics: Gross Tonnage 12,000; Length—492 ft.; Width—69 ft.; stabilizers; fully air conditioned; 8 passenger decks; 2 outside swimming pools; gymnasium/sauna; gambling; outside staterooms; inside staterooms; 400 dining room capacity; 115 theatre capacity.

Itinerary: 10-Day Cruises from Miami docking at Port Antonio, Cartagena, Panama, San Andres, Cozumel. Departure on Fridays. Air/Sea Package available from all major U. S. cities.

CUNARD LINE LIMITED

Queen Elizabeth Two transatlantic sailings between N. Y., Cherbourg and Southampton, 30 weeks beginning April. Fall, winter and occasional summer cruises in the Caribbean and Mediterranean; around the world cruises. Weekly Cunard Princess cruises year-round from Port Everglades, Florida. Cunard Countess cruises year round from San Juan to five Caribbean ports, including Caracas, Venezuela.

CUNARD COUNTESS

Sails from San Juan. Built 1976. Registry: Britain. Capacity: 750 Passengers; Normal Crew Size: 350 (British, except for dining room).

Specifics: Gross Tonnage 17,495; Length—536 ft., 10 in.; Width—74 ft., 10 in.; stabilizers; fully air conditioned; 8 passenger decks; 1 outside swimming pool; 2 elevators; gambling (slots, blackjack); outside staterooms; inside staterooms; 500 dining room capacity; 135 theatre capacity.

Itinerary: 7-Day Caribbean Cruises every Saturday from June through October. Port of Call: Caracas (Venezuela), Grenada, Barbados, St. Lucia, St. Thomas.

CUNARD PRINCESS

Leaves Fort Lauderdale. Built 1977. Registry: Britain. Capacity: 750 Passengers; Normal Crew Size: 350 (British, except for dining room).

Specifics: Gross Tonnage 17,495; Length—536 ft., 10 in.; Width—74 ft., 10 in.; stabilizers; fully air conditioned; 8 passenger decks; 1 outside swimming pool; 2 elevators; gambling (slots, blackjack); outside staterooms, inside staterooms; 500 dining room capacity; 135 theatre capacity.

Itinerary: 7-Day Cruises every Saturday June through October. Port of Call: Puerto Plata, San Juan, St. Thomas, Nassau.

QUEEN ELIZABETH 2

Sails from New York, Boston, Norfolk, Port Everglades. Built 1969. Registry: Britain. Capacity: 1,815 Trans-Atlantic; Normal Crew Size: 1,000 (British).

Specifics: Gross Tonnage 67,139; Length—963 ft.; Width—105 ft.; stabilizers; fully air conditioned; 13 passenger decks; 2 outside and 2 inside swimming pools; 13 elevators; gymnasium/sauna; gambling (casino w. slot machines, blackjack, and roulette); outside staterooms; inside staterooms; 834, 610, 102, 188 dining room capacity; 531 theatre capacity.

CARIBBEAN CRUISE SHIPS

Itinerary: Cruises vary in length from New York to the Caribbean. Some Ports of Call are St. Thomas, San Juan, Nassau, Martinque, etc.

EASTERN STEAMSHIP LINES
SS EMERALD SEAS
Leaves Miami. Built/Rebuilt 1944/1977. Registry: Panama; Capacity: 800 Passengers; Normal Crew Size: 400 (International).

Specifics: Gross Tonnage 24,458; Length—622 ft.; Width—75 ft.; 4 elevators; 7 passenger decks; 1 outside swimming pool; air conditioned; outside staterooms; inside staterooms; 465 dining room capacity; 158 theatre capacity.

Itinerary: Leaves every Monday for 4 night cruises to Nassau/Freeport. Also 3 night cruises every Friday to Nassau.

HELLENIC MEDITERRANEAN LINE
Services: San Juan to Caribbean; Piraeus to Greek Islands and Istanbul, Turkey.
MS AQUARIUS
From Piraeus. Built 1972. Registry: Greece. Capacity: 297 Passengers; Normal Crew Size: 125 (Greek).

Specifics: Gross Tonnage 4,800; Length—340 ft.; Width —45 ft.; stabilizers; fully air conditioned; 6 passenger decks; 1 outside swimming pool; 1 elevator; outside staterooms; inside staterooms; 180 dining room capacity.

Itinerary: 7-Day cruises December through April, San Juan to Caribbean.

HOLLAND AMERICA CRUISES
Services: Around the World, Singapore/Bali Alaska, Caribbean, Nassau and Bermuda.

SS ROTTERDAM

From New York and Port Everglades. Built/Rebuilt 1959/1969. Registry: Neth. Antilles. Capacity: 1,050 Passengers; Normal Crew Size: 560 (Dutch/Indonesian).

Specifics: Gross Tonnage 38,000; Length—748 ft.; Width—94 ft.; stabilizers; fully air conditioned; 11 passenger decks; 8 elevators; gymnasium/sauna; 1 outside and 1 inside swimming pool; outside staterooms; inside staterooms; 510 & 260 dining room capacity; 620 (Incl. Balcony) theatre capacity.

Itinerary: 7-Day Cruises to Nassau and Bermuda from June to August.

SS STATENDAM

Sails New York and Port Everglades. Built/Rebuilt 1957/1972. Registry: Neth. Antilles. Capacity: 800 Passengers; Normal Crew Size: 416 (Dutch/Indonesian).

Specifics: Gross Tonnage 24,500; Length—642 ft.; Width—79 ft.; stabilizers; fully air conditioned; 9 passenger decks; 3 elevators; 1 outside and 1 inside swimming pool; gymnasium/sauna; outside staterooms; inside staterooms; 438 dining room capacity; 330 theatre capacity.

Itinerary: 7-Day Bermuda Cruises from June through August. Also Grand Caribbean Cruises from New York or Port Everglades.

VEENDAM

Leaves Miami. Built/Rebuilt 1958/1972-73. Registry: Panama. Capacity: 666 Passengers; Normal Crew Size: 340 (International).

Specifics: Gross Tonnage 23,500; Length—617 ft.; Width—88 ft.; stabilizers; fully air conditioned; 7 passenger decks; 3 elevators; 1 outside and 1 inside swimming pool; gymnasium/sauna; outside staterooms; inside staterooms; 350 dining room capacity; 200 theatre capacity.

Itinerary: 14-Day Caribbean Cruises, Port of Calls Port-au-Prince, Montego Bay, Aruba, La Guaira, St. Thomas, etc. Departures every other Sunday.

VOLENDAM

Sails from New York and Miami. Built/Rebuilt 1958/ 1972-73. Registry: Panama. Capacity: 679 Passengers; Normal Crew Size: 340 (International).

Specifics: Gross Tonnage 23,500; Length—617 ft.; Width—88 ft.; stabilizers; 7 passenger decks; 3 elevators; fully air conditioned; 1 outside swimming pool; gymnasium/sauna; outside staterooms; inside staterooms; 350 dining room capacity; 200 theatre capacity.

Itinerary: 7-Day Cruises every Sunday to the Caribbean; 7-Day Cruises every Sunday to Bermuda.

HOME LINE CRUISES

Services Year-round cruises from New York; Caribbean cruises from Port Everglades, Fla. in winter.

DORIC

Sails from New York. Built/Rebuilt 1964/1976. Registry: Panama. Capacity: 720 Passengers; Normal Crew Size: 425 (Italian).

Specifics: Gross Tonnage 25,300; Length—629 ft.; Width—82 ft.; stabilizers; air conditioned; 10 passenger decks; 5 elevators; 2 outside and 1 inside swimming pools; gymnasium/sauna; outside staterooms; inside staterooms; 375 dining room capacity; 273 theatre capacity.

Itinerary: Weekly trips to Nassau and Bermuda leaving every Saturday. April to November. Winter Cruises to the West Indies.

OCEANIC

From New York. Built/Rebuilt 1965/1976. Registry: Panama. Capacity: 1,034 Passengers; Normal Crew Size: 600 (Italian).

Specifics: Gross Tonnage 39,241; Length—774 ft.; Width—97 ft.; stabilizers; air conditioned; 10 passenger decks; 4 elevators; 2 outside swimming pools; gymnasium/sauna; outside staterooms; inside staterooms; 575 dining room capacity; 420 theatre capacity.

Itinerary: Late Autumn and Early Winter Cruises to the West Indies; Weekly Cruises to Nassau and Bermuda.

NORWEGIAN CARIBBEAN LINES
(Klosters-Rederi A/S d/b/a/Norwegian Caribbean Lines)

Services: Cruises to Caribbean, Mediterranean, Black Sea, Scandinavia, North Cape, Baltic and Europe, Transatlantic.

Points of Departure: Port Everglades (Caribbean cruises) New York-London (air/sea cruises).

MS NORDIC PRINCE
Sails Miami. Built 1971. Registry: Norway. Capacity: 750 Passengers; Normal Crew Size: 320 (Norwegian Officers; Multinational Hotel Staff).

Specifics: Gross Tonnage 18,500; Length—550 ft.; Width—80 ft.; stabilizers; air conditioned; 8 passenger decks; 4 elevators; 1 outside swimming pool; sauna/massage center; outside staterooms; inside staterooms; 450 dining room capacity; 500 theatre capacity.

Itinerary: 14-Day cruise to the Caribbean with some Ports of Call: San Juan, St. Thomas, Guadeloupe, Aruba, Port-au-Prince, etc.

MS SONG OF NORWAY
From Miami. Built/Rebuilt 1970/1978. Registry: Norway. Capacity: 1,040 Passengers; Normal Crew Size: 400 (Norwegian Officers, Multinational Hotel Staff).

Specifics: Gross Tonnage 23,005; Length—635 ft.; Width—80 ft.; stabilizers; fully air conditioned; 8 passenger decks; 4 elevators; 1 outside swimming pool; outside staterooms; inside staterooms; 610 dining room capacity; 500 theatre capacity.

Itinerary: 7-Day Caribbean Cruises every Saturday, docking at Puerto Plata, San Juan, St. Thomas.

MS SKYWARD

From Miami. Built 1970. Registry: Norway. Capacity: 724 Passengers; Normal Crew Size: 300 (Mixed Crew, Norwegian Officers).

Specifics: Gross Tonnage 16,250; Length—525 ft.; Width—75 ft.; stabilizers; fully air conditioned; 8 passenger decks; 4 elevators; health club and sauna; 1 outside swimming pool; gambling (slot machines only); outside staterooms; inside staterooms; 452 dining room capacity; 190 theatre capacity.

Itinerary: Every Saturday 7-day cruises to Cape Haitien, San Juan, St. Thomas, Puerto Rico.

MS SOUTHWARD

Sails from Miami. Built 1970. Registry: Norway. Capacity: 738 Passengers; Normal Crew Size: 302 (Mixed Crew, Norwegian Officers).

Specifics: Gross Tonnage 16,607; Length—536 ft.; Width—75 ft.; stabilizers; fully air conditioned; 9 passenger decks; 4 elevators; 1 outside and 1 splash pool; health center and sauna; gambling (slot machines); outside staterooms; inside staterooms; 404 dining room capacity; 200 theatre capacity.

Itinerary: 7-Day cruises every Saturday to Cancun/Cozumel, Mexico; Grand Cayman Island; Ocho Rios and the Berry Islands.

MS STARWARD

Leaves Miami. Built 1968. Registry: Norway. Capacity:

742 Passengers; Normal Crew Size: 250 (Mixed Crew; Norwegian Officers).

Specifics: Gross Tonnage 16,000; Length—525 ft.; Width—75 ft.; stabilizers; fully air conditioned; 8 passenger decks; 4 elevators; health club and sauna; 2 outside swimming pools; gambling (slot machines only); outside staterooms; inside staterooms; 450 dining room capacity; 200 theatre capacity.

Itinerary: 7-Days: Port Antonia, Ocho Rios, Port-au-Prince, Nassau and the Berry Islands.

PAQUET FRENCH CRUISES
DOLPHIN (PAQUET/ULYSSES CRUISE)

Built/Rebuilt 1956/1973. Registry: Panama. Capacity: 683 Passengers; Normal Crew Size: 280 (International).

Specifics: Gross Tonnage 12,500; Length—501 ft.; Width—65 ft.; stabilizers, fully air conditioned; 7 passenger decks; 1 elevator; 1 outside swimming pool; gambling (full casino); outside staterooms; inside staterooms; 380 dining room capacity.

Itinerary: 7-16 Day cruises to Caribbean Islands, South America/Africa, Middle East in the Autumn, Turkey, Iceland/Ireland/Spain.

MERMOZ

From Toulon, Calais, Marseille, Miami. Built/Rebuilt 1957/1970. Registry: France. Capacity 550 Passengers; Normal Crew Size: 230 (French).

Specifics: Gross Tonnage 13,800; Length—530 ft.; Width—66 ft.; stabilizers; fully air conditioned; 5 passenger decks; 2 elevators; 2 outside swimming pools; gymnasium/sauna; outside staterooms; inside staterooms; 470 (plus 180 Grill) dining room capacity; 260 theatre capacity.

Itinerary: Frequently from Miami to the Bahamas.

CARIBBEAN CRUISE SHIPS

MS RENAISSANCE

Sails Port Everglades. Built 1966. Registry: France. Capacity: 350 Passengers; Normal Crew Size: 215 (French).

Specifics: Gross Tonnage 11,724; Length—492 ft.; Width—69 ft.; stabilizers; fully air conditioned; 1 elevator; 2 outside swimming pools; gymnasium/sauna; 8 passenger decks.

Itinerary: 12 and 14 day cruises to San Juan, Guadeloupe, St. Thomas. Santo Domingo, San Blas Islands, etc.

PRINCESS CRUISES

ISLAND PRINCESS

Leaves Los Angeles, San Francisco, Vancouver. Built 1972. Registry: Great Britain. Capacity: 622 Passengers; Normal Crew Size: 300 (British & Italian).

Specifics: Gross Tonnage 20,000; Length—550 ft.; Width—80 ft.; stabilizers; fully air conditioned; 7 passenger decks; 4 elevators; 2 outside swimming pools; outside staterooms; inside staterooms; 342 dining room capacity; 280 theatre capacity.

Itinerary: Varied cruises to Acapulco, Caribbean, South America, Mexico, Transcanal; summer offers cruises to Alaska/Canada; and fall has South Pacific cruises.

SUN PRINCESS

Los Angeles, San Juan, Vancouver. Built/Rebuilt 1972/1974. Registry: Great Britain. Capacity: 700 Passengers; Normal Crew Size: 324 (British).

Specifics: Gross Tonnage 17,000; Length—535 ft.; Width—75 ft.; stabilizers; fully air conditioned; 7 passenger decks; 4 elevators; 1 outside swimming pool; gymnasium/sauna; outside staterooms; inside staterooms; 400 dining room capacity; 186 theatre capacity.

Itinerary: Winter and Spring 7-Day Caribbean Cruise with Ports of Call: Curacao, Caracas, etc.; Summer-Fall Alaska/Canada Cruise; varied lengths with Ports of Call:

Victoria, Juneau, Ketchikan, Glacier Bay, Sitka, etc.

ROYAL CARIBBEAN CRUISE LINE
MS SUN VIKING

From Miami. Built 1972. Registry: Norway. Capacity: 750 Passengers; Normal Crew Size: 320 (Norwegian Officers, Multinational Hotel Staff).

Specifics: Gross Tonnage 18,500; Length—550 ft.; Width—80 ft.; stabilizers; air conditioned; 8 passenger decks; 4 elevators; 1 outside swimming pool; outside staterooms; inside staterooms; 450 dining room capacity; 500 theatre capacity.

Itinerary: 14-Day Cruises on Saturdays. Ports of Call: San Juan, St. Thomas, Martinique, Caracas, Aruba, Curacao, Port Antonio, Port-au-Prince.

SS NORWAY (formerly SS France)

Sails from Miami or Port Everglades. Registry: Norway. Capacity: 2,000 passengers; Normal Crew: 500 (Norwegian and European).

Specifics: Gross Tonnage 66,348; Length—1,035 ft.; Width—100 ft.; stabilizers; fully air conditioned; a deluxe one class cruise ship. The Norway features indoor and outdoor swimming pools, several night clubs, theaters, discos, gaming area, racquet and squash ball courts, including fully equipped hospital and dental facilities. Refurbishing changes include penthouses and outside cabins as well as expansion of the public areas for a fully one-class ship service.

Itinerary: Caribbean 7 Day service.

SS SUNDWARD II.

Sails from Miami. Built 1971. Registry: Norway. Capacity: 918 passengers; Crew 302 (West Indian and Norwegian).

CARIBBEAN CRUISE SHIPS

Specifics: Gross Tonnage 17,000; Length—484 ft.; Width—70.5 ft.; stabilized; fully air conditioned; a deluxe one-class service.

Itinerary: Caribbean 7-Day service.

Services: Year-round seven and 14-day cruises to the Caribbean from Miami.

ROYAL VIKING LINE

Services: Worldwide from all major markets—Mediterranean, North Cape, Caribbean Pacific and round-the-world cruises from east coast, west coast and European ports.

ROYAL VIKING SEA

Leaves San Francisco and Port Everglades. Built 1973. Registry: Norway. Capacity: 500 Passengers; Normal Crew Size: 300 (Norwegian & Mixed European).

Specifics: Gross Tonnage 22,000; Length—583 ft.; Width—83 ft.; stabilizers; fully air conditioned; 6 passenger decks; 5 elevators; 1 outside swimming pool, plus one dipping pool; gymnasium/sauna; outside staterooms; inside staterooms; 500 dining room capacity; 156 theatre capacity.

Itinerary: Most cruises between 10 and 39 days. Cruise Alaska/Canada; Around the World; British Isles/Norwegian Fjords; Caribbean; Mediterranean, etc.

ROYAL VIKING SKY

From San Francisco and Port Everglades. Built 1973. Registry: Norway. Capacity: 500 Passengers; Normal Crew Size: 300 (Norwegian & Mixed European).

Specifics: Gross Tonnage 22,000; Length—583 ft.; Width—83 ft.; stabilizers; 6 passenger decks; 5 elevators; fully air conditioned; 1 outside swimming pool with a dipping pool; gymnasium/sauna; outside staterooms; inside staterooms; 500 dining room capacity; 156 theatre capacity.

Itinerary: Varied length cruises. Cruises of Alaska/Canada; Around the World; Mediterranean, British Isles/Norwegian Fjords; Caribbean, etc.

ROYAL VIKING STAR

Sails from San Francisco and Port Everglades. Built 1972. Registry: Norway. Capacity: 500 Passengers; Normal Crew Size: 300 (Norwegian & Mixed European).

Specifics: Gross Tonnage 22,000; Length—581 ft.; Width—83 ft.; stabilizers; fully air conditioned; 6 passenger decks; 1 outside swimming pool; 5 elevators; outside staterooms; inside staterooms; 500 dining room capacity. 156 theatre capacity.

Itinerary: Worldwide cruising. Varied lengths of time. Cruises to Mediterranean, British Isles/Norwegian Fjords; Alaska/Canada; Around the World, etc.

SITMAR CRUISES

Services: Cruises from Port Everglades to the Caribbean —7, 10, 11, 14 days; from Los Angeles to Mexico—7, 10, 11 days; from San Francisco to Canada and Alaska—14 days; from Port Everglades, Los Angeles, San Juan and Acapulco—14-day Trans-Panama Canal.

TSS FAIRSEA

Leaves Los Angeles and San Francisco. Built/Rebuilt 1955/1971. Registry: Liberia. Capacity: 830 Passengers; Normal Crew Size: 500 (Italian).

Specifics: Gross Tonnage 25,000; Length—608 ft.; Width—80 ft.; stabilizers; fully air conditioned; 11 passenger decks; 3 elevators; 3 outside (1 for children) swimming pools; gymnasium/sauna; gambling (slot machines); outside staterooms; inside staterooms; 590 (two sittings) dining room capacity; 330 theatre capacity.

CARIBBEAN CRUISE SHIPS

Itinerary: Cruises range from 7 to 14 days. Cruises to Mexico docking at some ports: Acapulco, Puerto Vallarta, Mazatlan, etc. Also cruises to Canada and Alaska: Vancouver, Juneau, Sitka, Glacier Bay, etc.

TSS FAIRWIND

From Los Angeles, Port Everglades, and Fort Lauderdale. Built/Rebuilt 1956/1972. Registry: Liberia. Capacity: 830 Passengers; Normal Crew Size: 500 (Italian).

Specifics: Gross Tonnage 25,000; Length—608 ft.; Width—80 ft.; stabilizers; fully air conditioned; 11 passenger decks; 3 elevators; 3 (1 for children) outside swimming pools; gymnasium/sauna; gambling (slot machines); outside staterooms; inside staterooms; 590 (two sittings) dining room capacity; 330 theatre capacity.

Itinerary: 7-11 day cruises to Nassau, Cape Haitien, San Juan, St. Thomas, St. Maarten, Martinique, St. Lucia, etc. Also cruises to West Indies, South America, Mexico.

SUN LINE CRUISES
STELLA MARIS

Leave Venice and Nice. Registry: Greece. Built/Rebuilt 1960/1966. Capacity: 212 Passengers; Normal Crew Size: 100 (Greek).

Specifics: Gross Tonnage 4,000; Length—300 ft.; Width—45 ft.; stabilizers; air conditioned; 4 passenger decks; 1 outside swimming pool; outside staterooms; inside staterooms; 164 dining room capacity; 50 theatre capacity.

Itinerary: 7-Day Cruises in the spring and summer to the Aegean and Mediterranean. Some Ports of Call: Dubrovnik, Corfu, Elba, Costa, etc. and Tunix, Katakolon, Malta, etc.

STELLA OCEANIS

From Piraeus. Built/Rebuilt 1965/1967. Registry:

Greece. Capacity: 318 Passengers; Normal Crew Size: 140 (Greek).

Specifics: Gross Tonnage 6,000; Length—350 ft.; Width—53 ft.; stabilizers; air conditioned; 6 passenger decks; 1 elevator; 1 outside swimming pool; Monte Carlo Room; outside staterooms; inside staterooms; 200 dining room capacity; 75 theatre capacity.

Itinerary: 4-Day cruise every Monday from April to September. Ports of Call: Hydra, Santorini, Heraklion, Rhodes, Ephessos, Mykonos.

STELLA SOLARIS

Sails Piraeus. Built/Rebuilt 1951/1973. Registry: Greece. Capacity: 650 Passengers; Normal Crew Size: 310 (Greek).

Specifics: Gross Tonnage 18,000; Length—550 ft.; Width—72 ft.; stabilizers; air conditioned; 8 passenger decks; 3 elevators; 2 outside swimming pools; gymnasium/sauna; Monte Carlo Room; outside staterooms; inside staterooms; 420 dining room capacity; 275 theatre capacity.

Itinerary: 7-Day cruises leaving every Monday from April to September. Ports of Call: Heraklion, Santorini, Rhodes, Esphessos, Istanbul, Delos, Mykonos.

Appendix B

MAJOR CRUISE LINES

ADRIATICA LINE, 5 World Trade Center, New York, N. Y. 10048; 212-466-1370, 800-221-5252

AMERICAN CANADIAN LINE, P. O. Box 368, Warren, R. I. 02885; 401-245-1350, 800-556,7450

AMERICAN CRUISE LINES, Marin Park, Haddam, Conn. 06438; 203-345-8551, 800-243-6755

AMERICAN HAWAII CRUISES, One Embarcadero Center, Suite 611, San Francisco, Calif. 94111; 415-392-9400, 800-622-0666 (Calif.), 800-227-3666 (nationwide)

BAHAMA CRUISE LINE, 747 Third Ave., New York, N. Y. 10017; 212-371-6464, 212-246-7570, 800-223-0908 (nationwide) 800-522-5228 (N. Y.)

BERGEN LINE, 505 Fifth Ave., New York, N. Y. 10017; 212-986-2711

BRITISH COLUMBIA FERRY CORP., 1045 Howe St., Vancouver, B. C. Canada V6Z 2A9; 604-669-1211

CARNIVAL CRUISE LINES, 820 Biscayne Blvd., Miami, Fla. 33132; 305-377-4751, 800-327-7373

CHANDRIS, 666 Fifth Ave., New York, N. Y. 10019; 212-586-8370

COMMODORE CRUISE LINE, 1015 North America Way, Miami, Fla. 33132; 305-358-2622, 800-327-5617

COSTA CRUISES, 733 Third Ave., New York, N. Y. 10017; 212-682-3505

CUNARD LINE, 555 Fifth Ave., New York, N. Y. 10017; 212-880-7500

CYCLADIC CRUISES, 331 Madison Ave., New York, N. Y. 10017; 212-697-5648

DELTA QUEEN STEAMBOAT CO., 511 Main St., Cincinnati, Ohio 45202; 800-582-1888, 800-543-1949

DELTA STEAMSHIP LINES, One Market Plaza, San Francisco, Calif. 94106; 415-777-8300, 800-652-1426 (Calif.), 800-227-3676 (nationwide)

EASTERN STEAMSHIP LINES, 1220 Biscayne Blvd., Miami, Fla. 33101; 305-373-7501, 800-432-9552 (Fla.), 800-237-0271 (nationwide)

EPIROTIKI LINES, 551 Fifth Ave., New York, N. Y. 10017; 212-599-1750, 800-221-2470

HELLENIC MEDITERRANEAN LINES, 200 Park Ave., New York, N.Y. 10166: 212-697-4220

HOLLAND AMERICA CRUISES, 2 Penn Plaza, New York, N.Y. 10001; 212-760-3900, 800-522-6866 (N. Y.), 800-223-6655 (nationwide)

HOME LINES CRUISES, 1 World Trade Center, New York, N. Y. 10048; 212-432-1414

JUGOLINIJA, 19 Rector St., New York, N. Y. 10006; 212-248-4500

KARAGEORGIS CRUISES, 1350 Ave. of the Americas, New York, N. Y. 10019; 212-582-3007, 800-223-7892/3/4

KD GERMAN RHINE LINE, 170 Hamilton Ave., White Plains, N. Y. 10601; 914-948-3600; also 323 Geary St., San Francisco, Calif. 94102; 415-392-8817

K LINES-HELLENIC CRUISES, 645 Fifth Ave., New York, N. Y. 10022; 212-751-2435, 800-223-7880

LAURO LINE, One Biscayne Tower, Miami, Fla. 33131; 305-374-4120

MARCH SHIPPING, One World Trade Center, New York, N. Y. 10048; 212-938-9300, 800-221-3254

NILE RIVER CRUISES, 500 Fifth Ave., New York, N. Y. 10036; 212-840-5964, 800-223-6618

NORWEGIAN AMERICAN CRUISES, 29 Broadway, New York, N. Y. 10011; 212-422-3905, 800-221-2400

NORWEGIAN CARIBBEAN LINES, One Biscayne Tower, Miami, Fla. 33131; 1-800-432-9696 (Fla.), 800-327-7030 (nationwide)

PAQUET CRUISES, 1370 Ave. of the Americas, New York, N. Y. 10019; 212-757-9050, 800-221-2160 (west of Mississippi River, Ala., Fla., Miss.), 800-221-2490 (all other states)

POLISH OCEAN LINES, One World Trade Center, New York, N. Y. 10048; 212-938-1900

PRINCESS CRUISES, 2029 Century Park East, Los Angeles, Calif. 90067; 213-553-700, 800-421-0522 (except Calif.)

ROYAL CARIBBEAN CRUISE LINES, 903 South America Way, Miami, Fla. 33132; 305-371-4215

MAJOR CRUISE LINES

ROYAL CRUISE LINE, 1 Maritime Plaza, San Francisco, Calif. 94111; 415-956-7200

ROYAL VIKING LINE, One Embarcadero Center, San Francisco, Calif. 94111; 415-398-8000, 800-792-2970 (Calif.). 800-227-4246 (nationwide)

SITMAR CRUISES, 10100 Santa Monica Blvd., Los Angeles, Calif. 90067; 800-421-0880 (Calif.), 800-252-0301 (nationwide)

SUN LINE CRUISES, 1 Rockefeller Plaza, New York, N. Y. 10020; 212-397-6400, 800-223-5760

TIRRENIA LINE, 5 World Trade Center, New York, N. Y. 10048; 212-466-1370, 800-221-5252

WINDJAMMER CRUISES, P. O. Box 120, Miami Beach, Fla. 33139; 305-373-2090, 800-327-2600

Appendix C

CARIBBEAN CRUISE PORTS OF CALL

Acajutla	GUADELOUPE	Port-au-Prince
Acapulco	Guanaja Is.	Port Everglades
ANTIGUA	GUATEMALA	Port-of-Spain
ARUBA	HAITI	Providencia Is.
BAHAMAS	HONDURAS	Puerto Barrios
Balboa	Isla de Margarita	Puerto Cortes
Baltimore	JAMAICA	Puerto Limon
BARBADOS	KINGSTON	Puerto Morelos
BELIZE	La Guaira	Puerto Plata
BONAIRE	La Paz	PUERTO RICO
Cabo San Lucas	Los Angeles	Puerto Vallarta
Cap Haitien	Manzanillo	Roatan
Caracas	MARTINIQUE	ST. BARTHELEMY
Cartagena	Mazatlan	ST. JOHNS
Charleston	MEXICO	ST. KITTS
Coatzacoalcos	Mexico City	St. Lucia
COLOMBIA	Miami	ST. MAARTEN
COSTA RICA	Montego Bay	ST. THOMAS
Cozumel	Nassau	ST. VINCENT
Cristobal	NEVIS	SAN ANDRES
CUBA	New Orleans	San Blas Is.
CURACAO	NICARAGUA	San Juan
DOMINICAN REPUBLIC	Norfolk	San Francisco
ECUADOR	Ocho Rios	Santo Domingo
EL SALVADOR	PANAMA	Santo Thomas de Castilla
Fort-de-France	Panama	TRINIDAD
Freeport	PANAMA CANAL	UNITED STATES
Galapagos Islands	Playa del Carmen	VENEZUELA
Galveston	Pointe-a-Pitre	Vera Cruz
Grand Cayman	Port Antonio	Willemstad
GRENADA		

CARIBBEAN CRUISE PORTS OF CALL

Reprinted by special permission from the January-February 1980 issue of the OAG Worldwide Cruise and Shipline Guide. All rights reserved.

Appendix D

GOVERNMENT TOURIST OFFICES

ANGUILLA TOURIST INFOR-
MATION CENTER
39 W. 55th St.
New York, NY 10019
Tel. 212/586-2955.

ANTIGUA DEPARTMENT OF
TOURISM & TRADE OFFICE
610 Fifth Ave., Ste. 311
New York, NY 10020
Tel. 212/541-4117

ARUBA TOURIST BUREAU
576 Fifth Ave.
New York, NY 10036
Tel. 212/246-3030

BARBADOS TOURIST BOARD
800 Second Ave., 17th Floor
New York, NY 10017
Tel. 212/986-6516

BARBUDA DEPARTMENT OF
TOURISM & TRADE
610 Fifth Ave., Ste. 311
New York, NY 10020
Tel. 212/541-4117

BERMUDA DEPARTMENT OF
TOURISM
P.O. Box 465, Front Street
Hamilton, Bermuda
Tel. (809) 292-0023

BONAIRE TOURIST BOARD
685 Fifth Ave., Ste. 401
New York, NY 10022
Tel. 212/838-1797

BRITISH VIRGIN ISLANDS
INFORMATION BUREAU
515 Madison Ave.
New York, NY 10022
Tel. 212/371-6759

CAYMAN ISLANDS DEPT.
OF TOURISM
250 Catalonia Ave., Suite 604
Coral Gables, FL 33134
Toll Free: 800-327-8777
(except FL); FL 800-432-4858
(except Miami)

CUBA
c/o EMBASSY
388 Main St.
Ottawa, ON
Tel. 613/563-0141

CURACAO TOURIST BOARD
30 Rockefeller Plaza Mezzanine
  Fl. Room 50
New York, NY 10020
Tel. 212/265-0230

GOVERNMENT TOURIST OFFICES

DOMINICA TOURIST
ASSOCIATION
P.O. Box 73
Roseau, Dominica
Tel. 2351

DOMINICAN TOURIST IN-
FORMATION CENTER
485 Madison Ave.
New York, NY 10022
Tel. 212/826-0750

GRENADA TOURIST BOARD
866 Second Ave., Ste. 502
New York, NY 10017
Tel. 212/759-9675

GRENADINES TOURIST
BOARD
P. O. Box 834
Kingstown, St. Vincent, W.I.
Tel. 61224

GUADELOUPE TOURIST
BOARD
610 Fifth Ave.
New York, NY 10020
Tel. 212/757-1125

HAITI GOVERNMENT
TOURIST BUREAU
30 Rockefeller Plaza
New York, NY 10020
Tel. 212/757-3517

JAMAICA TOURIST BOARD
Peter Martin Assoc.
243 E. 61st St.
New York, NY 10021
Toll Free: 800-223-5225/6
(Northeast U. S.)

MONTSERRAT TOURIST
BOARD
P.O. Box 494, Station A
Toronto, ON M5W 1E4
Tel. 416/922-7318

NEVIS TOURIST INFOR-
MATION CENTER
39 W. 55th St.
New York, NY 10019
Tel. 212/586-2955

PUERTO RICO TOURISM CO.
1290 Ave. of the Americas
New York, NY 10019
Tel. 212/541-6630

SABA TOURIST OFFICE
445 Park Ave. Ste. 903
New York, NY 10022
Tel. 212/688-8350

ST. BARTHELEMY TOURIST
INFORMATION OFFICE
610 Fifth Avenue
New York, NY 10020
Tel. 212/757-1125

ST. EUSTATIUS TOURIST
OFFICE
445 Park Ave. Ste. 903
New York, NY 10022
Tel. 212/688-8350

ST. KITTS TOURIST INFOR-
MATION CENTER
39 W. 55th St.
New York, NY 10019
Tel. 212/586-2955

ST. LUCIA TOURIST
  BOARD
220 E. 42nd St.
New York, NY 10017
Tel. 212/867-2950

ST. MAARTEN TOURIST
  OFFICE
445 Park Ave. Ste. 903
New York, NY 10022
Tel. 212/688-8350

ST. MARTIN TOURIST BOARD
610 Fifth Ave.
New York, NY 10020
Tel. 212/757-1125

ST. VINCENT TOURIST
  BOARD
315 E. 72nd St.
New York, NY 10021
Tel. 212/628-8149

TRINIDAD AND TOBAGO
  TOURIST BOARDS
400 Madison Ave., Rms. 712-714
New York, NY 10017
Tel. 212/838-7750

TURKS & CAICOS INFOR-
  MATION OFFICES
Caribbean Tourism Assoc.
20 East 46th St.
New York, NY 10017
Tel. 212/682-0435

U. S. VIRGIN ISLANDS
  GOVERNMENT DIVISION
  OF TOURISM
10 Rockefeller Plaza, Suite 1001
New York, NY 10020
Tel. 212/582-4520

Appendix E
PASSENGER SHIP TERMINAL INFORMATION

Port of Miami

The New Port of Miami is now one of the finest in the world serving 23 major cruise ships and more than 1.5 million passengers annually. The proximity of all the beautiful, tropical islands, plus Florida's balmy weather year-round, has made Miami the leading port in the nation for cruise passengers. Port officials have begun an expansion program that will nearly double the size of the port and its current 17,000 daily passenger cruise capacity. Cruise ship berths will be expanded from nine to seventeen. By 1990 an estimated 4 million passengers will leave from Miami.

The New Port of Miami is located in tranquil Biscayne Bay facing the heart of Miami. The new cruise capital is only a few minutes from the Miami International Airport and from the famous resort hotels and motels in Miami and Miami Beach.

Passengers and visitors board the cruise ship through a terminal with spacious air-conditioned lounges and covered corridors to the ship's main lobby. Passengers arriving by limousine and taxi receive their luggage aboard ship . . . so do motorists who turn over their baggage at the boarding terminal to Port of Miami porters for shipboard delivery. Shipboard personnel deliver baggage to staterooms. Motorists then park and lock their cars in security parking lots only a few steps away, at a nominal daily fee.

Motorists drive onto the Port from Biscayne Boulevard (U.S. Highway #1) at Northeast 5th St., across a bridge onto the Port. Here signs by name of ship and pier number direct the motorist to his ship and parking area. Entrance to the Port is only a short distance from Highways #I-95, 395 and 836.

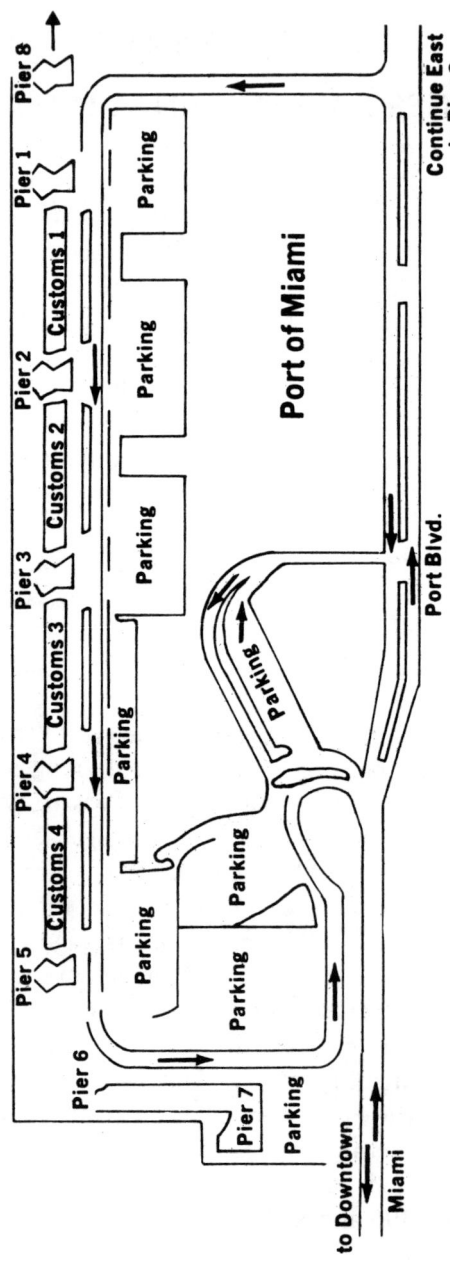

PASSENGER SHIP TERMINAL INFORMATION 319

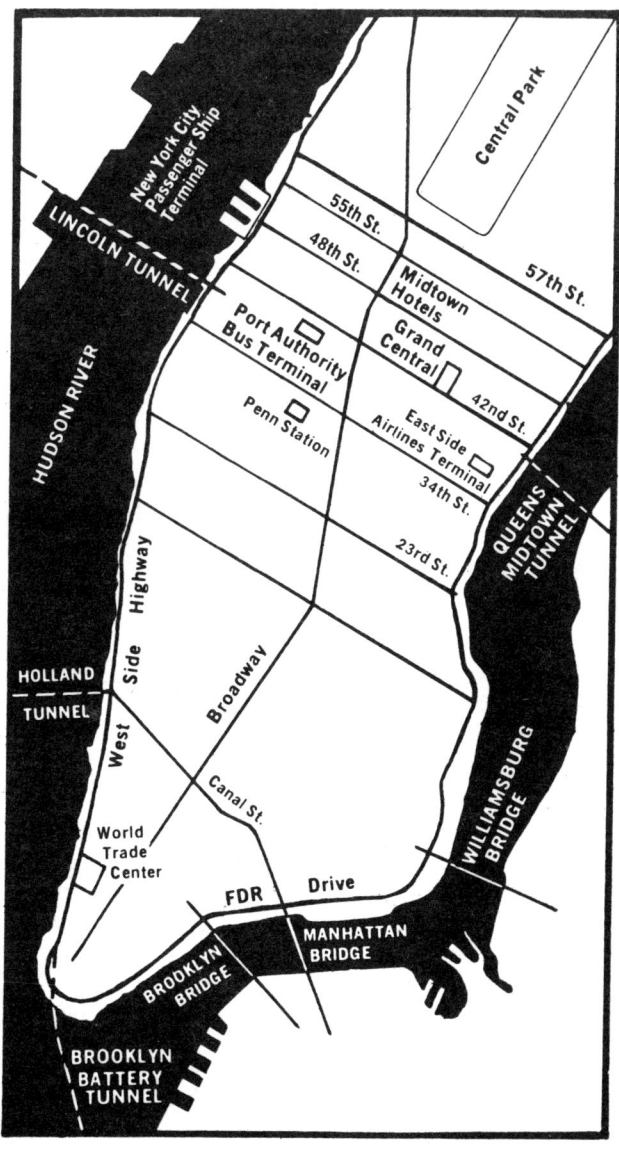

Reprinted by special permission from the January-February 1980 issue of the OAG Worldwide Cruise and Shipline Guide. All rights reserved.

PORT EVERGLADES

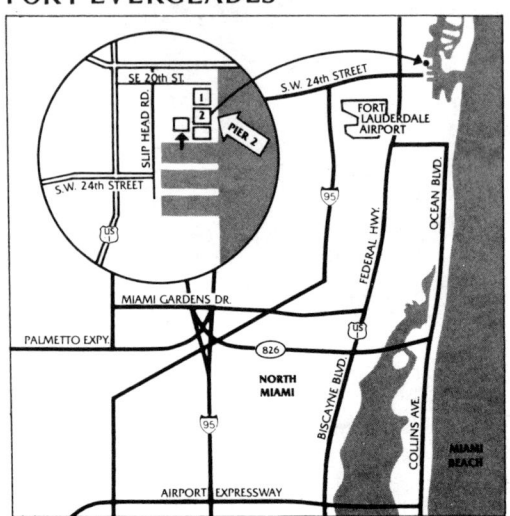

Port Everglades. Valet parking at $2.00 per day is available. Drive directly to Pier 2 and an attendant will take care of your car.

NEW ORLEANS

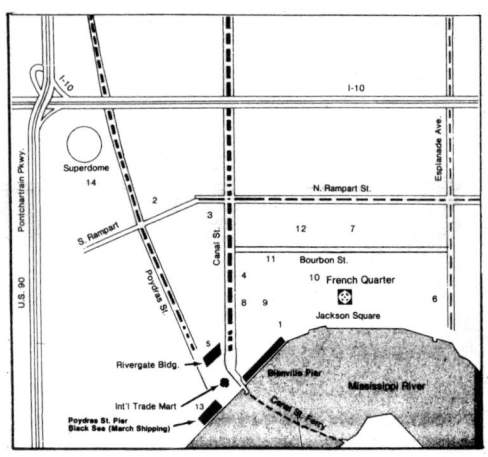

New Orleans. Bienville St. and Poydras St. Both piers flank the International Trade Mart at the foot of Canal St., Rivergate Center, just blocks from the French Quarter.

Reprinted by special permission from the January-February 1980 issue of the OAG Worldwide Cruise and Shipline Guide. All rights reserved.

LIBRARY OF DAVIDSON COLLEGE

Books on regular loan may be checked out for **two weeks**. Books must be presented at the Circulation Desk in order to be renewed.

A fine is charged after date due.

Special books are subject to special regulations at the discretion of the library staff.